John Fletcher's Chastity Plays
Mirrors of Modesty

John Fletcher's
Chastity Plays
Mirrors of Modesty

Nancy Cotton Pearse

Lewisburg
Bucknell University Press

© 1973 by Associated University Presses, Inc.

Associated University Presses, Inc.
Cranbury, New Jersey 08512

Library of Congress Cataloging in Publication Data

Pearse, Nancy Cotton, 1940–
  John Fletcher's chastity plays.

  Bibliography: p.
  1. Fletcher, John, 1579–1625. 2. Chastity in literature. I. Title.
PR2514.P4   822'.3   72-3258
ISBN 0-8387-1151-0

For my mother and father

Contents

Preface

The Beaumont and Fletcher canon contains over fifty plays, representing every conceivable dramatic genre and comprising the work of some dozen playwrights, yet all these plays are inadequately described by a half-dozen critical clichés. These fifty plays "lack moral fiber," they are "decadent," "sexy," "meretricious," or "mere entertainment" (as though that were a small accomplishment). We know, however, that these plays were immensely popular with Jacobean audiences, that Fletcher succeeded Shakespeare as chief playwright to the King's Men, and that Shakespeare himself sometimes collaborated with Fletcher (although a number of critics have done their best to expunge Fletcher from *The Two Noble Kinsmen* and *Henry VIII*).[1]

No other comparable body of Jacobean plays has produced literary criticism so little concerned to make distinctions between plays. Attempts to analyze these plays by groups have been made largely on the grounds of authorship. There are studies of the plays that Fletcher wrote alone, of the plays he wrote with Beaumont, and of the plays he wrote with Massinger. These studies tend to judge the plays on the basis of the merits of Fletcher's collaborator. As Beaumont has been much in favor for the last hundred years, the "fine" qualities of the Beaumont and Fletcher collaborations are, of course,

---

1. See, for example, Paul Bertram, *Shakespeare and the Two Noble Kinsmen* (New Brunswick, N.J., 1965). Arguments for and against Fletcher's participation in *Henry VIII* are summarized by R. A. Foakes in his edition of the play for the New Arden Shakespeare (Cambridge, Mass., 1957).

9

assigned to him. The fortunes of the Fletcher-Massinger plays tend
to depend on the value currently assigned to Massinger.[2]

The curious thing about these studies is their assumption that
Fletcher's contribution to that almost indissoluble mixture, a Jacobean collaboration, is the least important element, or, more invidiously,
that Fletcher is responsible for whatever flaws are detected in the
play. This procedure ignores completely the fact that the most con-
sistent and unifying factor in all these plays is Fletcher's hand.
Recently there has been a tendency for critics finally to acknowledge
that Fletcher was the leading author in the plays, and to refer to
the plays as Fletcherian. I have followed this practice in this study,
for it is clear that Fletcher was the dominant personality among
the collaborators.

The study that follows is an attempt to redress the balance of
opinion in Fletcher's favor. In pursuit of this aim, I have found it
necessary to attack head-on the "moral" objections to Fletcher, for
the alleged deficiency in Fletcher's morality is at the root of most
modern denigrations of his work. I have tried to show that objections
to these plays arise from Romantic misconceptions about their cultural
and literary antecedents. I have not attempted to discuss every play
in the canon; my procedure has been to select a group of plays that
have certain elements in common and that display as a group all the
features most objectionable to Beaumont and Fletcher critics. This
grouping of plays similar in technique and content seems to me more
important than grouping according to the identity of Fletcher's
collaborator.

As there is no modern critical edition of the entire canon, I have
tried to select for reference the best edition of each individual play.
The most useful is the Variorum edition, never completed, begun
in 1904 under the general editorship of A. H. Bullen. I have used,
where available, modern editions of individual plays, and I have

---

2. Some nineteenth-century critics saw Massinger as a monster, while
recent studies have seen him as a fine playwright and a stimulating moralist.
See T. A. Dunn, *Philip Massinger, The Man and the Playwright* (London,
1957); Philip Edwards, "Massinger the Censor" in *Essays on Shakespeare
and Elizabethan Drama,* ed. Richard Hosley (Columbia, Mo., 1962), pp.
341–50.

drawn also upon the edition of the dramatic works now in progress under the general editorship of Fredson Bowers. For the most part I have relied upon the ten-volume Cambridge edition (1905–1912), referred to in the notes as the Glover and Waller edition, which is a reprint of the Second Folio of 1679. All plays are dated according to Alfred Harbage, *Annals of the English Drama,* 2d ed. rev. Samuel Schoenbaum (Philadelphia, 1964). Attributions of authorship are based on Cyrus Hoy, "The Shares of Fletcher and his Collaborators in the Beaumont and Fletcher Canon," *Studies in Bibliography,* 8, 9, 11–15 (1956–1962), supplemented by G. E. Bentley, *The Jacobean and Caroline Stage,* 7 vols. (Oxford, 1941–1968), and E. K. Chambers, *The Elizabethan Stage,* 4 vols. (Oxford, 1923).

It would be impossible to express adequately my debt to Professor S. F. Johnson of Columbia University, who read this essay in manuscript and offered invaluable advice. I am indebted to Professors William W. Appleton and Elizabeth Donno for their stimulating suggestions. I should like also to thank my husband, Dr. Richard W. Pearse of Brooklyn College, for his suggestions and encouragement.

Acknowledgments

My thanks are due to the Cambridge University Press for permission to quote from *The Works of Francis Beaumont and John Fletcher,* edited by Arnold Glover and A. R. Waller, and from *The Dramatic Works of Beaumont and Fletcher,* edited by Fredson Bowers. Quotations from *The Works of Beaumont and Fletcher: Variorum Edition,* edited by A. H. Bullen, are by permission of G. Bell & Sons, Ltd. Quotations from Edmund Spenser's *Poetical Works,* edited by J. C. Smith and E. de Selincourt, are by permission of The Clarendon Press, Oxford.

John Fletcher's Chastity Plays
Mirrors of Modesty

1
Critical Attitudes toward
Beaumont and Fletcher

Reading the plays of John Fletcher, one encounters a prolific and competent poet, a good rhetorician, and a superb comic dramatist. Reading the criticism of these plays, one is repeatedly informed that Fletcher is a pornographer. For almost three hundred years it has been customary, indeed mandatory, to disapprove of Beaumont and Fletcher because of the allegedly low sexual morality of their plays. Ever since Richard Flecknoe in 1664 rebuked Fletcher for introducing obscenity into his plays and for violating decorum by seldom representing "an honorable woman without something of Dol Common in her,"[1] Beaumont and Fletcher have been considered talented but irreverent, even flagrantly obscene. Dryden, for example, asserted, "There is more bawdry in one play of Fletcher's, called *The Custom of the Country,* than in all ours together."[2] Dryden was responding with irritation and exaggeration to Jeremy Collier's attacks on the Restoration drama, but his statement has been canonized as a central tenet of Beaumont and Fletcher criticism.

Although the Beaumont and Fletcher plays, often in altered ver-

---

1. *A Discourse of the English Stage,* 1664. Quoted by Lawrence B. Wallis, *Fletcher, Beaumont and Company* (New York, 1947), p. 32.
2. "Preface to the Fables," *The Essays of John Dryden,* ed. W. P. Ker, 2 vols. (Oxford, 1900), 2:273.

sions,[3] continued to be performed throughout the eighteenth century, there were few significant critical comments on the plays until Coleridge, with his usual intuitive brevity, summed up the random disapproval of the preceding century and forecast the Victorian objections to the dramatists:

> Mem. To note how many of the Plays are founded on rapes—how many on unnatural incestuous passions—how many on mere lunacies. Then their virtuous women, either crazy superstitions of a merely bodily negation of a having been acted on, or Strumpets in their imaginations and wishes—or as in The Maid of the Mill, both at the same time.

> In Shakespear the mere generalities of Sex, mere words oftenest, seldom or never distinct images—all head-work, and fancy-drolleries—no sensation supposed in the Speaker, no itchy wriggling. In B. and F. the minutiae of a lecher.[4]

These censures became the commonplaces of criticism for a century. In particular, critics have echoed Coleridge's objections to the use of unpleasant and sensational situations in the plays. Typical is G. C. Macaulay's statement: "There too often occurs something essential to the plot, and not merely incidental in the dialogue, which justly offends a refined delicacy. Examples of this are afforded by the relations of Evadne and Amintor in The Maid's Tragedy, the incestuous passion of Arbaces in A King and No King, and the love of Leontius and Bacha in Cupid's Revenge."[5] For Charles Mills Gayley, A Wife for a Month illustrates Fletcher's "beastly perverseness of fancy, his prostitution of art to sordid sensationalism."[6]

Critics also follow Coleridge in denouncing Fletcher's portrayal

---

3. Described by A. C. Sprague in *Beaumont and Fletcher on the Restoration Stage* (Cambridge, Mass., 1926).

4. *Coleridge on the Seventeenth Century*, ed. Roberta Florence Brinkley (Durham, 1955), pp. 657, 658. I am ignoring in this study Coleridge's charge that Beaumont and Fletcher were servile divine rightists. Though the accusation was repeated by several generations of critics, it has been adequately laid to rest.

5. *Francis Beaumont* (London, 1883), p. 122.

6. *Beaumont, the Dramatist* (New York, 1914), p. 404.

of the virtuous woman, the chaste virgin or matron. Ladies of this type are censured for uttering "sentiments worthy of Diana in language unworthy of Doll Tearsheet."[7] A contradictory but equally frequent complaint is that the Fletcherian heroine is often so virtuous as to be unbelievable. I find this criticism first in Lamb, who thinks Fletcher's "flights of strained and improbable virtue" betray "an imperfect moral sensibility."[8] George Darley comments that Beaumont and Fletcher idealize so far as to "unnaturalize."[9] E. H. C. Oliphant feels that Fletcher's tragedies "do contain chaste, virtuous creatures, though there is something overstrained in their virtue."[10] *The Faithful Shepherdess,* a stylized idealization of chastity, is considered by W. W. Greg the worst offender in this regard among Fletcher's works: "This ideal which he sought to honor was one with which he was himself wholly out of sympathy. Consequently, in place of the supreme picture of womanly purity he intended, he produced what is no better than a grotesque caricature."[11] That Fletcher's chaste heroines are unnaturally idealized is true, but it is curious that the only reason advanced for this is Fletcher's "imperfect moral sensibility."

Because of such faults of situation and characterization, Beaumont and Fletcher have been held responsible for the "decadence" and decline of later Elizabethan drama. The most balanced statement of this idea is found in Alfred Harbage's *Shakespeare and the Rival Traditions.* Harbage sees Fletcher as one of a group writing for an *avant-garde* "coterie" at the private theaters and finds that among the "predecadent" coterie plays, Fletcher's "are distinguished by the substitution of ornament for fiber and of sophistic rhetoric for moral feeling."[12] This is a slightly softened version of the more usual supposition that Beaumont and Fletcher pandered to the base instincts of the corrupt and depraved Jacobean era. According to

7. Algernon Charles Swinburne, *Studies in Prose and Poetry* (London, 1894), p. 69.
8. *Specimens of the English Dramatic Poets,* 2 vols. (London, 1844), 2: 55.
9. *The Works of Beaumont and Fletcher,* 2 vols. (London, 1840), 1: xxv.
10. *The Plays of Beaumont and Fletcher* (New Haven, 1927), p. 42.
11. *Pastoral Poetry and Pastoral Drama* (London, 1906), pp. 273–74.
12. New York, 1952, pp. 304–5.

this theory, Beaumont and Fletcher were popular primarily because of their immorality, because "they raised the treatment of indecency to a fine art."[13]

In spite, however, of all the moral objections to Beaumont and Fletcher, many readers were genuinely attracted to the plays and often showed a sensitive appreciation of their lyric and dramatic skills.[14] An escape from this dilemma was found by crediting Beaumont with those scenes and characters which appealed to Victorian taste, and then excusing Beaumont while heaping condemnation on Fletcher.[15]

Only Swinburne among nineteenth-century critics attempted to defend Beaumont and Fletcher together. Calling Coleridge's remarks "captious if not rancorous," he has a good word even for *The Captain* (in which a wanton widow attempts to seduce her own father) and *The Custom of the Country* (which has a scene set in a male brothel), two plays that, more than any others, aroused the wrath of Victorian critics. He disagrees with Coleridge's description of Fletcher's subject matter:

> Among fifty-two plays there are exactly two which are founded upon rapes, *Valentinian* and *The Queen of Corinth;* there is not one which is founded on an incestuous passion, for the whole action of *A King and No King* hinges on the fact that Arbaces and Panthea are not brother and sister, but absolute strangers in blood; and if we except *The Mad Lover* and *The Nice Valor,* which may fairly be held liable to such a charge, I cannot discover an example of the "plays founded on mere lunacies."[16]

This is not entirely convincing, since in addition to the actual rapes in the two plays mentioned by Swinburne, there are threatened rapes in *The Faithful Shepherdess* and *The Little French Lawyer,* the

---

13. Quoted by O. L. Hatcher, *John Fletcher* (Chicago, 1905), p. 55.

14. See, for example, Gayley, p. 409. Predictably, the plays were bowdlerized, by Leigh Hunt. After his "Exclusion of Whatever is Morally Objectionable," there remained only a slender volume of lyrics, individual scenes, and "other Beauties." The material quoted is from the subtitle of Hunt's *Beaumont and Fletcher* (London, 1855).

15. See, for example, Macaulay, pp. 117ff.

16. *Studies in Prose and Poetry,* pp. 82–83.

queen's daughters have been raped before the opening of *Bonduca,* and rape is a frequent threat of lustful villains attempting to seduce innocent virgins. The rape of Lucrece is a frequent topic of discussion, as in *A Wife for a Month.* Incest is certainly suggested for four acts of *A King and No King,* and, as I have mentioned, Lelia in *The Captain* attempts to seduce her own father; moreover, the father of Monsieur Thomas cannot remarry for fear of committing incest because his son claims to have slept with all the available young girls in the county, and in *Women Pleased* Claudio disguises himself as a suitor to his married sister. Bacha, in *Cupid's Revenge,* attempts to seduce her former lover after he has become her stepson. Five of the plays represent abortive wedding-night encounters. No less than ten of Fletcher's virtuous women pretend, for various reasons, to be "Strumpets in their imaginations and wishes."

But Swinburne's real defense of the two dramatists is to picture them as eternal boys frolicking in a make-believe world of their own creation, where morality is irrelevant:

> There is the glory and grace of youth in all they have left us; if there be also somewhat too much of its graceless as well as its gracious qualities, yet there hangs about their memory as it were a music of the morning, a breath and savor of bright early manhood . . . which might charm asleep forever all thought or blame of all mortal infirmity or folly. For good or for evil, they are above all things poets of youth.[17]

A similar attitude appears in James Russell Lowell[18] and, several decades later, in Una Ellis-Fermor, who asserts that Beaumont and Fletcher are essentially not serious, that they do not raise "those issues touching the meaning of life and the destiny of man" which run through earlier Jacobean tragedy. Rather, they are to be credited with creating a "middle mood" in tragicomedy, a mood that pervades their tragedies and comedies as well. "Irresponsibility then is an essential part of their attitude, the irresponsibility which creates fairy-tales. . . ."[19] However, the notion of Beaumont and Fletcher

---

17. *Ibid.,* p. 76.
18. *Old English Dramatists* (Cambridge, Mass., 1892), p. 111.
19. *The Jacobean Drama,* 4th ed. (London, 1957), pp. 205–6.

as pure romancers was itself made the grounds for criticism. For Rupert Brooke their work was of "a fatally new kind" that led to the decline of the drama into "a sea of saccharine."[20] Thus, whether they created disgusting characters and situations or the unreal world of fairy-tale romance, they were held responsible for the decadence of the drama.

Since the Beaumont and Fletcher plays were not respectable as totalities, it is not surprising to find talented critics turning their attention for several decades to metrical and other tests of the composite authorship of this large and confusing canon. This textual criticism, valuable as it is, has not attempted to deal with the critical issues raised in the nineteenth century, while literary criticism as such has split into two distinct types in the last thirty years. One type simply ignores the moral objections to Fletcher and analyzes his considerable rhetorical skills; the other is traditional in that it is preoccupied with the issues raised by Coleridge.

Analysis of the Fletcherian plays as brilliant rhetorical constructs first finds expression in the 1940s. In 1947 Lawrence B. Wallis in *Fletcher, Beaumont and Company* argued that the structure of the plays is to be seen as determined by "emotional form" rather than by plot or characterization. This thesis was expressed more concisely and clearly some half dozen years before by Arthur Mizener in his brilliant essay "The High Design of *A King and No King.*" According to Mizener, Beaumont and Fletcher used the illusion of coherent narrative to further the effect of the emotional or psychological form, thus confusing critics who have mistakenly tried to find the meaning of a play in the pattern of the plot. Further, he feels that criticism has ignored the skill with which Beaumont and Fletcher project a light mood and a wide range of emotional effects because "moral shortcomings . . . are supposed to inhere in the mood" itself.[21]

This apprehension of Beaumont and Fletcher as practitioners of a brilliant rhetoric projecting complex emotional states has been the most fruitful contemporary approach to the plays. Eugene Waith uses this line of inquiry in *The Pattern of Tragicomedy in Beaumont*

---

20. *John Webster and the Elizabethan Drama* (London, 1916), pp. 71, 75.
21. *Modern Philology* 38 (1940–41) : 137.

and Fletcher, perhaps the best full-length critical work on the dramatists.[22] Waith finds a major influence on the style and substance of tragicomedy in the *Controversiae* of Seneca the Elder. Similarities in style are seen particularly in the striving after novelty in highly embellished debate about extreme and hypothetical situations. Waith finds such situations the key to the characterization in the typical Fletcherian play. Fletcher contrives confrontations between characters who are, or pretend to be, moral opposites; these characters are "protean" and may suddenly assume another role to prolong and intensify the situation.[23]

John F. Danby has another fresh approach to the plays.[24] He sees renaissance poets as socially "placed" in their relationship to patronage. Beaumont and Fletcher attempt to make the theater "literary," thus making it respectable as a patron. Danby's explorations of the social mechanics of this "assault on the playhouse" put in a new perspective the Victorian assumption of the pernicious influence of the Jacobean era. Moving to a discussion of aesthetics, Danby sees the Beaumont and Fletcher plays as organized, not around imagery narrowly conceived, but around hyperbole and conceit:

The main poetic feature of Beaumont and Fletcher is their adaptation to the stage of the sonneteer's material and the sonneteer's "conceit." The primary affiliation of their drama is with the Sidneians and the metaphysicals. . . . Their words are stretched in the frame of their situations, and it is the frame which gives the manifoldness of "wit." Their achievement was to make dramatic situation perform the work of metaphysical conceit.[25]

This thesis enables Danby to present a fresh analysis of the wedding-night scene between Evadne and Amintor in *The Maid's Tragedy,*

22. New Haven, 1952. This paragraph is summarized from chapters 2 and 3.

23. Waith does not mention Coleridge, but this is obviously his suggestion as to why Fletcher makes his virtuous women pretend to be whores, i.e., in order to prolong debate.

24. *Poets on Fortune's Hill* (London, 1952); reprinted in 1964 as *Elizabethan and Jacobean Poets.* This paragraph is a summary of chapters 6 and 7.

25. *Ibid.,* p. 257.

a scene traditionally cited as "objectionable"; Danby describes the scene as a series of "moral puns" that play with the traditional petrarchan values.

In general, these recent critics argue that the desire for rhetorical display determines content; extreme issues—rape, adultery, impotence—are introduced primarily as topics for brilliant and clever debate.

A more traditional group of recent critics, those who concern themselves with theme and content as well as form and style, continue to express the feeling that some values (chastity, for example) are ethically perverted when debate about them is allowed. Since the Victorian criticisms, characteristically social rather than aesthetic, boil down, fundamentally, to an objection to Fletcher's representation of the relationships between the sexes, it is curious to find these criticisms repeated when the social values which produced Coleridge's strictures have so largely disappeared from our society, and when "shocking" subjects are no longer unfamiliar on the stage. But that is exactly what we do find. As recently as 1960 Robert Ornstein in *The Moral Vision of Jacobean Tragedy* deplores Fletcher's "calculated prurience" and "ethical frivolity," and finds his heroines morally ambivalent. "The climactic moments of Fletcher's tragicomedies occur more often than not in boudoirs when honor or courtly love is in rhetorical question. The chaste heroine lures her would-be lover on only to insist upon her virtue when we can no longer believe in it."[26]

Surprisingly, only one recent critic, Clifford Leech, has made a significant post-Freudian attempt to justify a group of plays full of "sensational" sexual situations. Leech defends Fletcher from the charge of using salaciousness for its own sake and tries to make a case for him as a thoughtful and "disturbing" playwright. According to Leech, Fletcher shows a "genuine interest in the novel twistings of the human situation"[27] and this leads him repeatedly to the sexually charged scene. He seeks to explore the abnormal, the peripheral in life; it is for this reason, paradoxically, that he repeats

---

26. Madison, Wis., 1960, p. 163.
27. *The John Fletcher Plays* (Cambridge, Mass., 1962), p. 22.

himself, for abnormal behavior tends to follow recognizable patterns. Leech's attempt to make Fletcher into a proto-Freudian and therefore into a writer more acceptable to modern taste is not convincing. Fletcher's characters are, as the nineteenth century saw, extremely idealized and make conventional moral responses rather than pathological emotional ones to the extreme situations in which they find themselves. Leech is accurate, however, when he points out the persistent preoccupation in the plays with the preservation of virginity. This same preoccupation is found in the late Shakespeare and is one of the points of contact between Shakespearean romances and Fletcherian tragicomedy. A. H. Thorndike's long-debated suggestion that Beaumont and Fletcher were the innovators of the new romanticism, rather than Shakespeare,[28] Leech finds academic. Rather, he suggests that the emphasis on virginity in both groups of plays "emerged from something deeper than would be implied by a mere borrowing."[29] This is a very viable suggestion, and it will be one of the purposes of this study to explore the nature of the "something deeper."

The tendency of modern criticism of Fletcher to split into two schools—one concentrating on rhetorical form, the other on theme and content—indicates that neither approach has been wholly satisfactory. A synthesis of these is the purpose of William W. Appleton's *Beaumont and Fletcher: A Critical Study*. Appleton, after discussing the relationships between the tensions and paradoxes of tragicomedy and Jacobean society, goes on to assert that Fletcher, basically an entertainer, is forced to repeat his successes, and this leads to the search for the sensational and outré to give interest to familiar dramatic patterns. Appleton denies that Beaumont and Fletcher emphasize the theme of rape to the extent that Coleridge believed, but "no one can deny that it powerfully attracted them. . . . The extremities of chastity and lust, moralizing and pornography, inexorably appealed to them."[30] He finds the heroines morally ambivalent, the language often gross and direct, misogyny ubiquitous, women and

---

28. Thorndike advanced this thesis in *The Influence of Beaumont and Fletcher on Shakespeare* (Worcester, Mass., 1901).
29. Leech, p. 161.
30. London, 1956, p. 60.

erotic situations given a decided prominence. Appleton is right; these elements do exist in the plays. And they continue to be the thorn in the side of Fletcherian criticism.

But how did they affect the Jacobean audience? This is surely the question to ask. What did Jacobeans think of Fletcher's preference for themes such as rape, incest, impotence? Why did they prefer heroes and heroines of incredibly idealized virtue? What was their response to a chaste heroine who suddenly pretended to be a whore?

The first place to look for answers to these questions is in Jacobean criticism of Beaumont and Fletcher—in the commendatory verses printed in the First Folio of 1647. In startling contrast to all subsequent critics, the authors of these verses praised Fletcher's plays for their beneficent didactic influence. The plays inculcated virtue, and they did so in a specific way: they taught chastity. Roger L'Estrange, for example, praises the plays because they teach young girls to beware of the oaths of false lovers:

> The Credulous, bright Girle, that beleeves all
> Language, (in Othes) if Good, Canonicall,
> Is fortifi'd, and taught, here, to beware
> Of ev'ry specious bayte, of ev'ry snare
> Save one: and that same Caution takes her more,
> Then all the flattery she felt before.
>
> (p. xxix)[31]

Even the less respectable ladies in the audience were moved, according to Henry Harington, to give over looseness, and even prostitution:

> Some, I dare say, that did with loose thoughts sit,
> Reclaim'd by thee, came converts from the pit.
> And many a she that to be tane up came,
> Tooke up themselves, and after left the game.
>
> (p. liii)

---

31. The citations in the text refer to vol. 1 of *The Works of Francis Beaumont and John Fletcher,* ed. Arnold Glover and A. R. Waller, 10 vols. (Cambridge, 1905–1912).

Jasper Maine agrees:

> They who possess a Box, and halfe Crowne spent
> To learne Obscenenes, returned innocent,
> And thankt you for this coznage, whose chaste Scene
> Taught Loves so noble, so reform'd, so cleane,
> That they who brought foule fires, and thither came
> To bargaine, went thence with a holy flame.
>
> (p. xxxvi)

Robert Stapylton describes Fletcher's chief purpose in terms that suggest the morality play:

> But his maine end does drooping Vertue raise,
> And crownes her beauty with eternall Bayes;
> In Scaenes where she inflames the frozen soule,
> While Vice (her paint washt off) appeares so foule. . . .
>
> (p. xxi)

"None writes lov's passion in the world, like" Fletcher, according to Robert Herrick (p. xli), and William Habington commends his portrayal of passion as particularly moral:

> Thou warmst the Lover; how severely just
> Thou wert to punish, if he burnt to lust.
> With what a blush thou didst the Maid adorne,
> But tempted, with how innocent a scorne.
>
> (p. xxvi)

And the playwright is praised for displaying, in a manner appropriate for a bishop's son, the proper workings of poetic justice:

> Thy Phancy gave no unswept Language vent;
> Slaunderst not Lawes, prophan'st no holy Page,
> (As if thy Fathers Crosier aw'd the Stage;)
> High Crimes were still arraign'd, though they made shift
> To prosper out foure Acts, were plaugu'd i'th Fift. . . .
>
> (p. xliii)[32]

---

32. Harington (p. liii) also comments on Fletcher's proper use of poetic justice.

L'Estrange affects surprise that the plays of Beaumont and Fletcher are being revived in print because "The Palate of this age gusts nothing High;/That has not Custard in't or Bawdery" (p. xxviii). John Earle also commends Fletcher because his wit is "untainted with obscenity" (p. xxxiii).

Perhaps the most puzzling to a modern reader of all the Folio verses are those of Richard Lovelace, who singles out for praise in a marginal note the now infamous *Custom of the Country* and its infamous male brothel scene. Lovelace apparently feels that Fletcher could represent any subject in such a way as to avoid offense:

> Heare ye foule Speakers, that pronounce the Aire
> Of Stewes and Shores, I will informe you where
> And how to cloathe aright your wanton wit,
> Without her nasty Bawd attending it.
> View here a loose thought said with such a grace,
> Minerva might have spoke in Venus face;
> So well disguis'd, that t'was conceiv'd by none
> But Cupid had Diana's linnen on;
> And all his naked parts so vail'd, th' expresse
> The Shape with clowding the uncomlinesse;
> That if this Reformation which we
> Receiv'd, had not been buried with thee,
> The Stage (as this work) might have liv'd and lov'd;
> Her lines; the austere Skarlet had approv'd,
> And th' Actors wisely been from that offence
> As cleare, as they are now from Audience.
>
> (p. xxv)

The Folio verses are quite positive in their opinion and commendation. When all allowances are made for exaggeration in response to Puritan attacks on the stage, it is hard to believe that this mass of praise is due solely to a Jacobean taste for depravity not since equaled in Western culture. It is far more reasonable to assume that some component of the so-called Elizabethan world picture has been lost to us, and that this loss makes us unable to see the didactic qualities in the Fletcherian plays.

Surely the next step is to analyze the plays to see if, and how, they can be said to inculcate chastity; that will be my purpose in chapter 2. If Fletcher intended to glorify chastity, then we must dismiss the idea that those sensational threats to chastity—rape, incest, and so forth—were used either solely for debate, as the students of rhetoric would have it, or solely for the creation of erotic and pornographic situations, as the Coleridgeans contend.

2

The Defense of Chastity

The allegedly immoral Fletcher wrote two plays specifically labeled as morality plays. He and either Beaumont or Field each contributed two playlets to *Four Plays, or Moral Representations, in One* (*c.* 1608–1613).[1] Fletcher's contributions are *The Triumph of Death* and *The Triumph of Time*. One can easily ignore the latter, a dull and old-fashioned morality with Anthropos surrounded by characters named Desire, Vain Delight, Honesty, Simplicity, and so forth. On the other hand, *The Triumph of Death* is a significant, if not very successful play; it also is a morality play, but it is given a veneer of realism. It compresses a complex plot into one quarter the length of a normal play, and this brevity exposes characteristic Fletcherian themes very baldly. The play is a brief commentary on the text that the rewards of sin are death; the specific sin involved is lust.

1. Glover and Waller, vol. 10. Because there are no act or scene divisions, citations in the text refer to page numbers. I am somewhat hesitant about using the *Four Plays* as paradigms, both because they are among the least important of the Beaumont and Fletcher plays and because the auspices of their production, if any, are unknown. (See W. J. Lawrence, "The Date of *Four Plays in One," TLS* [11 December 1919], p. 740, for the suggestion that the play was performed at court either for the celebration of the wedding of Princess Elizabeth and the Elector Palatine or for some other court wedding.) These disadvantages, however, are outweighed by several other considerations. Since all the plays discussed in this study show marked similarities in their affinities with morality-play structure, the *Four Plays* are an instructive starting point in that they are explicitly designated as morality plays. These playlets are additionally useful as paradigms because their brevity exposes characteristic themes clearly.

Fletcher's source is William Painter's *Palace of Pleasure,* Tome I, novella 42.[2] In this story, Didaco, a wealthy nobleman, loves the poor and orphaned Violenta. When she refuses his passionate entreaties and offers of money, he at length agrees to marry her. Violenta, coming to dote on her husband, is easily persuaded to keep their marriage a secret. Eventually he tires of her and makes a second, bigamous marriage. Violenta realizes that she cannot make her marriage public because she has no witnesses to the ceremony and the identity of the officiating priest is unknown to her; she determines to revenge herself and then die. An old woman named Janique agrees to help her in return for a rich sum of gold. Violenta murders her betrayer; she confesses her crime and is condemned to be beheaded. By the conclusion of the story, the character of Violenta has shifted from that of betrayed maiden to bloody revenger. Not content with stabbing her seducer some ten or twelve times, she rips out his deceitful eyes, tongue, and heart. Fletcher changes the story to de-emphasize the cruel revenge of the heroine and to give greater prominence to her betrayal and abandonment. And the fickle bigamist is made over into a diabolic and lustful villain.

Fletcher's heroine, now called Gabriella, has been secretly married to Lavall, the chosen heir of the childless Duke of Anjou. Lavall tells her that the marriage must be kept secret lest he be disinherited; actually he is already betrothed to Hellena,[3] chosen for him by his royal patron. Gabriella realizes, however, that he no longer loves her. Formerly he had made passionate suit to her until she "came fairly off with honor'd Marriage," although the ceremony has linked her only "to this man's Lust" (p. 335). When she learns of Lavall's bigamous marriage with Hellena, she dispatches her betrayer; after revealing all to the Duke, she commits suicide. Her devoted assistant Maria follows suit; her loyalty, a change from the mercenary motivation of Janique in Painter, emphasizes that Gabriella is able to inspire devotion.

<hr/>

2. Ed. Joseph Jacobs, 3 vols. (London, 1890). Some minor details (e.g., the false report of Perolot's death at Orleans) suggest *The Atheist's Tragedy.*
3. The name Hellena may have been selected to suggest a comparison between Gabriella and Oenone, abandoned by inconstant Paris for another Helen.

This Italianate revenge tragedy Fletcher transforms into an allegory. Gabriella is the Mankind figure of a morality play; she is torn between good and evil spirits represented by her husband Lavall (i.e., Love-All=promiscuous lust) and her old and dear friend Casta (=Chastity), Fletcher's most significant addition to the cast of characters. Lavall is a "damn'd divell," "the Devil," a "leacher Lord," "Devil Lord, the damn'd Lord of all lewdness" (p. 345). He is a "salt-itch,/ For whom no cure but ever burning brimstone/ Can be imagin'd" (p. 349). According to the courtiers, he is possessed by an evil spirit:

> The Devil follows him; and for a truth, Sir,
> Appears in visible figure often to him. . . .
> (p. 338)

Lavall calls this spirit "devil lust." This "most deboist and barbarous" villain (p. 337) is "the base dishonor of a thousand women" (p. 354):

> His appetite to Women (for there he carries
> His main Sail spread) so boundles, and abominably,
> That but to have her name by that tongue spoken,
> Poisons the virtue of the purest Virgin.
> (p. 338)

In contrast, "Heaven reigns within Casta" (p. 340), who is more than once called a "saint." She is "blessed, Blessed Sweetness, Divine Virgin" (p. 341), "full of forcible Divine perswasion" (p. 344). Her allegorical function is underlined by the fact that the play becomes a struggle, not between Gabriella and Lavall, but between Lavall and Casta.

Before the "secret love" between Gabriella and Lavall, "no two women in the world more lov'd" (p. 343) each other than she and Casta. Gabriella's first love, Perolot, is Casta's brother. But since her secret marriage, Gabriella has not dared to see her old friend, for "Casta is quick, and of a piercing judgement,/ And quickly will find out a flaw" (p. 343). Gabriella has lost touch with her good angel, Chastity, and Chastity's representative, Perolot. This is an allegorical representation of Gabriella's loss of honor in the loveless marriage with Lavall. The first direct encounter between the good and evil spirits occurs midway in the playlet. Lavall catches sight of Casta and is inflamed by her beauty but realizes that she is "too full of grace" for him. But Lavall's "evil spirit" materializes and urges him to rape her. Chastity, however, has mystical powers: Casta's reappearance exorcises the demon, who vanishes with the cry, "Her virtue, like a spell, sinks me to darkness" (p. 341).

Lavall nonetheless resolves to have Casta. He agrees to visit Gabriella as a ruse, making it a condition of his visit that Casta shall also be there. Allegorically, then, Lust seeks to defile Chastity. Unless this allegorical meaning is perceived, Lavall's visit to Gabriella makes no sense. For the scene that, in narrative terms, should be a confrontation between the heroine and her betrayer (as in the original story), becomes a confrontation between Lavall and Casta. Arriving at Gabriella's house, Lavall completely ignores her and forces his attentions on her friend. He urges Casta to sit by him, eliciting the comment, "By the Devil?" (i.e., Sit next to the Devil?) (p. 349). The villain likens himself to "lustie Tarquin/ Turn'd into flames with Lucrece coy denyals." Casta cries out, "O help me Justice:/ Help me, my Chastitie" (p. 350). At this point Gabriella murders her betrayer, saying, as she strikes the final blow, "This for Casta" (p. 353). Allegorically speaking, this final stroke is the heroine's revenge for her injured chastity.

Gabriella, as is traditional in a revenge action, dies, in this case by her own hand. It is significant, however, that she commits suicide because she desires to be with her dead sweetheart Perolot, rather than because of any shame she might feel as a murderess. Indeed, the Duke, when he hears her motives, forgives the murder of his heir and urges her to live. As this is a chastity morality, "Thou shalt not commit adultery" is given priority over the injunction "Thou shalt not kill."

The Triumph of Death, then, is an allegorical play in which the opposing forces that contend for the soul are Chastity and Lechery. Enough veneer of Italianate romance is added to make the whole more palatable to Jacobean taste. In fact, the play is best interpreted in much the way Bernard Spivack interprets *Othello* in *Shakespeare and the Allegory of Evil* (New York, 1958), that is, as a morality play brought up to date. This type of play is common in the Fletcherian canon; when Fletcher uses this model, the opposing forces are always the same—chastity and lust.

I have seen no discussion of *The Triumph of Death* as a moral allegory, though the nature of the play is unmistakable. I have seen, on the other hand, criticism that places Casta among the unnaturally virtuous heroines of Fletcher.[4] But if my evaluation of the nature of the play is correct, then it would be surprising to find Casta anything other than unnaturally idealized, for she is not intended as a realistic character at all. Casta is a Virtue, a component of the personality of the heroine, Gabriella. Whenever Fletcher presents a lady of this type, the reader would do well to suspect a moral allegory, particularly when a character like Casta is found in a play that deals, as does this one, with extremities of virtue and vice.

One other aspect of this playlet deserves attention as typically Fletcherian. This is the passage in which Casta's father suggests that she leave her "solitary life at home" for preferment at court. Anyone familiar with Jacobean drama is familiar with the convention by which the court is presented as the very quintessence of iniquity. An invitation to court, therefore, is by definition a threat to the chastity of a lady.[5] A Fletcherian heroine faced with such an invitation responds, without hesitation, with a refusal to be prostituted to the lust of great men. Casta's response is typical:

> When shall I pray again? (a Courtier)
> Or when I do, to what God? what new body
> And new face must I make me, with new manners?
> For I must be no more my self. Whose Mistriss
> Must I be first? with whose sin-offering season'd?
> And when I am grown so great and glorious

---

4. Oliphant, p. 42.

5. Robert Brustein, "Italianate Court Satire and the Plays of John Marston," Ph.D. diss. (Columbia University, 1957), demonstrates in his chapter on "The Court Lady" (pp. 153–211) that, in the opinion of most satirists and moralists, a lady at court was *ipso facto* in a state of sin. This attitude gives special point to the conventional use of the invitation or summons to court as a trial of a heroine's chastity.

With prostitution of my burning beauties,
That great Lords kneel, and Princes beg for favours,
Do you think I'll be your Daughter, a poor Gentlemans,
Or know you for my father?

(p. 340)

Since Casta is undeniably Chastity incarnate, this speech cannot be interpreted otherwise than as exemplary. It is clearly designed as instruction for young ladies faced with the temptation of greatness, yet heroines who give similar speeches in the same situation are criticized for "immodest" language.[6] But such heroines clearly were not considered by Fletcher and his audience to be immodest because they are aware of and denounce the temptations of court life. Rather, this sarcastic speech, coming from the bashful and cloistered Casta, is to be seen as an example of the "innocent scorn" of temptation praised by Habington in the Folio commendatory verses (above, chap. 1).

The question of the heroine of unbelievable virtue and her appearance of immodesty needs further exploration. There is another type of nonrealistic characterization, besides the abstracting of character in moral allegory, that produces the same effect. This is the presentation of a character as an exemplum. *The Triumph of Honor,* another of the *Four Plays in One,* can be studied as an example of this technique.

This "moral representation" explicitly celebrates valor and clemency in the persons of Sophocles, Duke of Athens, and Martius, a Roman general, and chastity and constancy in Dorigen, the wife of Sophocles. The first half of the playlet displays the workings of masculine honor. General Martius captures Athens, but Duke Sophocles' noble behavior as a captive moves him to clemency and admiration. The two men become fast friends and strive to outdo each other in courtesies. Martius spares Sophocles' life and restores his dukedom; Sophocles gives Martius a victory triumph and welcomes him as a guest to Athens.

Unfortunately, however, Martius has also been impressed with

---

6. For an example, see Eugene M. Waith, "A Tragicomedy of Humors: Fletcher's *The Loyal Subject," MLQ* 6 (1945) : 309.

the beauty of Dorigen. Torn between love for his friend and lust for his friend's wife, he tries to preserve his "fame and nature":

> Shall I thus fall? I will not; no, my tears
> Cast on my heart, shall quench these lawless fires:
> He conquers best, conquers his lewd desires.
>
> (p. 303)

The conquest of passion is conceived of as being greater than the conquest of a city, as in Lyly's *Campaspe*. But Martius fails to achieve this nobler victory; thus the burden of restraint falls on Dorigen.

The emphasis of the play now shifts to the display of feminine honor. When Martius reveals his lust to her, Dorigen defends her chastity in a speech of twenty-three lines, urging him to remember the gods, friendship, hospitality, piety, and his own fame. Sophocles, she says, will doubt her fidelity before he doubts Martius's honor. She suggests that this attempted seduction is merely a pretense on his part in order to discover if his friend's wife is faithful:

> Sure thou but tri'st me out of love to him,
> And wouldst reject me, if I did consent.
>
> (p. 304)

Chastity, as in *The Triumph of Death*, is seen as such a supreme virtue that the lack of it destroys all other good qualities:

> O Martius, Martius, wouldst thou in one minute,
> Blast all thy Laurels, which so many years
> Thou hast been purchasing with blood and sweat?
>
> (p. 304)

The length and vehemence of this speech in defense of chastity are typically Fletcherian.

At this point the play becomes a retelling of Chaucer's *Franklin's Tale*. When Martius, although he knows Dorigen "confut'st divinely," nevertheless renews his illicit overtures, she makes a scornful vow:

> These rocks we see so fix'd, shall be removed,
> Made champion field, ere I so impious prove,
> To stain my Lords bed with adulterous love.
> (p. 304)

Martius turns for help to his brother Valerius, who in his youth
learned magical skills. Valerius has suspected Martius's lapse from
virtue and confirms his suspicions by a stratagem that has bothered
readers. He pretends to his brother that he himself lusts for Dorigen,
and immediately elicits the proof of his suspicions when Martius is
inflamed to jealousy. Valerius describes his action as searching his
brother's wound; he is trying to show his brother his faults by
letting him see how heinous his own behavior looks in another. He
then uses this little charade as a text for a lecture:

> Far, far be such love from Valerius,
> So far he scorns to live to be call'd brother
> By him that dares own such folly and vice.
> . (p. 305)

Martius recognizes his own folly but cannot control his passion. So
Valerius, as a temporary expedient to prevent his brother's suicide,
creates the magical illusion that the rocks have been removed; he
prays, however, that Diana will continue to "fortifie" Dorigen's
mind.

Dorigen, when the rocks are removed, stands "constant and
chaste . . . 'gainst gods" as against men:

> Hence, lewd Magician; dar'st thou make the gods
> Bawds to thy lust; will they do miracles
> To further evil? or do they love it now?
> Know, if they dare do so, I dare hate them,
> And will no longer serve 'em.
> (p. 308)

But her husband commands her to fulfill her vow; worse, he suspects
the whole tale as a ruse on her part to conceal an affair with Martius.
This ignoble jealousy she punishes by pretending that she has antici-

pated his command and has already complied with Martius's desires. This pretense of wantonness parallels Valerius's earlier pretense to his brother. The purpose of both is to shame vice with its own image.

Expecting his magnanimous refusal, Dorigen now offers herself to Martius as a gift from Sophocles, but Martius does not respond with magnanimity. Disappointed by both the men who love her, Dorigen proposes the ultimate resistance:

> See, thou ungrateful, since thy desperate lust
> Nothing can cure but death, I'll die for thee,
> Whilst my chaste name lives to posterity.
>
> (p. 310)

Her threat of suicide at last arouses Martius's better nature; he praises Dorigen as the "Angel" of her sex, and as the instrument of his reformation: "O my mirror!/ How perfectly thou shew'st me all my faults" (p. 310). On the heels of Martius's reformation comes Sophocles' redemption; he rushes in prepared to die to revenge his wife's chastity. There follows a scene of mutual repentance and forgiveness, after which Diana descends with the "moral":

> Let her [Dorigen] triumph; with her, her Lord, and friend,
> Who, though misled, still honor was their end.
>
> (p. 311)

Womanly honor, chastity, thus comes off a great deal better than masculine honor, valor and clemency.

One has only to look at the source of this plot in Chaucer, or at one of the numerous medieval or Renaissance versions of the same story, to realize what a radical change has been made in the theme. Chaucer presents a conundrum of courtesy; a deadlocked situation is resolved by magnanimity. The husband's courtesy in sending his wife to fulfill her promise is matched by the courtesy of the lover in sending her back untouched, and the magician is equally magnanimous in refusing to accept his promised fee. Chaucer leaves the reader to make a decision as to which of the three was most courteous: "Lordynges, this question, thanne, wol I aske now,/ Which was the mooste fre, as thynketh yow?" Although Chaucer gives a good deal of space to Dorigen's thoughts and feelings, the emphasis of the story falls upon the actions of the men, rather than upon the plight of the woman. The emphasis is reversed in the Fletcherian version. The plight of Dorigen, described in the dramatis personae of the Second Folio (1679) as "the example of Chastity," is clearly the focus of attention. The deadlocked situation is broken by her willingness to die for her honor rather than by the courtesy of the men. Indeed, this latter quality is notably absent. Chaucer's courtly lover is turned into a lustful seducer, and his courteous husband is given a fit of ungovernable jealousy. The change in their names tends to abstract them to representatives of Roman valor (Martius) and Athenian wisdom (Sophocles), both of which appear very shabby in their confrontation with feminine chastity. This is given specific emphasis in the play by Dorigen's exclamation, "O wretched men!/ With all your valour and your learning, bubbles" (p. 309). The metamorphosis of the story from a trial of courtesy to a trial of chastity is rather remarkable, and, at the same time, typical of the Beaumont and Fletcher canon. The same process occurs in the change of Heywood's *The Royal King and the Loyal Subject* into Fletcher's *The Loyal Subject* (see below, chap. 9).

The stock themes and situations in *The Triumph of Honor,* which Fletcher repeatedly employs in order to glorify chastity, have been misunderstood by critics. One device we have already noticed is the pretense of wantonness used to reform wantonness in another by holding a mirror up to vice. This type of behavior is the basis for Coleridge's charge that Fletcher's heroines are "strumpets in their imaginations and wishes," or, as it has been stated more recently, that Fletcher delights "in the piquant flavor of situations where chaste men and women are made to 'talk bawdy.' "[7] But there is not an example of this behavior in a Fletcherian play that is used gratuitously; it is always intended to act as a spur to reformation or as a test of behavior.

Another convention is the emphasizing of exemplary behavior, such as Dorigen's, by contrasting it with a corrupt and sensual society, as Fletcher does with Casta in *The Triumph of Death.* Because of

7. *Ibid.*

the space devoted to Sophocles and Martius, this is not possible within the brief scope of *The Triumph of Honor*.[8] The same purpose is served, however, by the frame play that encloses the *Four Plays*. The four "triumphs" are dramatic sports for the wedding celebration of Emmanuel of Portugal and Isabella of Castile. The grave king and queen praise Dorigen's behavior in the playlet; the comments of the merry and frivolous courtiers in the stage audience provide the contrasting milieu of easy virtue, a milieu in which ladies entertain their lovers in coaches and prostitutes are not shamed by the legal punishment of public carting:

> Frigoso. How many of our wives now adays would deserve to triumph in such a Chariot?
> Rinaldo. That's all one; you see they triumph in Caroches.
> Frigoso. That they do, by the mass; but not all neither; many of them are content with Carts.
>
> (p. 312)

This type of joking, intended for a comment on the extraordinary quality of Dorigen's behavior, is rather too often taken as a personal expression of Fletcher's misogyny. Instead, it is simply a part of the thematic structure of the play, contrasting the display of Athenian virtue in the golden age of Greece and Rome to the fallen "now adays." Misogynistic characters abound in Beaumont and Fletcher, but misogynists as such are either villains or objects of satire.

Also illustrated in this play is another theme unrecognized by critics, that of the reforming power of chastity. Repeatedly one encounters the charge that Fletcher allows easy repentance to sordid villainy, that the villains' "sudden conversions . . . make us wonder whether in his heart Fletcher felt any difference between a satyr-like lust and a chaste love. . . ."[9] Presumably the repentance of Martius would fall into this category. But Fletcher emphasizes not

---

8. A burlesque of the love triangle is intended in the subplot, in which a corporal and a sutler fight over a laundress. But this subplot is so truncated and incoherent that it fails of its purpose.

9. Paul Elmer More, "Beaumont and Fletcher—II," *The Nation* (1 May 1913), p. 437. The criticism appears first in Coleridge, p. 669. Cf. also Gayley, p. 403; F. H. Ristine, *English Tragicomedy* (New York, 1910), p. 117; J. A. Symonds, *In the Key of Blue* (London, 1893), p. 221.

the internal process of repentance, but the external cause of repentance: chastity is portrayed as a holy virtue with the power to subdue and reform lust.

It is clear that those plays in which Fletcher and his collaborators glorify chastity and display exemplary virtue are those plays which anger critics. A play like *The Beggar's Bush,* which does not mention chastity, is lavishly praised for its genuinely fine qualities; a play like *A Wife for a Month,* in which chastity is the only topic, is thoroughly damned because its fine qualities are supposedly made subservient to the interests of pornography. But, again, the conventions that Fletcher uses to present chastity are intended to have a moral rather than a pornographic effect. The critical misunderstanding arises from the fact that Fletcher begins with a set of basic premises and attitudes about chastity and lust that neither modern nor Victorian nor (to a large extent) Restoration critics share. Chapters 3, 4, and 5 will discuss the nature of these premises and attitudes. It is sufficient for the moment to note that chastity was a common moral and literary topic in Elizabethan and Jacobean times and that Fletcher considered it important enough to embody in a whole series of plays. These plays have so much in common that I propose to call them the chastity plays. Besides those plays already discussed, the following use chastity as a major motif: *The Captain, The Coxcomb, Cupid's Revenge, The Custom of the Country, The Faithful Shepherdess, The Humorous Lieutenant, The Knight of Malta, The Little French Lawyer, The Lovers' Progress, The Loyal Subject, The Maid in the Mill, Thierry and Theodoret, Valentinian, A Wife for a Month.* Chastity is a minor theme in *The Double Marriage, The Honest Man's Fortune, The Woman Hater,* and *Women Pleased. A King and No King, The Maid's Tragedy, Philaster,* and *The Queen of Corinth* are somewhat anomalous, but have some claim to be considered as chastity plays.[10] Precisely these plays, making up almost half the Beaumont and Fletcher canon, have earned Fletcher his reputation as an immoralist.

---

10. These plays, here listed alphabetically by groups, are listed chronologically in Appendix A, which gives additional information about their authorship and auspices and also indicates the location in this essay of the extended discussion of each play.

These plays are alike in that they deal centrally or peripherally with the trials of chastity. These trials are introduced to elicit a lengthy set speech in defense of chastity, as, for example, Dorigen's speech to Martius. It is this set defense of feminine honor that is the single most prominent characteristic of the Fletcherian chastity play. A number of stock plot situations are used to elicit such speeches. Actual threats to honor are a summons to court and attempts at seduction, rape, and sometimes incest. Situations that cast suspicion upon the chastity of the heroine, and therefore demand a statement of principle from her, are jealousy, slander, pretended wantonness, and the impotence of her husband. Misogyny may be used for the same purpose, or may be part of the sordid milieu that enhances, by contrast, the virtue of the heroine. There is a natural tendency to employ the more extreme of these devices because they provide a greater contrast to the virtue they threaten. This list coincides exactly with the list of "sensational" and "objectionable" situations that critics have attacked.

Any of these stock situations may be used in a convention that seems the oddest of all to post-Jacobean critics, the chastity test. In a test of chastity, as distinguished from a trial of chastity, a character will simulate one of the real dangers to honor, that is, he may pretend to rape or seduce the heroine, merely in order to test her virtue. The tester's purpose is to allow the lady to prove her innocence; a chastity test, then, is the action of a good man.

A fully developed example of a chastity test appears in the earliest Beaumont and Fletcher play, *The Woman Hater* (1606).[11] This comedy was apparently written originally by Beaumont, but both Cyrus Hoy and the play's most recent editor see Fletcher's hand (as either reviser or collaborator) in the scenes that present the chastity test.[12] The part of the plot that concerns us shows the misadventures of the high-spirited Oriana, secretly beloved by the Duke of Milan, when she runs afoul of Gondarino, a famous misogynist. Oriana is

---

11. Ed. George Walton Williams, *Dramatic Works*, vol. 1.
12. Cyrus Hoy, "The Shares of Fletcher and his Collaborators (III)," *SB* 11 (1958):98. Hoy concludes that before the play was printed Fletcher revised five scenes—III.i; IV.ii-iii; and V.ii,v. G. W. Williams, *Dramatic Works*, 1:151, finds Fletcher's work also in III.iii and V.i.

so amused at Gondarino's extravagant misogyny that she pretends to be in love with him in order to provoke him. Gondarino is so outraged that he decides to revenge himself horribly on Oriana as a warning to her entire sex. In pursuance of this plan, he slanders her chastity to the Duke.

Gondarino is forced to a more dastardly plot when the lovesick Duke echoes Othello's "Be sure thou provest my love a whore." The Duke warns the slanderer, "Looke it/ Be true you tell mee, or by our countries Saint/ Your head goes off" (III.i.204–6). In order to manufacture the necessary ocular proof, Gondarino confesses his villainy to Oriana and, pretending remorse, persuades her to retire, for her "honors safetie," to a private house of his, until he can undo his slander. Actually he lodges her in a bawdy house. (The motif of the virgin in a brothel, a theme as ancient as New Comedy, was receiving a rather full treatment about this time in Shakespeare's *Pericles*.) Gondarino now fetches the Duke and points out Oriana sitting at the window of the brothel. He is not convinced that this makes her a prostitute, and his examination of Gondarino's servants confirms his suspicion that Oriana was brought to the house against her will. Gondarino remains vehement in his accusations, and demands the ultimate examination:

> . . . if you hope to trie her truly, and satisfie your selfe what frailtie is, give her the Test: . . . put her too'it without hope or pittie. . . .
>
> (V.ii.49–52)

So much suspicion has been cast upon Oriana's honor that she can be cleared only by a test of her chastity.

The courtier Arrigo puts Oriana to "the Test," while the Duke and Gondarino watch from above. Arrigo announces to Oriana that the Duke has condemned her to death because of Gondarino's accusations that she is unchaste. In the courtier's admonitions to her, Beaumont again draws on *Othello*, this time from Desdemona's death scene:

> Lady, your praiers may doe your soule some good,

> That sure your body cannot merit by 'um:
> You must prepare to die.
>
> (V.iv.15–17)[13]

Oriana's defense of her chastity is succinct (later heroines greatly amplify her brief lines):

> Tell him the child, this present houre brought forth
> To see the world, ha's not a soule more pure,
> More white, more virgin then I have.
>
> (V.iv.32–34)

Arrigo then offers to save her if she will lie with him. She is still firm:

> Before I would win life, with the deare losse
> Of honour, I dare finde meanes to free my self.
>
> (V.iv.57–58)

She remains firm when Arrigo threatens to enjoy her "though it be betweene the parting of thy soule and body." "Ile guard the one, let heavens guard the tother" (V.iv.69–71) is her final resolution. At this moment the Duke stops the test from above. Arrigo's language emphasizes that the test has been a formalized piece of playacting:

> Lady, the scene of blood is done;
> Ye are now as free from scandal, as from death.
>
> (V.iv.75–76)

Oriana's honor is clear and her reward is marriage to the Duke.

Beaumont here uses the chastity test, already a familiar convention of stage and story, in a very unobjectionable way. The "Test" is very clearly announced and circumscribed, and I have not seen any objections to this play on the grounds of its use of this subject. It is when

---

13. Cf. *Othello,* V.ii.26–33. All citations of Shakespeare refer to the *Complete Works,* ed. Hardin Craig (Chicago, 1951). I should not be surprised if Beaumont and Fletcher, in the vindication of Oriana, intended a spoof on Othello's failure to allow Desdemona a chance to prove her innocence. There are enough verbal echoes of the earlier play to suggest this, and Beaumont throughout *The Woman Hater* has the fun of a young man laughing at what he obviously considers the excesses of an older, established playwright.

this convention is used as a bit of dramatic shorthand, when the audience is expected to recognize a seduction speech as a test without elaborate announcement, that critical confusion arises.

This occurs in *The Honest Man's Fortune* (1613), a collaboration by Fletcher, Field, and Massinger.[14] Here the trials of chastity provide a very minor part of the action. The play as a whole deals with the exemplary virtue and patience of Lord Montague when he loses all his worldly possessions in a spiteful and unjust lawsuit by the Duke of Orleans. Orleans, like Shakespeare's Leontes, is motivated by an unfounded jealousy of his devoted wife. He has persuaded himself that Montague, who loved the Lady of Orleans before her marriage, has cuckolded him. Now that he has ruined Montague, he intends to divorce his wife. When her brother Amiens draws his sword to defend her innocence, the Lady, in a surprising reversal, amazes her husband and brother by confessing to adultery. The lie is successful in its intention, to stop the duel, but the enraged Orleans sneers at this explanation, refusing to trust a woman who "prefers any defence/ Before the safety of her honor" (p. 217). Cast out into the street, the Lady sees Amiens dueling over her honor with Montague. She stops this fight with assertions of her honesty. Amiens, too, reviles his sister for her virtuously intended lie, and he also leaves her to the streets. Abandoned by husband and brother to probable starvation, the unfortunate Lady now faces a climactic trial: Montague, whom she once loved and still admires, begins to woo her lustfully.

The Jacobean audience would immediately have recognized this as a chastity test. Instead of berating her with threats and suspicions, Montague, being a virtuous man, allows the Lady to vindicate herself. Though Montague does not warn the audience in advance of his intentions, they have other indications of his purpose. Most important, the hero has been strongly delineated for over half an act as nearly perfect in virtue, not the sort of man to turn adulterer.

---

14. Glover and Waller, vol. 10. (There are no scene divisions; citations in the text refer to page numbers.) A slightly different version is edited by J. Gerritsen (Groningen, Djarkarta, 1952). His substantive text is MS Dyce 9, the promptbook prepared in 1625 to replace an earlier, lost promptbook.

Second, in an earlier meditation on chastity, he has exclaimed:

> What an honest work it would be; when we find
> A Virgin in her poverty, and youth
> Inclining to be tempted, to imploy
> As much perswasion, and as much expence
> To keep her upright, as men use to do upon her falling.
>
> (p. 209)

He has thus already been characterized as a protector of feminine honor. Further, he has just been seen defending with his sword this particular lady's honor. Because of these incidents, the audience is assured of Montague's virtue and perceives that he is making trial of the Lady with his lascivious talk.

She meets the test successfully, asserting her resolve to be chaste in spite of her helpless poverty:

> Lady.   How
> You think me altered, that you promise your
> Attempt success I know not; but were all
> The sweet temptations that deceive us set
> On this side, and on that side all the [wantes][15]
> These neither should persuade me, nor these force.
> Mont.   Then misery may waste your body.
> Lady.   Yes, but lust shall never.
>
> (pp. 219–220)

The Lady's virtue would be seen by the audience as very great indeed. Oriana was faced with either death or dishonor, and, for a romantic heroine, the choice is a simple one. The Lady of Orleans remains loyal to the husband who has cruelly abandoned her, even when she is faced with a temptation from a man she once loved. Montague's fervent praise of her continence and fidelity is clearly the direction of the audience's feelings:

> I have found you still as uncorupted as I left you first.
> Continue so; and I will serve you with
> As much devotion as my word, my hand

---

15. I have adopted the reading "wantes" from Gerritsen's edition in place of the Ff "waiters."

Or purse can show you. . . .

(p. 220)

Whereupon, he relieves her poverty until she later reclaims her husband by her Griselda-like devotion, assuming that he but makes "passionate triall" of her "suspected patience" (p. 236).

In this play, the test serves two obvious purposes. It clears Montague as well as the Lady from Orleans' base suspicions. It helps to characterize Montague as an "honest man" in that he allows a suspected lady to clear herself and then relieves her poverty; this places him in sharper contrast to his enemy, Orleans. But A. W. Ward puts a very different construction upon Montague's behavior in this scene:

> Montague "the honest man" may preserve a dignified and cheerful demeanor under misfortune; but his virtue has its seamy side . . . he had at an earlier stage of his career sought to console himself by sin for misfortune.[16]

Ward may be confused not only because Montague does not announce a test, but also because the climate of Beaumont and Fletcher criticism makes critics eager to find corroborating evidence of Fletcher's immorality.[17] It is doubtful that a Jacobean would have made this mistake.

---

16. *A History of English Dramatic Literature to the Death of Queen Anne,* 2d. ed. (London, 1899), 2: 688.

17. There is do doubt that the climate of Beaumont and Fletcher criticism causes even the soundest scholars to misread the text. To take another example from this same play, Harbage, p. 214, cites Laverdine, a character in the subplot, as an example of an overt homosexual, a character type he finds common in the coterie drama: "Laverdine pursues with overt intentions the page Veramour until the latter proves to be a woman." This is precisely the opposite of what actually occurs in the play. Laverdine, struck with the exemplary fidelity that Veramour displays toward his master, concludes that the page must be a lovelorn girl disguised in order to be near the object of her affections. Laverdine pursues Veramour under the impression that the page is a girl and immediately gives up his suit when Veramour proves that he is indeed a boy. What homosexual joking there is in this episode is intended to burlesque the stage convention of the girl page. This dramatic convention is specifically mentioned when Veramour proves himself to be a boy; with amusement he says, "I took example by two or three Plays, that methought/Concerned me" (p. 277).

When one begins to compare examples of this convention of the chastity test in the various plays of the canon, Fletcher's intentions become clear. Nevertheless, the perception of a convention as such may not make it the more palatable to the reader who wonders why a heroine must always be tested, why chastity must constantly be proved in action. The reason for this is not Fletcher's personal misogyny, nor his projection of the attitude of a social class, but the religious, social, and literary antecedents of the heroine of militant chastity. I shall explore these antecedents in the next three chapters.

3

Religious and Social Attitudes
toward Chastity

The Reformation glorified marriage at the expense of celibacy, with
the result that the earlier idealization of virginity was displaced by
the idealization of chastity—constancy, physical and emotional—of
husband and wife.[1] Virginity was still valued, but as a state preserved
for the prospective husband rather than as a gift consecrated to
Christ.

The causes of this change in attitude are complex and have been
studied elsewhere. C. S. Lewis, for example, sees the new feeling for
marriage as a reconciliation of the ascetic demands of the medieval
church and the romantic aspirations of medieval courtly love.[2] Another factor was the rise of capitalistic economic organization and
the consequently heavier emphasis on the family as an economic
unit,[3] and still another, the humanist ideals of education for women,
which were producing a new woman fit for fuller companionship
with man.[4]

---

1. Chilton Latham Powell, *English Domestic Relations 1487–1653* (New
York, 1917).

2. *The Allegory of Love* (Oxford, 1936). Lewis's thesis is amplified by
Francis Lee Utley, *The Crooked Rib* (Columbus, 1944).

3. Louis B. Wright, *Middle-Class Culture in Elizabethan England* (Ithaca,
1935), chap. 5 and passim; Alice Clark, *Working Life of Women in the
Seventeenth Century* (London, 1919).

4. Carroll Camden, *The Elizabethan Woman* (Houston, 1952), chap. 2.

Furthermore, marriage was seen to be more important when the Renaissance turned from medieval otherworldliness and began to look at the condition of man in this world. The Renaissance man looked at the world through medieval spectacles (as numerous recent historical and literary studies have made abundantly clear), but he did look at the world, as well as at the heavenly city. This vision can be seen very clearly in Erasmus's *Encomium Matrimonii,* translated by Richard Tavernour (London, 1536). Erasmus praises marriage as an institution introduced by God in paradise because of man's need for companionship. Marriage satisfies the social as well as the sexual desires that God has given man. Erasmus is writing to urge a friend to forsake his vow of bachelorhood and create posterity, and he anticipates his reader's religious scruples by reminding him that men are not gods:

> But virgynite (ye wyll say) is a dyvyne thynge, an angelycall thyng. Trewthe it is, but, on the contrarysyde, wedlocke is an humane thynge. I nowe speke to a man beynge my selfe a man. (sigs. C2ᵛ–C3ʳ)

Christ was a virgin, of course, but Christ was a god and did many things for men to wonder at rather than imitate.

Whatever the precise causes of the new idealization of marriage, the determination of Protestants to promulgate this ideal is remarkable.[5] Nothing is more striking than their elevation of the misogynistic St. Paul, who introduced asceticism into the Christian church,[6] as

On the general subject of changing attitudes toward marriage, see Lawrence Stone, *The Crisis of the Aristocracy 1558–1641* (Oxford, 1965). In his chapter on "Marriage and the Family" Stone makes the important point that the new ideals of marriage, originally middle-class and puritan in origin, had to a large extent permeated the thinking of the aristocracy. The idea that the Jacobean upper classes were much more lax in their sexual and marital habits than were the bourgeoisie is largely a result of the greater publicity given to the private lives of the nobility. The supposition of the laxness of the upper classes has been reinforced by Harbage's *Shakespeare and the Rival Traditions.* However, Harbage collects some useful information about Elizabethan attitudes in his chapters on "Sexual Behavior" and "Wedded Love."

5. See William and Malleville Haller, "The Puritan Art of Love," *The Huntington Library Quarterly* 5 (1941–42):235–72.

6. Katherine M. Rogers, *The Troublesome Helpmate* (Seattle, Wash., 1966), pp. 7ff.

the patron saint of matrimony. Everywhere one finds quoted the apostle's statement that marriage is an honorable state among men (Hebrews 13:4), a statement incorporated into the Anglican marriage ceremony.[7] Protestant divines seldom mention that Paul also said, "It were good for a man not to touch a woman (I Corinthians 7:1).[8] Equally interesting is the change in the emphasis read into Paul's comment that celibacy is a gift of God (I Corinthians 7:7). The marginal gloss in the 1560 Geneva Bible (the edition most familiar to the average Elizabethan) points out that the "gift of continencie" comes by "a peculiar grace of God" to only a few; marriage is necessary for those men who do not have this gift.

Queen Elizabeth, of course, was looked upon as one of the gifted in the Pauline sense. As Virgin Queen, she seems during the transition of the English Church from Catholicism to Protestantism to have taken the place in popular affection of the Virgin Mother. Elizabeth, however, was also the "Queen of Chastity," who was faithful to her wedded spouse, England, and who kept a stern (if not always disinterested) eye on the morals of her courtiers and attendants.[9] However the Elizabethans idolized their virgin queen, they nonetheless believed that the duty of the generality of mankind was to marry. Marriage was the most honorable institution, for it alone of human laws and institutions was established directly by God himself, in paradise, rather than through his usual intermediaries, prophets and princes.[10]

---

7. Powell, pp. 20–21, discusses the origin of the modern marriage ceremony.

8. This pronouncement is very carefully glossed in the marginal notes of the Geneva Bible (1560). The reader is instructed to interpret "good" as "expedient," for "mariage bringeth many griefes with it, and that by reason of the corruption of our first estate." Thus is the sting taken out of St. Paul's preaching.

9. See E. C. Wilson, *England's Eliza* (Cambridge, Mass., 1939), p. 134, for a discussion of the use of poetic imagery suggesting an identification between Elizabeth and Mary. Pp. 4–6 and 124–35 discuss the conception that Elizabeth was married to her kingdom; chap. 5 deals with the idealization of Elizabeth under the figure of Diana. See also Utley, p. 84.

10. As clearly stated in the Anglican marriage ceremony. Amplified and explained in "A Preparative to Marriage" by the popular preacher Henry Smith, *The Works of Henry Smith,* ed. Thomas Fuller, 2 vols. (Edinburgh, 1866), 1:5ff.

From the point of view of this study, the most important aspect of the growing emphasis on marriage was the correspondingly greater emphasis on chastity, particularly as a virtue proper to woman. In theory, the sixteenth century did not acknowledge the acceptability of a double standard of sexual morality, but it did place a higher value on the chastity of the woman than on that of the man. This emphasis was partly due to physiology, the hymen being a special sort of possession; as Marlowe writes, "Jewels being lost are found againe, this never,/ T'is lost but once, and once lost, lost for ever" (*Hero and Leander,* ii.85–86). The emphasis on female chastity was also partly social and economic; the first duty of the wife was to protect the sanctity of the marriage bed and thus guarantee to her husband that his children were actually his own issue. Women supposedly needed special exhortation to chastity, because it was a commonplace that they have stronger passions and weaker wills than men.[11] Because of this universally acknowledged weakness of the feminine sex, a truly chaste woman was considered a jewel above price. The exaggerated praise of a chaste woman as a miracle, which seems to the modern reader to be based on an essentially misogynistic premise, was, for the Elizabethan, based on a premise taken to be a matter of fact. The Bible assured him that woman was the weaker vessel. And so the sixteenth-century woman was continually exhorted to be chaste by a host of didactic writers in treatises on marriage, courtesy books, devotional works, pamphlets in praise of women, sermons, and, at the turn of the century, Theophrastian characters. The bulk of this literature is so repetitious that a few examples will illustrate the temper and tendency of the whole.[12]

Edmund Tilney's *A brief and pleasant discourse of duties in Mariage, called the Flower of Friendshippe* (London, 1568) is one of the most agreeable of the treatises on marriage.[13] Tilney creates a frame for his discussion: a company of ladies and gentlemen gath-

---

11. Powell, pp. 148–49, discusses this traditional view.
12. It was repetitious, of course, because it was all based on the teachings of the Bible and of the church fathers.
13. For a thorough survey of domestic conduct books, see Powell, chaps. 4–6. I have chosen to discuss Tilney's work because it has some literary merit and because of his long association with the drama as Master of Revels.

ered in an arbor eagerly embrace a proposal that they discuss marriage, "bicause no friendship, or amitie is, or ought to be more deere, and surer, than the love of man and wyfe" (sig. C3^r). The duties of a husband are enumerated by the first day's speaker, who declares that the worst crime a man can commit against his wife is adultery, but gambling and drinking to excess are equally likely to alienate her love. The duties of the wife, outlined by the second day's speaker, have only one end: The woman must "above all imbrace chastitie. For the happinesse of matrimonie, doth consist in a chaste matrone. . . ." (sig. D4^r). Chastity is "the chiefest dowrye, the greatest inheritaunce, and the [most] precious Jewell" that a woman can bring to her husband (sig. D7^v). The wife "must not onely be good, but likewise must apeere so" (sig. E2^v). Thus the greatest help to marriage is shamefastness, "the onely defence that nature hath given to women, to keepe their reputation, to preserve their chastitie, to mainteine their honor, and to advance their praise" (sig. D7^v). Lest the reader should miss the point, even after several pages to this effect, a marginal note instructs him, "The happinesse of mariage consisteth in a chast wife" (sig. D4^r).

Sermons and devotional literature drove home the same lesson. Thomas Bentley's *Monument of Matrons* (London, 1582), dedicated to Queen Elizabeth, is an example of a specialized devotional book, one compiled specifically for women. The title page explains its division into "seven several Lamps of Virginitie, or distinct treatises; whereof the first five concern praier and meditation: the other two last, precepts and examples . . . compiled . . . out of the sacred scriptures, and other approovd authors. . . ." Section five, or the Fifth Lamp of Virginitie, contains model prayers, remarkable for length and vehemency, asking God for the gifts of silence, shamefastness, and chastity. There are prayers for maidens, which beg for deliverance from vice lest the speaker "prove a member of the Divell, by following the works of the flesh, and losing that inestimable treasure of great price, mine honestie, chastitie, and virginitie" (V.3).[14] There are prayers for matrons, asking for strength "to live

---

14. Each section of Bentley's work is paged separately; citations in the text refer to section and page.

chastlie and purelie in holie matrimonie, and to avoid the filthie lusts of whoredome" (V.35). The most extraordinary is "A lamentation of anie woman, virgin, wife, or widowe, for hir virginitie or chastitie, lost by fornication or adulterie." The intensely emotional abasement of this thirteen-page prayer (V.13–26) is quite typical. If Bentley's repentant reader found herself in need of further expiation, she would also find, on succeeding pages, "Another on the same subject" (six pages in length), "A praier of Marie Magdalens repentance," and "Another praier of the woman taken in adulterie." Mary Magdalene's example showed that God could forgive unchastity (after extensive and rigorous spiritual mortification of the sinner), but *The Monument of Matrons* as a whole makes it clear that man and society expect chastity as a norm of conduct.

This is the lesson inculcated by Renaissance courtesy books and theoretical treatises on women. Ruth Kelso, after an exhaustive examination of the treatises on women written in Europe between 1400 and 1600, concludes that there was "no formulated ideal for the lady as such, distinguished either from the gentleman or from any other woman. . . . The lady . . . turns out to be merely a wife." Naturally enough, then, chastity is the moral quality most praised in her. Kelso goes on to observe that, although the maid is "warned on all sides" against unchastity, little practical advice is offered.[15]

Perhaps moralists thought they were filling this gap with the examples of good wives held up for emulation in pamphlets in praise of women.[16] The same exemplary ladies reappear in tract after tract as illustrations of woman's reason, fortitude, military prowess, ability to govern, constancy, and chastity. Sir Thomas Elyot's *Defence of Good Women* (1540) is very comprehensive in this respect. Among women distinguished as constant wives he cites Panthea, Portia, Paulina (wife of Seneca), and Ligarius's wife—because they all

---

15. *Doctrine for the Lady of the Renaissance* (Urbana, Ill., 1956). Quotations are from pp. 1, 51.
16. The genre is an old one, going back to Boccaccio. Utley gives an analytical index of such works in English before 1568. The genre continues well into the seventeenth century; for bibliography see C. S. Lewis, *English Literature in the Sixteenth Century* (Oxford, 1954).

committed or tried to commit suicide at their husbands' deaths. Oenone remained continent and constant to Paris after he abandoned her, and she died of grief when he was slain by Achilles. Penelope replaces Griselda as the *nonpareil* of wifeliness:

> Ought the unchastitie of any woman to be so remembered, as the continence of queene Penelope oughte to be honored, who in the absence of Ulixes her husbande, the space of .xx. yeres, kept her honour and fame uncorrupted, notwithstandinge that with many diverse wowers she was dayely assaulted, but by no maner of meane moughte she be founden, by dede word nor countenance in her chast purpose unconstant.[17]

With a sublime disregard for repetition, moralists and pamphleteers extolled the same ladies from one end of the sixteenth century to the other. In 1599 Nicholas Breton in "The Praise of Vertuous Ladies" inveighs against those who

> will say women are unconstant; but I say not all: for Penelope, and Cleopatra, Lucretia, with divers more too long to rehearse, shall stand for examples of such constancie, as no man (ever) more constant.[18]

Women who have been unchaste and unconstant (for this sublunary world is by no means perfect) merely serve as foils to the shining qualities of ladies who have been chaste.[19]

The result of this mass of teaching was that feminine "honor" and "honesty" came to be considered almost exclusively as sexual purity.[20] Furthermore, to be "honorable" a woman must "not onely be good, but likewise must apeere so," for her "good name is the flower of estimation, and the pearle of credit"[21] and is, of course,

---

17. Sir Thomas Elyot, *The Defence of Good Women,* ed. E. J. Howard (Oxford, Ohio, 1940), pp. 19–20.

18. *Works in Verse and Prose,* ed. A. B. Grosart, 2 vols. (Edinburgh, 1879), 2:58.

19. Elyot, pp. 24–25. The sentiment is frequently expressed; see, for example, Barnaby Rich, *The Excellency of Good Women* (London, 1613), sig. B2ʳ.

20. C. B. Watson, *Shakespeare and the Renaissance Concept of Honor* (Princeton, 1960), p. 159. Watson discusses, pp. 437ff, Shakespeare's use of this concept.

21. Tilney, sig. B2ᵛ.

inextricably linked with the good name of her husband. The reputation for chastity is as important as chastity itself, and a good name is like physical virginity: once lost, it is impossible to recover. "A woman that is once tainted in her honour, must be driven to a harde course of recovery, she must rubbe off the skinne to wipe out the spot."[22] A matron kept her good name through shamefastness or through a love of honor, which, as C. B. Watson points out, is merely the reverse side of the same coin.[23]

Chastity, then, is woman's only honor, and she is responsible for protecting that honor. This was the view of the ordinary Elizabethan, and it is precisely the view of woman that informs the Fletcherian chastity plays. It is apparent, however, that Fletcher presents a chaste heroine with an emphasis differing from that of an Elizabethan playwright of, say, the 1590s. One reason is due to the manner in which chastity was idealized. In order to glorify chastity, the sixteenth century also vilified lust. This intense vilification had the authority of the Church.

The central document for study of this topic is "A Sermon agaynst whoredome and uncleannesse" (called in the running title "A Sermon against Adultery"), which appeared in all editions of the official Anglican *Book of Homilies*.[24] The homilies were designed to be read regularly in church to supplement the preaching of the less learned clergy. As church attendance was required, as a test of recusancy,[25] each English churchgoer must have heard the *Book of Homilies* through many times. The influence of the homilies in the dissemination of official doctrine can hardly be overestimated. Certainly, the arguments and examples of the sermon against adultery were used by every writer on the subject and even reappeared unchanged in

---

22. Rich, sigs. C3r–C3v.
23. Watson, p. 159.
24. Citations in the text refer to the edition of 1576. The "Sermon Against Adultery" was included in Tome 1 of the *Homilies*, which was first published in 1547. Tome 2 (1563) added "Of Matrimony"; this later homily is primarily taken up with advice about household management.
25. J. Gairdner, *The English Church in the Sixteenth Century* (London, 1902) and W. H. Frere, *The English Church in the Reigns of Elizabeth and James I* (London, 1904).

fiction and verse. Because of its position as a *summa* of lechery, this homily must be examined in detail.

The sermon begins with the announcement that whoredom is the chief sin of contemporary life:

> above other vices, the outragious seas of adultery (or breaking of wedlock), whoredome, fornication and uncleannesse, have not onely brast in, but also overflowed almost the whole world . . . so abundantly, that through the customable use thereof, this vice is growen into suche an height, that in a maner among many, it is counted no synne at all, but rather a pastime, a dalliaunce, and but a touch of youth. (sig. K7^r)

Therefore it is necessary to declare "howe odious, hateful, and abominable it is, and hath alway ben reputed before GOD and all good men . . ." (sig. K7^r). Christ confirmed the seventh commandment and forbade even lustful thoughts. Lustful sins corrupt

> both the body and soule of man, and make them, of the temples of the holy ghost, the fylthy dunghyl, or dungeon of all uncleane spirites, of the house of God, the dwellyng place of Satan. (sig. L1^r)

John the Baptist, aware of the enormity of this sin, rebuked Herod for committing adultery. If adultery were a merely venial pastime, "truely John had ben more then twyse madde, if he woulde have had the displeasure of a kyng, yf he woulde have been cast in prison, and lost his head for a trifle" (sigs. L1^v–L2^r).

Part II of the sermon depicts whoredom as a "most fylthie lake, foule puddle, and stynkyng synke, whereunto all kyndes of synnes and evylies flowe" (sig. L4^r). Whoredom, in effect, is the *radix malorum*:

> For hath not the adulterer a pryde in his whoredome? . . . Is not the adulterer also idle, and delighteth in no godly exercise, but onely in that his most fylthie and beastly pleasure. . . . Doeth not the whoremonger geve his mynde to gluttonie, that he may be the more apt to serve his lustes and carnall pleasures? Doeth not the adulterer geve his mynde to covetousnesse . . . that he may be

the more able to maynteyne his harlottes. . . . Swelleth he not also with envie agaynst other, fearyng that his pray shoulde be allured and taken away from hym? Agayne, is he not ireful, and replenished with wrath and displeasure, even agaynst his best be-loved, if at any time his beastly and devylish request be letted? What sinne, or kynde of sinne is it that is not joyned with forni-cation and whoredom? It is a monster of many heades. . . . If one several sinne bringeth damnation, what is to be thought of that sinne whiche is accompanied with all evyle, and hath wayting on it whatsoever is hateful to God, damnable to man, and pleasant to Satan? (sigs. L4ʳ–L4ᵛ)

Lechery, then, leads to all the other deadly sins; it also leads to worldly misery. Through whoredom man and woman lose their good name, their patrimony and substance, their health, strength, wits, beauty, and youth. Whoredom is the cause of syphilis ("the french pockes, with other divers diseases"), bastards, manslaughter, divorce.

In Part III the homilist launches into an exposition of the acts of God and the laws of men against adultery. God destroyed Sodom and Gomorrah for their "uncleannesse" and smote Pharaoh and his house with plagues because he defiled Abraham's wife, Sara. God sent the Flood "to shewe howe greatly he abhorreth adultery, whore-dome, fornication and al uncleannes":

Manslaughter was committed before, yet was not the worlde de-stroyed for that: but for whoredome, all the worlde (fewe only except) was overflowed with waters, and so perished. (sig. L6ᵛ)

Pagans, who have been without this evidence of God's judgments, have nevertheless, guided only by the law of nature, seen fit to inflict grievous punishments for adultery. The Lepreians punished adultery with public carting; the Locrensians, with blinding. Adultery was a capital crime among the Romans, Egyptians, Arabians, Athenians, "Tartarians," and Turks. Certainly Christians should be shamed by these examples. There are, however, remedies for this sin and means of avoiding it; the chief of these remedies is, of course, a chaste marriage.

The "Sermon Against Adultery" is by no means extreme, for the period, in its condemnation of lechery; it is only exceptionally comprehensive. The elevation of lechery to such a prominent place among the Seven Deadly Sins is ubiquitous in the latter half of the sixteenth century. In contrast, in the Middle Ages lechery ran a poor and rather venial seventh in the lists of deadly sins. In Elizabethan catalogues it is usually found listed in the second or third place after pride. Typical is the enumeration of deadly sins in Arthur Dent's *The Plaine Mans Path-way to Heaven* (1601), an influential devotional treatise: "Of the signs of damnation there are nine: Pride, Whoredom, Covetousness, Contempt of the Gospel, Swearing, Lying, Drunkeness, Idleness, and Oppression."[26] This list has a definitely middle-class bias, but all classes tended to put lechery high on the list of deadly sins. The concept of lechery as the root of all evil was also standard during the period. Fletcher's lecherous villains, so often taken as grotesque and prurient caricatures, are only rather literal exempla of current theory. His audiences assumed with the Homilies that a lecherous man would also be proud, envious, wrathful, avaricious, slothful, and gluttonous.[27] The extreme opposition of chastity and lechery in Elizabethan theory was an outgrowth, then, of the vigorous idealization of marriage. The opposition of extremes of lust and chastity, it is universally agreed, is the fundamental mechanism of many of Fletcher's plays.

Before Fletcher began to write, however, a change in temper and emphasis is perceptible in theorizing about women and marriage as the English Renaissance shifts from the Elizabethan to the Jacobean mood. The change stems partly from the increasing divergence between real life and the rigid, ascetic rules laid down for wives by the theoreticians. In theory, the chaste and obedient wife stayed

---

26. Quoted by Wright, pp. 253–54. The tract went through twenty-five editions by 1640.

27. The reverse is also assumed to be true. It is common in the drama to find a proud, gluttonous, or avaricious character who is given the added failing of lechery, even when his lechery may not materially affect events in the play. See, for example, the discussion of *The Loyal Subject* below, chap. 9. Similarly, stage tyrants are almost invariably addicted to lechery. The original formulation of the definition of a tyrant was that he substituted "lust for law." Originally the phrase denoted the substitution of self-will for considerations of the general good of the commonwealth. Gradually, however, "lust" in this context comes to be interpreted so that it indicates, sometimes exclusively, sexual lust.

within her home to protect her fame and honor and to manage her family's domestic affairs. The actual Elizabethan matron, to the uneasiness of the average Elizabethan male and the outrage of Puritan zealots, was quite a different creature, so different, indeed, that a continental proverb described England as "a paradise for women."[28] Married women, to the surprise of foreign visitors, went abroad as they chose and without chaperones. They chose their own company and pastimes, painted their faces, and wore clothes as elaborate as they could afford, sometimes even adopting masculine fashions.[29] Indeed, the many social, religious, economic, and political upheavals of Elizabethan England were having a revolutionary effect on the status of women in all classes of society.

Learned ladies of the aristocracy—Lady Jane Grey, the Countess of Pembroke, the Countess of Westmoreland, the three daughters of Sir Antony Coke, Elizabeth herself—are often cited as examples of the new woman of this period. More important, however, than the fashionable Latin and Greek learning of the upper-class lady was the general literacy of large numbers of women. Little girls frequently attended the elementary schools and, in some cases at least, were admitted to the grammar schools; there seems to have been at least one boarding school in London for young girls.[30] Women were not only literate but formed a large enough part of the book-buying public to make it worthwhile for writers and printers to cater to their tastes.[31]

Women of any class could view with pride a throne occupied by a female prince. The competence and stature of Elizabeth as a ruler did much to elevate and dignify the position of women in society.[32] Elizabeth was not the first female head of state, however. In the middle of the century, the rule of Mary Tudor in England and the regency of Mary of Guise in Scotland and of Catherine de

---

28. Violet A. Wilson, *Society Women of Shakespeare's Time* (London, 1924), p. 1. Wilson gives a number of thumbnail biographies of well-known Elizabethan women.

29. Powell, pp. 174–76; Wright, pp. 466ff.

30. Camden, pp. 47–48.

31. Wright, pp. 103–14; Utley, p. 84.

32. Camden, p. 56; Wallace Notestein, "The English Woman, 1580–1650," in *Studies in Social History*, ed. J. H. Plumb (London, 1955), p. 102.

Medici in France flew in the face of St. Paul's teaching in 1 Timothy 2:12 that women should not hold positions of authority over men.[33] John Knox was so provoked that he wrote *The first Blast of the Trumpet against the Monstrous Regiment of Women* (1558). Amusingly enough, Knox had to recant when, in the very year of the publication of his pamphlet, Elizabeth became the protector of Protestantism in Europe.[34]

This Protestantism, incidentally, changed the status of women as much by its emphasis on individual conversion as it did by its emphasis on the dignity of marriage. Since women had been grudgingly admitted by the early Church Fathers to have souls, their souls were as susceptible to individual calls from God as were the souls of men. It was not inconceivable that a wife might have a call or conversion which preceded or differed from that of her husband.

> Wives were commanded to obey their husbands, but, like all subjects of higher powers, they were commanded first to obey God. . . . But, since God communicated by his word and through conscience as freely with wives as with husbands, such an admission was the camel's head of liberty within the tent of masculine supremacy.[35]

More extreme Protestants, the separatist sects—Brownists, Baptists, Independents, Millenarians, Familists, Seekers, Ranters, and above all the Quakers—not only laid great emphasis upon the spiritual equality of the sexes but also admitted women to an equal share in church government. "The orthodox arguments and texts for woman's exclusion from church office had been identical with those for her subordination in general. It was impossible now to attack the one without weakening the other."[36]

Economic factors also caused a widening gap between the ideal woman of theory and the real woman of Elizabethan life. Women of the upper mercantile classes were apparently the most emanci-

---

33. Powell, pp. 171–72.
34. Rogers, pp. 135–37.
35. Hallers, p. 252.
36. K. V. Thomas, "Women and the Civil War Sects," *Past and Present,* no. 13 (April 1958), p. 57.

pated.[37] They assisted their husbands in their shops, and usually the wife, rather than the son, inherited and ran the family business. Guild membership was open to women in certain cases.[38] The rise of capitalism, which was responsible for a heavier emphasis on the family as an agency for the accumulation and preservation of capital, at the same time caused disturbing changes in the family at the upper levels of society. The accumulation of wealth meant, in many cases, a growing idleness among rich aristocrats and "city madams" as household supervision was turned over to hired servants.[39] This resulted not only in the decline of "housekeeping," a decline much lamented in Elizabethan literature, but also in the growth of a "society" of the wealthy,[40] detached from the duties of their country estates and clustering in London, in spite of royal edicts to the contrary. Court ladies, detached from their traditional vocation in the home, frequently became targets of satire and abuse.

These court ladies were not assisted in a reorientation of values by the example of the childish new queen, Anne of Denmark, or by the nouveau riche court of James I. James himself was extremely ambivalent in his feelings toward women, lecturing them on properly chaste behavior while at the same time cultivating equivocal and intense attachments to male favorites.[41] Elizabeth had insisted, not always successfully, on rigid standards of behavior for her maids of honor; the Jacobean court created an unhealthy atmosphere for women. A familiar illustration is the often quoted description of the entertainment at Theobald's for the visit in 1606 of King Christian of Denmark. The court ladies portraying Faith, Hope, and Charity in a masque before the king were so drunk that they ended the evening sick and "spewing in the lower hall." Not without cause did Sir John Harington moralize on the occasion:

Such things greatly astonish those courtiers who knew the good

---

37. Notestein, p. 97.
38. Clark, p. 196 and passim; Wright, p. 204.
39. Clark, p. 41.
40. Notestein, p. 104.
41. D. H. Willson, *King James VI and I* (New York, 1956), passim.

order, sobriety and discretion of the old Queen's time, so that in secret they say that the Danes have again conquered England, such is the beastliness, riot and excess at Court.[42]

The year before, in 1605, the appearance of the queen and her ladies in the *Masque of Blackness* had elicited similar disapproval from spectators: "Their apparel was rich but, some said, too light and courtesan-like for such great ones."[43] Thus the rich and idle ladies of the aristocracy are censured and, in satiric literature, the court lady becomes almost synonymous with the whore.[44]

This view seemed to be confirmed by the various scandals that rocked the Jacobean court. Not the least dramatic was the divorce in 1605 of Penelope Devereux from her husband, Lord Rich, and her immediate remarriage, Lord Rich still living, with her lover, the Earl of Devonshire. While she was still Lady Rich, Penelope Devereux had borne five children to the Earl.[45] The great scandal of James's reign, however, was the trumped-up divorce of Frances Howard, Countess of Essex, and the subsequent disclosure of her complicity in the poisoning of her lover's disapproving friend, Sir Thomas Overbury. The king himself took a rather unadmirable role in the quasi-legal divorce proceedings, as he wished the countess to be free to marry his favorite, Robert Carr.[46] The Countess of Essex represents, of course, an extreme of behavior. Nonetheless, her notorious life was taken as an object lesson by a generation that idealized the retiring, dependent woman but, to its distress, could not ignore the many factors working in society for the greater personal freedom of all women and the debauchery of some. It is small wonder that the age-old controversy over the nature of woman, a controversy that had been relatively undistinguished and quiescent in the six-

---

42. Quoted by G. B. Harrison, *A Jacobean Journal* (London, 1941), p. 325. This opinion is the more interesting in that it comes from Harington, translator of Ariosto and author of the robust *Metamorphosis of Ajax*.
43. *Ibid.,* p. 181.
44. Rogers, chap. 3. Brustein, p. 155, points out that "in the satiric view court ladies were considered the worst female offenders of the day."
45. Harrison, pp. 251–57.
46. Willson, pp. 336ff.

teenth century, took on a new acrimoniousness in the Jacobean period.[47]

A sense of unease and disillusionment concerning women makes itself felt about the turn of the century. Eudo C. Mason has written about what he calls the "sex nausea" that appears shortly before 1600 in Shakespeare's tragic plays and in Jacobean tragedy generally. Mason attributes this to a "reaction after excess," presumably referring to the platonic idealization of love in the sixteenth century.[48] There are surely other factors. The intense idealization of marriage is one; another, the increasingly felt discrepancy between the ideal woman of theory and the actual woman of Elizabethan and, more, of Jacobean life. Another would be the logical (but unforeseen) consequences of that religious and social theory which made such a fearsome monster of the sin of lechery.

The denunciation of lechery and its elevation to the *radix malorum* were doubtless a result partly of the increasing moral earnestness of the Reformation. The voluminous number of tracts addressed to an audience of women suggests, however, that much of this vituperation was intended to frighten female readers and auditors into compliance with a patriarchal family structure. Apparently, however, all this propaganda had an unexpected effect on masculine attitudes. By painting lechery in such lurid colors in order to admonish the weakness of women, men had created a picture of a temptation that seemed far too strong for naturally weak women to withstand. The lecturers were trapped by these circular implications of their initial premises; lectures designed to frighten women began to frighten men. One of the few who ridiculed the logical absurdity to which

---

47. Wright, p. 481. There had been, during the Elizabethan period, a general softening of satiric attacks on women. John Peter, *Complaint and Satire in Early English Literature* (Oxford, 1956), p. 114, notes "a strong tendency, during the latter half of the sixteenth century and the first decade of the seventeenth, to review their position, so long accepted, of moral inferiority to men." Utley, p. ix, observes that "after the second third of the century of Elizabeth it is unusual for any artist of the stature of Chaucer or Dunbar to devote himself to the *querelle des femmes* in anything more than an epigram or digression."

48. "Satire on Women and Sex in Elizabethan Tragedy," *English Studies* 30 (1950):1-3.

the narrowing definition of feminine honor had led was Barnaby Rich. In *The Honestie of This Age* (1614) he wrote:

> In former ages there were many imperfections attributed to women that are now accounted no defects at all, neyther are they thought to bee any scandals to their reputations. . . . Is shee not to be charged with the abuse of her bodie, it is well, shee is honest, what care we for the deformities of the minde.
> Will you see now a womans honestie is pent up in a little roome, it is still confined but from her girdle downewards.
> Is not this a happie age for women. Menne have manie faults whereby to taynt their credites; there is no imprefection in a woman but that of her bodie, and who is able to prove that.[49]

This disgruntled ridicule was not, however, characteristic of the general response to the new mores.

Much more typical is an increasing earnestness and anxiety over female chastity. Illustrative is Sir Thomas Overbury's enormously popular character of *A Wife* (London, 1614). As his title indicates, Overbury's ostensible purpose in this verse character is a description of a good wife. Overbury's poem, however, is markedly different from the earlier speculations on the married state by such writers as Erasmus and Tilney, for whom marriage is the flower of friendship. Overbury's work shows the anxiety of a society that has made a bogey out of lust; his poem does not describe a companion but offers advice to men on keeping a wife chaste. *A Wife* begins conventionally enough with praise of marriage, but the nature of the praise has changed. Marriage is not described as a higher form of friendship but as a "medicine" for lust (sig. B2^r), for within marriage "the very act is Chastity" (sig. B1^v). Lust, rather than a solitary life, is the opposite of marriage (sig. B2^r). With marriage equated to chastity and predicated as the opposite of lust, the qualities demanded in a good wife are consequently much narrowed. Tilney had required chastity as the *sine qua non* in a wife, but had also discussed the necessity for obedience, household skills, and a pleasant disposi-

---

49. Ed. Peter Cunningham, Percy Society Reprints 11 (London, 1844): 15–16.

tion. For Overbury, chastity alone makes a good wife. Consequently, a man must choose a wife for her virtue, knowledge, and discretion.

Each of these qualities, moreover, has a specific application. For example, virtue, "that active gentry" (sig. B2ᵛ), is more important than high birth, because goodness keeps a wife chaste:

> By Good I would have Holy understood,
> So God Shee cannot love, but also mee
> The law requires our words and deeds be good,
> Religion even the Thoughts doth sanctifie:
>   And she is more a Maide which ravish't is,
>   Then She which onely doth but wish amisse.
>   (sig. B3ᵛ)

"Lust onely by Religion is withstood" (sig. B3ᵛ). Similarly, knowledge, while it gives woman greater scope of conversation, is chiefly requisite because it will "her inborne vertue fortifie./ They are most firmly good, that best know why" (sig. B4ʳ). Discretion is equally necessary because good name is as important as good life and because the husband's good name is dependent upon his wife's:

> To keepe their Name when 'tis in others hands
> Discretion askes, their Credit is by farre
> More fraile then They, on likely-hoods it stands,
> And hard to be desprov'd Lust's slanders are.
>   Their Carriage, not their Chastity alone,
>   Must keepe their Name chaste from suspition.
>   (sig. B4ᵛ)

Overbury's poem implies an audience exclusively male; the work is actually a marriage treatise, but the subject is no longer reciprocal conjugal duty but women in general, who have become an inexplicable "They" who control masculine honor. Anxiety over the natural frailty of "Them" permeates the poem to such an extent that it becomes an uneasy meditation on lust and chastity. The anxiety is produced by the consideration that women are morally weaker than men but have stronger desires and appetites,

yet on their hands

> The Chastity of men doth often lie:
> Lust would more common be then any one,
> Could it like other sinnes be done alone.
>   (sig. C1^v)

It is frightening that men must trust their honor to the keeping of such frail creatures. This anxiety creates a new attitude toward jealousy. The jealous husband had been almost immemorially (and of course continued to be) an object of ridicule or contempt. With the idealization of married companionship, some sensible advice was given to the suspicious husband: William Massie, for example, in a marriage sermon delivered in 1586, points out that "in no wise" may a wise husband be jealous about the honesty of his wife, for jealousy "either needes not, or bootes not."[50] It is foolish to be jealous of a good wife and useless to be jealous of a bad, for a bad woman has incalculable wiles and will get her own way in spite of any surveillance. Overbury's advice differs and is typical of a change in attitude noticeable at the turn of the century. For a husband

> To barre the meanes is Care, not Jelousie.
> Some lawfull things to be avoyded are,
> When, they occasion of unlawfull be.
> Lust ere it hurts is best descride afarre.
>   (sig. B4^r)

The jealous husband is now only "careful"; not to take reasonable precaution is as contemptible as to be unreasonably jealous. Earlier attitudes, of course, persisted side by side with this increasing masculine anxiety. Nonetheless, Overbury seems to express a feeling that was growing, especially among members of his own class, with its heavy emphasis on honor. Some of his lines have the ring of a *cri de coeur:*

> This misery doth Jelousie ensue,
> That we may prove her false, but cannot True.
>   (sig. B3^v)

---

50. *A Sermon Preached at Trafford* (Oxford, 1586), sig. C2^r.

This "misery" is, of course, the plight of Othello, and must have been the feeling of many a Jacobean cavalier. A woman may be taken in the act of adultery, but how can a wife be taken in the act of chastity?

It was exactly this jealous misery that Overbury's contemporary Fletcher assuaged in his plays about chastity. I do not think it has been noticed how many of Fletcher's heroines are wives, and wives who are taken, so to speak, in the act of chastity. The endlessly repeated trials and tests of chastity in the Fletcherian plays are used to show the fidelity and integrity of constant wives. The overwhelming popularity of Fletcher—despite his artistic inferiority to Shakespeare, Jonson, and other of his fellow playwrights—is readily understandable when one considers how many of his plays gave a soothing, wish-fulfilling reassurance to audiences indoctrinated with a horror of wifely unchastity and the dishonor it brought to the husband. In their preoccupation with marital situations, the Fletcherian chastity plays are much more akin to the sentimental domestic dramas of the eighteenth century than to the Restoration plays with which they are so often compared.

It may be objected to the thesis presented in this chapter that the drama in seventeenth-century Spain, a country virtually untouched either by the Reformation or the Counter-Reformation, places an even higher value on female honor than the Beaumont and Fletcher plays, here assumed to be a product of Reformation thought. This is only apparently true. The real emphasis in such plays as *The Star of Seville* and *The Surgeon of His Own Dishonor* is placed upon the honor of the man. If the hero even suspects that another man has admired his wife, sister, daughter, or sweetheart, not only must the offending rival be eliminated, and that secretly, but also the woman. The woman is equally responsible, even if she has done nothing more than be so beautiful as to attract attention. The basic premises of such plays are clearly the same as those of the medieval misogynists who reviled women and their beauty as the primary cause of their own lusts. The English plays are in marked contrast to the Spanish in this respect. Fletcherian heroines themselves defend their own honor.

Before looking at the Fletcherian plays themselves, however, it is necessary to go back and pick up another thread of the discussion. The immediate antecedents of the improbably chaste Fletcherian heroine, who defends her honor against an improbably lustful villain, are to be found as much in fiction and verse as in social theory, in the numerous stories of chaste wives that had wide circulation in the fifty or sixty years before Fletcher began to write, and it is to these tales we shall turn next.

4

Mirrors of Modesty

In 1578 Thomas Salter addressed a little tract called *The Mirrhor of Modesty* to "all Mothers, Matrones, and Maidens of Englande." The tract offers advice about the training and education of young girls that will best keep them virginal while they are single and chaste after they are married. To achieve this desired result, Salter urges that

> our wise matrone shall reade, or cause her maidens to reade, the examples and lives of godly and vertuous ladies, whose worthy fame and bright renowne yet liveth, and still will live for ever, which shee shall make choice of, out of the holy Scripture, and other histories, both auncient and of late dayes; whiche bookes will not onely delight them, but as a spurre it will pricke and incite their hartes to follow vertue, and have vice in horror and disdaine . . . for you shall never repeate the vertuous lives of any suche ladies as Claudia, Portia, Lucretia, and such like were, but you shall kindle a desire in them to treade their steppes, and become in tyme like unto them, and to disdayne and have in horrour those that to the contrarye pas the course of their lives in wickednesse.[1]

Similarly, when Geoffrey Fenton in 1567 dedicated his *Tragicall Discourses* to Lady Mary Sidney, he recommended the study of history as beneficial for a woman:

---

1. Ed. J. Payne Collier in *Illustrations of Old English Literature* (London, 1866; repr. New York, 1966), 1:11. Each item in Collier's collection is paged separately.

what stoare of examples are there to instructe her in her dutie, eyther for the maried to kepe her fayth to her husband, with Lucretia, or the unmaried to defend her virginitye, with Virginya. (I.4)[2]

He recommends his own translations of Italian novelle on the same grounds:

For heare maye bee seene such patternes of chastetye, and maydes so assured and constant in vertue, that they have not doubted rather to reappose a felicitye in the extreme panges of death then to fall by anye violent force into the daunger of the fleshlye enne-mye to theyr honour. (I.8)

It is impossible to say whether or not English girls were in actual fact brought up on such stories, but there is no doubt that both these writers express a favorite Renaissance theory—that the most efficacious instruction is instruction by example.[3] In the effort to instruct women to be chaste, English writers supplied printers with scores of stories and narrative poems describing the lives of virtuous virgins and wives.

There were many women who were extolled for their loyalty to their husbands, women such as Portia, Camma, Cornelia, Alcestis. To the Renaissance mind, however, three wives, more than any others, represented exemplary chastity. These were Penelope, Lucrece, and Susanna, parallel examples drawn from Greek, Roman, and biblical story. Their stories were told repeatedly, and other chaste heroines were perceived by Elizabethans in terms of their resemblance to these three great achetypes. Such stories of triumphant chastity, especially as shaped by Robert Greene and by the verse narratives of the 1590s, are the immediate antecedents, in form as well as in content, of the Fletcherian chastity play. The discussion that follows will not be concerned necessarily with the source or origin of these stories, but with the fact that fiction and verse cultivated the popular

2. All in-text citations of Fenton's *Tragicall Discourses* refer to volume and page numbers in the reprint of the 1567 edition in The Tudor Translations, gen. ed. W. E. Henley (London, 1898; repr. New York, 1967).
3. Discussed at some length by Hardin Craig in *The Enchanted Glass* (Oxford, 1935), pp. 231 ff.

taste for chaste and beleaguered heroines for several decades before Fletcher began to write.

Penelope

Penelope, faithful to Ulysses during his twenty-year absence from Ithaca, was the archetype of the faithful wife. She is frequently alluded to in lyric verse as the exemplar of conjugal fidelity.[4] The disquisition on dancing in John Davies's *Orchestra* is occasioned by Penelope's refusal to dance with Antinous in Ulysses' absence.[5]

Peter Colse's *Penelope's Complaint* (London, 1596), which claims the *Odyssey* as its source, depicts the Homeric heroine in some detail. Colse writes a verse complaint in which Penelope tells her own story; she, and not Ulysses, is the central character, and all the episodes that do not concern her directly are omitted.[6] While Colse's Penelope is still mourning the departure of Ulysses, the suitors arrive as permanent houseguests, but with a striking change in motivation. In the *Odyssey* the suitors desire Penelope chiefly as a political pawn; she is the key to control of the kingdom of Ithaca. Though she is as "lovely as Artemis or golden Aphrodite," she is not an object of romantic or sexual desire, but of ambition. On those rare occasions on which Homer's heroine addresses the suitors directly, she reproves them for their atrocious manners, their boorish behavior, and their

---

4. See, for example, *A Gorgeous Gallery of Gallant Inventions,* ed. Hyder E. Rollins (Cambridge, Mass., 1926), pp. 15, 64, 88; *Tottel's Miscellany,* ed. Hyder E. Rollins, rev. ed. (Cambridge, Mass., 1965), 1:201, 219.

5. Davies's opening stanzas deliberately mislead the reader as to the poem's content:

> Where lives the man that never yet did hear
> Of chaste Penelope, Ulysses' queen?
> Who kept her faith unspotted twenty year,
> Till he return'd, that far away had been . . . .

Davies is apparently taking advantage of the popularity of the Penelope story in order to entice his audience to read further. The quotation is taken from E. M. W. Tillyard's edition of *Orchestra* (London, 1947), p. 15.

6. *Penelope's Complaint* presents some problems of interpretation because of its relationship to the puzzling poem, Willobie's *Avisa;* see below, chap. 5. The discussion in the text ignores the topical allusions, if any, to be found in this work and concentrates on those elements which the poem shares with other narratives of Penelope's life.

conspiracy to murder Telemachus. Colse changes the emphasis entirely. There is no mention of the political ambitions of the suitors; rather, they are "leachers vile" who desire to corrupt Penelope. The nurse Euryclea warns her, "Be charie of thy chastitie/Which sutors seeke so shamefully" (sig. G1ʳ). The maidservants, who in Homer complaisantly become mistresses to the suitors, in Colse complain bitterly to their mistress of the "helhounds" who have defiled them and made them pregnant. When Colse's heroine confronts her suitors, it is to defend in lengthy speeches her chastity against their attempted seductions. We find speeches with such titles as "Antinous interrupting her sighing, offereth his suit," "Her answer to her wooers," "The speech of her wooers," "Her answer to her sutors." Antinous, the ringleader as in Homer, suggests to her that Ulysses is a traitor to love and not worth her sighs; he offers to supply her husband's place (sigs. C3ʳ⁻ᵛ). She vows to die a "martir's death" before she breaks her marriage vow. The issue is specifically adultery, because Colse's Penelope, unlike Homer's heroine, is in no doubt about Ulysses' being alive. Indeed, she eventually writes to him about her troubles (her letter is borrowed from the *Heroides*),[7] although earlier she had hesitated to do so for fear of "putting him in a jelousie."

Penelope "bewailes the want of Ulysses in the night" but is too chary of her honor to supply his place from among her suitors. Colse gives Penelope a very sensual nature in order to make her twenty-year continence seem the more heroic. Ulysses' pretense of madness to avoid military service was motivated not by a prophecy that he would be long away, but by his desire to dally at home with his young wife. After his pretense is exposed, Ulysses spends his last days at home devising new "nuptial sports" with Penelope, who declares, "By day I shal his presence misse:/ Much more, his absence in the night" (sig. B2ʳ). Colse is not being prurient; he is making a rough-and-ready attempt at introducing the kind of motivation that he thinks will sharpen the moral lesson of Penelope's life. This point is worth noting, because Fletcher's heroines have been

---

7. Douglas Bush, *Mythology and the Renaissance Tradition in English Poetry* (Minneapolis, 1932; repr. New York, 1957), p. 311.

accused of prurience because of their similar references to "nuptial joys."[8] Colse and Fletcher, in making their heroines speak in this way, are both trying to make the same point, that is, the more keenly a woman appreciates "nuptial sports," the more self-denying is her refusal to take a lover.

At one point, indeed, Colse's Penelope "debateth with her selfe of marriage," but this is largely a rhetorical exercise and a device that allows her to express at length her resolve to remain faithful:

> No, no, my constant chastitie,
> The world throughout about shal ringe
> In prayse of chast Penelope,
> From time, to time, shal al men sing. . . .
>   (sig. E1ᵛ)

This leads her to a three-stanza speech entitled "her commendation of chastity"; the opening stanza is typical:

> O Chastitie, the cheefest kay,
> Of womens worthie treasury;
> A vertue that's of virgines gay,
> The pure and redoubted dowry.
> A poesy springing for aye,
> A floure that never can decay.
>   (sig. E1ᵛ)

Such a speech would be inconceivable in Homer's tale of adventure.

Another interesting change in the story, and one that is a commonplace in Elizabethan literature, is the emphasis placed on the faithless Helen as a foil for the faithful Penelope. In the *Odyssey* Helen appears briefly in Book IV during Telemachus's visit to the court of Menelaus. She has settled down to married life and appears as the gracious and busy hostess; her role in the Trojan War is hardly alluded to. The foil set up for Penelope in the *Odyssey* is Clytem-

---

8. For a particularly virulent attack on language of this sort, see Robert Boyle, "On Massinger and *The Two Noble Kinsmen*," *The New Shakespeare Society Transactions* 8, 1st ser. (1882):371–99. Boyle accuses the First Queen in *The Two Noble Kinsmen* of "gloating over her unclean reminiscences" (p. 383).

nestra; this contrast is drawn several times, most specifically by the
spirit of Agamemnon in Book XXIV when he hears the story of
the suitors when they arrive in Hades:

> "Unconquerable Odysseus!" the soul of Agamemnon cried. "Ah,
> happy prince, blessed in Icarius' daughter with a wife in whom all
> virtues meet, flawless Penelope, who has proved herself so good
> and wise, so faithful to her wedded love. . . . What a contrast
> with Clytemnestra and the infamy she sank to when she killed her
> wedded lord!"[9]

The point of the contrast is loyalty. Clytemnestra is not mentioned
by Colse; because his theme is chastity, Helen offers a better contrast. He writes speeches for his heroine with the titles "She accuseth
Hellen of Light consent," "She controlleth Hellen for her ill example," "Against Paris and his treacheries." With remarkable fore-
knowledge, Penelope declares that Helen's bad example has created
"a thousand Bridewell birds" (i.e., London prostitutes; Bridewell was
the Elizabethan prison for whores) and is responsible for the bad
behavior of the infamous Messalina and of Joan of Naples (sigs.
B4^{r-v}). Penelope boasts that if the "leacher" Paris had been her
guest instead of Helen's, she would have flayed his face with her
fingernails:

> Then should sir Paris soone have felt,
> The furie of my chast desires,
> Ulysses seene how I had delt,
> The dole that lawles love requires.
> (sig. C1^v)

This chaste fury makes Colse's Penelope seem like a tasteless virago
when compared with Homer's Penelope, who is described by the
epithets "wise" and "prudent."

However foreign she may be to our taste, Colse's heroine is intended as an exemplum for his time. The subtitle labels the poem
as "a mirrour for wanton minions" that will teach them proper
behavior, and the envoy draws a moral not too unexpected for a

---

9. Trans. E. V. Rieu (London, 1946), p. 356.

version of the *Odyssey* that excludes Odysseus except as the agent of destruction for the suitors:

> Lo Ladies, Jove reserves a friend,
> For those that tender chastitie,
> But Leachers brought to dolefull end,
> Amidst their chief securitie:
> Penelope for bale had blisse,
> When villanes vengeance could not misse.
>
> (sig. H4ʳ)

Colse's poem is bad verse and badly over-moralized. Greene gives a much more charming version of the Greek matron in *Penelope's Web* (1587), but his Penelope is the same self-consciously virtuous exemplum. The title page tells us that we may find in this work "a Christall Myrror of faeminine perfection," and in his dedication to the Countesses of Cumberland and Warwick, Greene describes his purpose as follows:

> Homer penned his Odissea comprehending the life of Ulisses because he was wise. And I . . . have attempted the discourse of Penelopes Web, for that she was chast, that as divers reading the Poets works did imitate his wisedome and spoke well of his pollicie: so some by glancing at this toy may take a president of her chastitie. (V.142) [10]

Greene uses Penelope's work on the great web to avoid the importunity of her suitors as the basis of a frame narrative for a group of short stories. At night she sits up with her nurse and three maids unweaving the work she had done by day. They while away the time with a discussion of love, commending that affection which, like Penelope's, is founded upon virtue rather than fancy. This is the love that keeps her chaste and constant. The first maid tells her mistress that "in requitall of such constant affection, the Gods in justice must crowne you with immortalitie, and the world reward you with fame and honour" (V.154). Another maid compares

---

10. All in-text citations of Greene's works refer to volume and page numbers in his *Life and Works,* ed. A. B. Grosart, 15 vols. (London, 1881–86).

Penelope's fidelity to that of the Roman matrons Macrina and Lucrece, both of whom, while their husbands were away at war, occupied their free hours with spinning, "by such huswifery to avoyde the allurements of vanitie":

> I am sure Madame the report of your chastitie, being once spred abroade, the Gretians are as prodigall in prayses as the Romanes, and blind Homer shall be as ready by his pen to make your chastitie immortall, as ever was any of their babling Poets. (V.158)

Adroitly and modestly, Penelope turns the conversation to more general topics, and after her nurse describes good and bad marriages, she asserts that any husband, however bad, can be reformed by the good behavior of his wife, especially if she is obedient, chaste, and silent. To prove her point, she tells three stories on consecutive nights to illustrate these womanly virtues.

Penelope prefaces each of her stories with a pleasantly schoolmarmish lecture on the quality to be illustrated, citing the opinions of philosophers and examples from ancient story. In the lecture on chastity, Greene has Penelope mention familiar examples of continence—Alexander, Portia, Cyrus, and Panthea—as well as cite the opinions of Euboides, Socrates, Plato, Julius Caesar, Epictetus, Euripides, Crates, and Marcus Aurelius. All the ancients agree that "the greatest fortresse and defence that nature had given to a woman for the preservation of her reputation and honour, was Chastitie: which lost and vyolated, there remaineth nothing but shame and infamie" (V.198–99). The astonishing length and chronology of this speech are typical; Greene was well aware of the popularity of such lengthy defenses of feminine honor. Greene's theme is exactly the same as Colse's, but his Penelope, domestic and careful for the moral welfare of her charges, is a far more appealing character.

The Penelope pattern, then, gives us a wife who by industry and the use of her wits protects her chastity in her husband's absence. This is the pattern we find in the story of Ulrico and Barbara in Tome II, novella 28 of Painter's *Palace of Pleasure* (1567) and in George Whetstone's adaptation of the same story in *The Rock of Regard* (1576). The third section of Whetstone's work is entitled

"The Arbour of Vertue," and contains a verse narrative of "the chaste and honourable life of a Bohemian Ladie" and two Hungarian barons that "wagerd the spoile of her Chastitie" (p. 145).[11] This tale is, of course, the source of the *Cymbeline* wager plot, but its interest for our discussion lies in the fact that both Painter and Whetstone perceive the heroine as a latter-day Penelope. Painter begins his novel with a paean of praise for Barbara:

> Penelope, the woful Wife of absent Ulisses, in hir tedious longing for the home retourne of that hir adventurous knight, assayled wyth Carefull heart amid the troupe of amorous Suters, and within the Bowels of hir royall Pallace, deserved no greater fame for hir valiaunt encountries and stoute defence of the invincible, and Adamant fort of hir chastity than this Boeme Lady doth by resisting two mighty Barrons, that canoned the Walles, and well mured rampart of hir pudicity. (III.195)[12]

Ulrico, Barbara's husband, wishes to go to war to improve his fortunes, but fears to do so lest neighboring gentlemen "no doubte would swarme togyther in greater heapes then ever dyd the wowers of Penelope, within the famous graunge of Ithaca, the house of Wandering Ulisses" (III.199). Whetstone's Ulrico is similarly "in a jealous feare" lest his wife be unfaithful in his absence:

> I call to mynd fayre Helens moode, who trudg'd with Trojan
>   knight,
> When as her lord was forst from home with forreine foes to fight.
> The ruffling rout at Ithaca, Ulysses farre from home,
> Doth force a thousand fearefull thoughts within my head to rome:
> Then Penelopes constancie this dread would gladly weare,
> She plaste alone, without her leake, afresh doth raise my feare.
>   (p. 153)

In both versions Ulrico is reassured by Barbara and leaves for the wars, first securing from a magician a picture of his wife that has

---

11. In-text citations of Whetstone's *Rock of Regard* refer to page numbers in the edition by J. P. Collier (London, 1870).

12. All in-text citations of Painter's *Palace of Pleasure* refer to volume and page numbers in the edition of Joseph Jacobs, 3 vols. (London, 1890).

marvelous properties: If it turns yellow, Ulrico will know that his wife is tempted; if black, that her honor is lost.

Ulrico is successful in the wars against the Turks, and is honored in the Hungarian court. After a two-year absence from home, he is chided by Alberto and Udislao, who doubt that his wife can still be faithful. They wager their lands that, within two months, one or both shall enjoy the lady. Alberto travels to Bohemia, woos Barbara, and for his pains is clapped into prison by his hostess and made to spin flax to earn his food. Udislao meets the same fate. Ulrico is enriched with the gain of their lands, and the King of Hungary banishes the presumptuous barons. The chaste lady, according to Whetstone, receives everlasting fame:

> Faire Barbara, for foyling them, did to her honour mount:
> She was the chiefe about the queene in credite and account.
> Whereas she lived many dayes, and helde her wishe at will,
> Nowe being deade, in worthy fame, her vertues liveth still.
>
> (pp. 171–72)

Thus chastity not only is vindicated but also is rewarded with fame and fortune.

In considering the relationship of a story such as this to the Fletcherian chastity play, two details deserve special attention. The first is that Barbara, clever as Penelope with her never-finished web, uses a ruse to entice the knights into prison. She pretends to each to feel love for him so that he is fooled into making an assignation with her; the place picked for the meeting turns out to be a locked and barred room. This deserves mention because the Fletcherian heroine is reproved for leading her suitors on (see, for example, Ornstein's comment above, chap. 1). The attitude indicated by Whetstone, however, an attitude that also appears in Fletcher, is that a man who attempts to seduce a chaste lady is a despicable scoundrel, and therefore any means used to expose him, even a pretense of wantonness by the heroine, is justified. More important, the witty ruse is itself one of the major sources of the appeal of the story. Elizabethan audiences delighted in the sight of cleverness used to overcome the superior force of a villain.[13] A familiar example is *Measure for Measure,* in which the mainspring of the action is the application of "craft against vice" (III.ii.291). It is not only permissible, but admirable, for naturally weak woman to use her wits against the vice of a lustful villain.

The second important point to notice about this story is that Ulrico's magic picture of his wife turns yellow during the time when Alberto and Udislao pay court to her, the change in color indicating, according to the magician's instructions, that Barbara is tempted.[14] Clearly the word *tempted* in this trial of chastity does not have the meaning of "inclining toward evil," for Barbara at no time wavers in her fidelity to Ulrico. Rather, *tempted,* when used of a chaste lady, means "exposed to temptation" or "offered a temptation," which means, of course, provided with an opportunity to prove her chastity. This point is important, for heroines in stories and plays of chastity are tempted in this latter sense; their constancy is spotless, but it is circumstances that give them occasion to prove this.

"The Lady of Bohemia" shows how various can be the stories modeled on the Penelope pattern. Only the basic situation of the wife resisting seduction during her husband's absence need be present. Fletcher uses the Penelope pattern in *The Knight of Malta, The Double Marriage, Valentinian, The Humorous Lieutenant,* and *The Honest Man's Fortune.*

Susanna

Another story pattern congenial to Reformation tastes is found in the Apocryphal History of Susanna, which also describes righteousness vindicated. Susanna is wife to Joachim, a rich man of greatest honor among the Jews in Babylon. She is "a very delicate woman, and beauteous to behold" (verse 31), and her beauty inflames the

---

13. See Jean E. Johnson, "The Persecuted Heroine in English Renaissance Tragicomedy," Ph.D. diss. (Columbia University, 1969), p. 41, for a more extended discussion of this attitude.

14. Yellow was the color traditionally associated with jealousy. The change in the picture reflects the feelings of the fearful viewer (Ulrico) rather than a change in the feelings of Barbara.

lust of two Elders, ancients chosen to be judges over the people. They conspire together to attempt to seduce Susanna after dinner when she is accustomed to walk in her garden. Their threats to her and her refusal should be quoted in full, because they are the kernel of so many future speeches of seduction and refusal:

> Behold, the garden doors are shut, that no man can see us, and we are in love with thee; therefore consent unto us, and lie with us.
> If thou wilt not, we will bear witness against thee, that a young man was with thee: and therefore thou didst send thy maids from thee.
> Then Susanna sighed, and said, I am straitened on every side; for if I do this thing, it is death unto me: and if I do it not, I cannot escape your hands.
> It is better for me to fall into your hands, and not do it, then to sin in the sight of the Lord.
>
> (verses 20–23)

Brief as is this treatment of a highly dramatic situation, it gives us elements that recur again and again: A beautiful woman chooses infamy rather than the spiritual death that will follow adultery, for sin, however secret, cannot be hidden "in the sight of the Lord." Unjust judges described their lust as love, they offer secrecy in return for intimacy, and they threaten to use their greater power and prestige against her. It is interesting to notice that the promise of secrecy, which is a virtue in the hero of a tale of courtly love, is the language of a villain in a tale of chaste love.

The Elders carry out their threats and slander Susanna, who is brought to trial and condemned to death as an adulteress. Susanna's only defense is a short speech reposing her trust in God:

> Then Susanna cried out with a loud voice, and said, O everlasting God, that knowest all things before they be:
> Thou knowest that they have borne false witness against me, and behold, I must die; whereas I never did such things as these men have maliciously invented against me.
> And the Lord heard her voice.
>
> (verses 42–44)

The Lord raises up the young Daniel to judgment, who confutes the

Elders by examining them separately and leading them to give con-
flicting evidence. The judges are put to the death they had prepared
for their victim. Susanna is praised by all her kindred because "there
was no dishonesty found in her" (verse 63), and Daniel's reputation
is launched. Interest is equally divided between Susanna's virtue and
Daniel's exploit.

The Susanna pattern shows us a beautiful and chaste woman who
resists seduction, who is slandered by villains of greater authority
and credit, and who reposes her trust in God and is vindicated in
this life—a very dramatic story, and one that allows for endless
variation and expansion.

In England the story of Susanna early found expression in a morality play, Thomas Garter's *The Most Virtuous and Godly Susanna*
(1563–1569).[15] Already, in this early version, there is a slight shift
in emphasis. In the apocryphal narrative the focus is largely upon the
actions of the judges and upon Daniel's cleverness. Garter shows a
slightly more spirited Susanna, a wife who can banter and tease her
husband. She has need of spirit, because the attempt on her chastity
is the premeditated plan of Satan and his Vice, Ill Report. Satan has
a particular grudge against Susanna because she has so far resisted
his attempts to overthrow her godliness by tempting her with six of
the Seven Deadly Sins; now he means to assault her with "filthy
lustes of fleshly men" (l. 176). His agents, the unjust judges, are
named Voluptas and Sensualitas, in that curious manner of the
hybrid morality play in which the characters are seen as historical
personages and, at the same time, as representatives of abstract
qualities. When the Elders accost Garter's Susanna in the garden,
she passively places her trust in God, but, in addition, she gives her
would-be seducers a lecture:

You are of age, and know right well, that no such sinne should be,
You know also God doth it curse, and eake our lawe on earth,

---

15. First printed in 1578; in-text citations refer to the facsimile edition
prepared by B. Ifor Evans and W. W. Greg in The Malone Society
Reprints (Oxford, 1936). An earlier (lost) Susanna play was written in
England by Ralph Radcliff during the first half of the century; this version
was probably a Latin play written for performance by students (Jean
Johnson, p. 152).

Doth recompense such sinners to, with sharpe and cruell death.
And therefore good my friend I say, doe leave as you begon,
And I will holde me so content, and hyde what you have done.

(ll. 754–58)

The lecture that condemns lust and offers silence as a reward for reformed behavior appears in other versions of Susanna.

Garter's play, except for incidental expansions (low comic scenes with the Vice, a tirade against court life delivered by Susanna's servants, a scene of domestic teasing between Susanna and Joachim), generally follows the biblical narrative. There are some changes, however, that are important for our consideration of the Susanna pattern as a forerunner of the chastity play. First, the emphasis, as already noticed, tends to fall more on the heroine than upon Daniel. The Prologue describes the argument in such a way as to show this shift in emphasis: "Of Susans lyfe the story is, what trouble she was in,/ How narrowly she scaped Death because she would not sinne" (ll. 10–11). Second, the Prologue very explicitly announces the moral to be drawn from these events, namely, "how prone God is to helpe such as are just" (l. 8). Moreover, these matters are like a "myrrour" (l. 20), because "ensample good, is meete in these our dayes" (l. 22). This pattern, of slandered chastity vindicated by providential events, appears in Fletcher in *The Knight of Malta, The Humorous Lieutenant, The Lovers' Progress, Philaster,* and, with modification, in *The Faithful Shepherdess. The Woman Hater,* discussed in chapter 2, is a humorous inversion of the pattern: Gondarino slanders Oriana's chastity, not because she refuses to lie with him, but because she appears to wish to. Garter's *Susanna* is also very important as an antecedent to Fletcher because it portrays an attempted seduction as a full-scale contest between cosmic forces of good and evil, between Satan and his agents on the one side, and, on the other, the godly representatives of the Lord. This morality pattern we have already seen in Fletcher in *The Triumph of Death.* The idea is fundamental in Fletcher.

Many other versions of Susanna intervene between Garter and Fletcher and serve to refine the story and demonstrate its possibilities. In 1566 Tome I of Painter's *Palace of Pleasure* contained two Susanna stories—Novel 41, "A Ladie Falslie Accused," and Novel 45, "The Duchess of Savoy." The lady of Novel 41 is married to a French lord who has the unusual habit of collecting lions. Her husband's steward, false as are most stewards in literature, becomes enamored of his mistress and woos her to satisfy his base desires. The indignant lady, far more verbal than her prototype, denounces his lust in a lengthy speech, threatening him with death if he approaches her again. She does not mention the matter to her husband; like Garter's Susanna, she intends to remain silent if her wooer behaves. Painter here has an interesting digression of several pages that deserves attention in that it explains the rationale behind this behavior. He commends her silence, contrasting her with those women who disturb their husbands over trifles, women "that care not to moleste theyr husbands, for the first Flie that buzzeth before their eyes, conceyving a frivolous and sodaine opinion of their chastitie, not so much assailed, or to sharpely defended, chaunting glorious Hympnes and high prayses of their victorie" (I.206); it is better to remain silent and avoid scandal. We remember Colse's Penelope, fearful of writing to Ulysses about the suitors, lest she put him "'in a jelousie." Painter continues his admonition:

> And truly that woman deserveth greater glorie, which of herselfe defendeth her honestie, and quencheth the flames livelye kindled in the hartes of other, with the coldnes of continencie, by that meanes vanquishing two, then she doth, which manifesting the vice of an other, discloseth as it were, a certaine apparaunce of her frailtie, and the litle reason wherwith she is indewed, to vanquish him that confesseth to be her servaunt, and whose wil dependeth at her commaundement. (I.206–7)

Unfortunately for Painter's lady, though her behavior is appropriate in the circumstances, the steward renounces the role of the courtly lover abashed by his mistress's rebuke.

Instead, his love turns to hate, and, like Garter's Voluptas and Sensualitas, he uses "divelish invention" (I.207) to revenge himself by slander. He persuades the court fool, a simple-minded boy, to hide under the lady's bed at night and then to steal out of her chamber at dawn. Securing reliable witnesses of this suspicious behavior, the "divelish counsaylour" accuses the lady of adultery to his master. The French lord behaves much as Othello does. With his "eyes rolling in his heade" (I.210) (cf. Desdemona's "you are fatal then/When your eyes roll so" V.ii.6–7), he turns on the steward, threatening, "If my wyfe be slaundred, and accused wrongfully, assure thy selfe that I will be revenged uppon thee" (I.210). Being "lyke to runne out of his wittes" (I.211), he refuses to hear any defense of the lady, and, only allowing her time to "provide for her soules health" (I.212), he condemns her to be thrown to his lions. The lady can only fortify herself "in the hope of the mercifull hande of Almightye God" (I.212), to whom she addresses two lengthy prayers, reminding Him that He "diddest discharge Susanna from the slaunder of the perverse and adulterous Judges" (I.213). And the Lord hears her voice.

> the goodnesse of God, who is a just Judge, and suffreth his owne elect to be proved to the extremitie, of purpose to make their glorie the greater, and the ruine of the wicked more apparaunt, manifested there an evident miracle. (I.213)

The lions, "cruell and capitall enemies of adulterie, amonges themselves" (I.204), not only do not harm the lady, but they fawn upon her with great affection. The steward immediately confesses his villainy and is torn to pieces by the same lions.

The lady forgives the rash sentence of her remorseful husband in a speech that sums up the mystique of chastity literature:

> I rejoyce in resistaunce of the assaultes of love, and death to guarde and kepe my chastitie pure and inviolable; and may serve for example to every honourable Ladie, being assailed with suche strong and mightie adversaries, to kepe them selves honest. For the croune is not due but to her that shall lawfully combate to the ende. (I.215–16)

Chastity is a gift of grace, but it must be proved by trial to win the crown. The trial of chastity is clearly the center of interest in this version of Susanna. The miracle of the lions removes the need for a Daniel altogether, and the storyteller can concentrate almost exclusively on the feelings and attitudes of his heroine, beseiged, as in Garter's play, by forces conceived of as "divelish."

The variety of the materials that can be shaped to this pattern of the beautiful lady falsely accused of adultery is shown by Painter's version of "The Duchess of Savoy." This is, in actuality, a story of courtly love rather than chastity tried and proved, but the author nonetheless draws a parallel with Susanna. The Duchess of Savoy, sister to the King of England, is married to a white-haired old Duke whose part in the story is almost nonexistent. The Duchess hears of the unequaled beauty of Lord John of Mendozza, and in order to see him makes a feigned pilgrimage to the Spanish shrine of St. James. She is not disappointed when she meets Mendozza, and even promises obliquely to become his mistress on her return trip from the shrine. This assignation is prevented by the arrival of her unsuspecting husband, who, worried that she travels so lightly accompanied, has overtaken her by sea to assure her of safe conduct home. The Duchess is overcome with remorse, perceiving that "God had withstanded her lascivious wil" (I.301), and returns home, determining henceforth to be a good woman. Shortly, the Duke of Savoy goes to war, leaving the Earl of Pancalier as his lieutenant-general. The Earl woos his mistress, meets a sharp rebuke, and changes his love into hatred. "By the instinct of the devil," he devises a complicated plot that allows him to accuse the Duchess of adultery with his own nephew. The circumstantial evidence is so strong that she is condemned to be burned alive if a champion does not appear to do battle for her innocence. Needless to say, Mendozza appears in disguise and in mortal combat defeats the Earl of Pancalier and vindicates the Duchess's honesty. And much later, after the Duke of Savoy conveniently dies in the wars, Mendozza and the Duchess are married and live happily ever after.

The Duchess of Savoy is certainly a different type of heroine from Susanna, yet the Duchess's trial scene is molded to the biblical pattern. The Duchess, unaware of the identity of her champion and convinced that Mendozza has abandoned her to an infamous death, reposes all her trust in God for vindication, praying:

O Lorde God, which art the very veritie it self, and knowest the bytternesse that I fele in my harte, to see my self falsely accused, shew forth now the treasure of thy grace upon me wretched Princesse: and as thou diddest deliver Susanna from her trouble, and Judith from Holofernes, deliver me from the hande of a tiraunt: who like a lion hungrie for my bloud, devoureth both myne honour and life. (I.321)

The Lord raises up a very convenient Daniel indeed in a lover in disguise (a device that Fletcher uses in *The Lovers' Progress* and *The Knight of Malta*). Yet this is felt to be an exemplary tale, for the heroine had reformed before the false accusation and considers it a punishment for her earlier hypocrisy. The Duchess of Savoy is not uncommonly cited by Renaissance writers as a modern precedent of chastity. Thomas de la Peend, for example, tells her story in "The moste notable historie of John Lord of Mandosse" (London, 1565). He announces in the argument that his poem will tell of a duchess falsely accused of adultery: "But God, which still defendeth ryght,/ From deathe hath her delyvered" (sig. B3ᵛ). One of George Pettie's chaste heroines, when considering the evil that may be done by a lustful villain, calls to mind "the Erle of Pancalier . . . who when the duchesse of Savoy would not yeeld to his lasscivious lust, wrought sutch wyles, that she was condemned for adultry, and judged to suffer most shamefull death by burning."[16]

A more conventional but more verbal Susanna appears in Greene's expansion of the apocryphal tale in *The Myrrour of Modestie* (1584).[17] The title page advertises that the reader will find

as in a perfect Glass howe the Lorde delivereth the innocent from

16. George Pettie, *A Petite Pallace of Pettie His Pleasure*, ed. Herbert Hartman (London, 1938), p. 27.

17. Greene's dedication of his tale of Susanna to the Countess of Darby is an earlier version of the dedication to *Penelope's Web:* "The Poet Homer . . . tooke paines to pen the travels of Ulisses bicause he was wise, and I have applied my small skill to levell out the life of Susanna, bicause she was chast. He sought to pleasure others by the shewe of Ulisses wisedome, and I (if I might) to profite all by Susannas chastite. Divers followed Ulisses steps, (although they suspected it for a fained tale) then I hope most will treade Susannas trace, in that they knowe it an unfeined truth" (III.7).

all imminent perils, and plagueth the bloudthirstie hypocrites with deserved punishments. Shewing that the graie heades of dooting adulterers shall not go with peace into the grave, neither shall the righteous be forsaken in the Daie of trouble. (III.3)

The most interesting feature of Greene's version, for our purposes, is his great expansion of the speeches exchanged between Susanna and the Elders when they surprise her in the garden. The first Elder begins the assault with a seduction speech rather than with threats. He flatteringly describes the great love her beauty has aroused and promises secrecy if she will submit to them: "That sin which is secretlie committed is alwaies halfe pardoned: she liveth chastelie enough that liveth warely" (III.19). Moreover, their great credit will prevent any suspicion, and her own pleasure will be served in the acquisition of two "trusty freends." In a speech that runs to four pages, Susanna denounces their lust and defends chastity, reminding them that no secret can be kept from God. Here is one of those lengthy and rhetorically elaborate speeches in defense of chastity that are one of the key features of the Fletcherian chastity play.

The evil judges are not convinced, even when they hear Susanna "cunninglie to confute their devilish conclusions" (III.24). The second Elder renews the assault with threats to bear false witness against her as an adulteress. He reminds her that Bathsheba could not resist the lust of King David or prevent him from murdering her husband. Susanna denounces this sophistry for another two pages and meditates upon her dilemma, but concludes by reposing her trust in God. The rest follows as in the Apocrypha, with the interesting variation that, at the trial, Daniel delivers a long lecture on lust to each of the Elders, a variation again in the direction of rhetorical elaboration of attitudes toward lechery and chastity.

Besides its lengthy speeches, Greene's version has another interesting feature in its comparison of Susanna's garden to Eden. This garden is so pleasant that it seems "a second paradise" (III.12), and the first Elder seems to the heroine to be a "subtill serpent" (III.19). The "mischevous pretence of these subtill serpentes" (III.26) proceeds from their "devillish imagination" (III.17). The implied comparison of seduction and the original temptation of Eve is a commonplace in chastity literature. Seducers, especially bawds, are frequently likened to serpents.

Greene uses both the Penelope and Susanna stories again in his semi-autobiographical *Never Too Late* and its sequel, *Francesco's Fortunes* (1590).[18] In the first part, the hero, Francesco, leaves his wife, Isabel, in Caerbranck and makes a business trip to Troynovant, where he becomes infatuated with a courtesan named Infida and for many years prodigally wastes his substance on her. During his absence Isabel conducts herself in so exemplary a manner that she wins "great commendations of all for her loyaltie and constancie" (VIII.95). She is confident of reclaiming Francesco, and writes to him as follows:

> If Penelope longde for her Ulysses, thinke Isabel wisheth for her Francesco, as loyall to thee as she was constant to the wily Greeke, and no lesse desirous to see thee in Caerbranck, than she to enjoy his presence in Ithaca, watering my cheekes with as manie teares, as she her face with plaints, yet my Francesco, hoping I have no such cause as she to increase her cares: for I have such resolution in thy constancie, that no Circes with all her inchantments, no Calipso with all her sorceries, no Syren with all their melodies could pervert thee. (VIII.97–98)

Francesco is moved, but, catching sight of Infida, he returns to his folly, vowing, "I will not leave this Troy for the chastest Penelope in the world" (VIII.100). As soon as his purse is empty, however, the courtesan casts him aside, and *Never Too Late* ends with Francesco repenting.

He is still repentant at the opening of the sequel, *Francesco's Fortunes,* but, too ashamed to return home, he regains his wasted money by writing plays, and acquires fame in the bargain. The

---

18. The autobiographical elements include Francesco's desertion of his wife and child, his long liaison with a courtesan (Greene had an illegitimate child by the sister of Cutting Ball, the captain of a gang of thieves), and his success as a playwright. It would be gratifying to know that Greene's wife actually lived the life of a modern-day Susanna, so that she might be included in the following chapter on chaste English heroines, but nothing is actually known of her beyond the facts that her name was Dorothy and that she came originally from Lincolnshire. (Biographical information on Greene is from the annotated life by Nicholas Storojenko, included by Grosart in Vol. 1 of his edition of Greene's works.)

courtesan, hearing of his new wealth, renews her enticements, but the now-reformed Francesco despises her. Meanwhile, Isabel also shows fortitude in the face of temptation. Bernardo, an old magistrate of her city, attempts to seduce her with a speech of two pages, and Isabel defends her honor for four pages using language that indicates the parallel with Susanna and the unjust judges: "Hath God placed you as a Burgomaster of this Citty, and so a Judge over his people to punish sinne, and will you maintaine wickedness?" (VIII.149). Bernardo threatens to send her to prison "and cause some Ruffian in the citie to sweare, that since the absence of thy husband Francesco, he hath lien with thee, and for coyne used thee as his concubine" (VIII.154).

Isabel spits in Bernardo's face and is sent to prison; at her trial she is judged guilty. She still reposes her trust in God, however, praying out loud and remembering how He shrouded "Sussanna from the treacherie of the two Elders in raysing up young Daniel to maintaine her right" (VIII.162). Dispensing with Daniel, God causes the perjured witness to recant suddenly and miraculously; Isabel is freed, and Bernardo is deposed from office and forced to pay Isabel a great fine. "Thus was Isabel delivered from her enimies, and reckoned more famous for hir chastitie through al Caerbranck" (VIII.164). This ordeal, besides bringing Isabel fortune and fame, also brings the return of her much-longed-for Francesco. News of her fortitude reaches him in Troynovant when a gentleman at an inn recounts the tale of Isabel as "a myrrour of chastitie" (VIII.164). Francesco repents and goes home and is instantly forgiven by Isabel for his six-year absence.

Lucrece

The story of Lucrece, the third of our exemplary matrons, was enormously popular during the Middle Ages and the Renaissance. Versions of her history were available in Livy, Ovid, Plutarch, Valerius Maximus, St. Augustine, the *Gesta Romanorum,* Boccaccio, Gower, Chaucer, Lydgate, Ser Giovanni Fiorentino, Bandello, Painter, Shakespeare, Middleton, and Heywood. Ballads about

Lucrece were entered on the Stationers' Register in 1568 and 1569.[19]
In 1574 the narrator of Richard Robinson's long poem *The Reward
of Wickednesse* is conducted on a tour of hell by Morpheus and
meets Tarquin, who tells the story of Lucrece to his visitors. The
ravisher praises his victim lavishly, urging that her life be considered
an exemplum:

> But al you Ladies, Wives, and Maides eache one,
> Of what degree or yet estate you be:
> No doubte although Lucretia bee gone,
> As myrrour maye remaine, this storye when you see.
> So may you learne the gifte of chastitye,
> > What love you ought your husbandes for to beare,
> > In spending of her daies, the profe doeth plaine apeare.
> > > (sig. F1^r)

Lucrece is exemplary because she prefers death to dishonor and
because of her love for her husband Collatine. The latter point is
clearly proved when Collatine and the other Roman lords, after
boasting of their wives, return secretly from the battlefield at Ardea
to find all the Roman matrons dancing and carousing, all except
Lucrece, who is found among her maids, spinning to pass the time
until her husband returns.

Lucrece provides the basic story pattern of the chaste woman who
commits suicide after being raped by a tyrant. Certain features of
the story, especially as they are amplified in Shakespeare's version,
become more or less permanently attached to this pattern. Among
these are the entry by night of the ravisher to the victim's bed-

---

19. The versions of Lucrece are discussed in the New Variorum edition
of Shakespeare, *The Poems*, ed. Hyder E. Rollins (Philadelphia, 1938),
pp. 416ff. Thomas Middleton's *The Ghost of Lucrece*, ed. J. Q. Adams
(New York, 1937), is noteworthy because it is a celebration of chastity in
verse written in the decade before the appearance of *The Faithful Shepherdess*, Fletcher's first play. Heywood's play *The Rape of Lucrece* (1606–
1608) defies classification. His Lucrece is a self-conscious exemplum, but
the pathos of the scenes in which she appears is undercut when the singing
peer Valerius breaks into a ribald song about the rape, beginning, "Did he
take fair Lucrece by the toe, man" (IV.vi). Actually, however, Lucrece plays
a very minor role in the play, which is, as a whole, concerned with the
adventures of the entire family of Tarquin the Proud and which is pre-
dominantly martial in tone. A Latin play, *Lucretia*, performed 11 February
1605 at St. John's College, Oxford, is unfortunately lost.

chamber with a drawn sword, the threat of the ravisher to slander
his victim's chastity unless she gives in, the pleadings of the victim
to be spared, the lament of the ravished woman, the impotent grief
of the husband, and the political downfall of the tyrant. For our
purposes in the discussion of the development of narrative patterns
for rape, the key event of the story is Lucrece's suicide.[20]

Lucrece's suicide is necessitated by a basic assumption about rape
that is often implied but seldom made explicit in the various versions
of the story. A ravished woman cannot go on living without running the risk of producing a bastard, or, equally important, without
arousing the suspicion that she in some degree was a willing accomplice in her own rape. This attitude grows out of that basic premise
about women, noted in chapter 3, that they have weaker wills and

---

20. St. Augustine in *The City of God* (trans. Marcus Dods, New York,
1950) has an important discussion of Lucrece's suicide. In his discussion of
the sin of self-murder, Augustine confronts the extreme case of suicide after
rape and declares that suicide is unnecessary in these circumstances because
purity is a virtue of the soul and therefore cannot be destroyed by the
violation of the body. Nonetheless, the victim of this crime if she is a "pure
spirit from which modesty has not departed" will feel "shame, lest that act
which could not be suffered without some sensual pleasure, should be believed to have been committed also with some assent of the will. . . . And
consequently, even if some of these virgins killed themselves to avoid such
disgrace, who that has any human feeling would refuse to forgive them?"
(pp. 21–22). A case in point is Lucrece. Augustine argues that either she
was chaste, in which case her suicide was foolish and unnecessary, or she
enjoyed her ravishment, in which case she slew herself from a feeling of
guilt. As we know her to have been chaste, continues Augustine, her suicide
was prompted by "the overwhelming burden of her shame. She was ashamed
that so foul a crime had been perpetrated upon her, though without her
abetting; and this matron, with the Roman love of glory in her veins, was
seized with a proud dread that, if she continued to live, it would be supposed
she willingly did not resent the wrong that had been done her. She could
not exhibit to men her conscience, but she judged that her self-inflicted punishment would testify her state of mind. . . ." (p. 25). Christian women
are not faced with this dilemma because they can exhibit their consciences
to God. Thus Augustine tactfully avoids either condemning or praising
Lucrece.

John Donne's *Biathanatos,* a defense of suicide (written in 1608 but not
published until 1646), takes St. Augustine to task for even raising the issue
as to whether or not self-murder is permissible when chastity is at stake
(p. 150). Donne points out (pp. 148–49) that the church has canonized and
the church fathers have praised such martyrs as St. Pelagia who, in order
to preserve her chastity, drowned herself. The 1646 edition of *Biathanatos*
has been reproduced in facsimile by the Facsimile Text Society (New
York, 1930).

stronger desires than men. They are therefore likely to protest much
but to enjoy being forced, since force will clear them from blame.
Moreover, once a woman loses her honor, even if by force, she is
likely to sink into a life of sin. This is the argument of many a
villain in Elizabethan fiction who is meditating rape. For example,
a young man considering rape in Fenton's *Tragicall Discourses*
argues to himself that his intended victim "peradventure after the
first taste of the plesant jewstes of love, wil slacke the bridle of her
rigour, and converte the harde and angrye clymate of her invincible
humor into a disposicion of lesse difficultie, and she easier hereafter
to be intreated" (II.85). Suicide, then, is doubly necessary for the
ravished woman; not only does it clear her from suspicion but it also
prevents degradation into a life of sin thereafter.

Chaucer implies as much in his version in *The Legend of Good
Women*. His Lucrece commits suicide so that her husband will not
have the infamy "for hir gylt ne for hir blame." Chaucer is careful
to point out the correct interpretation of the story: "I telle hyt, for
she was of love so trewe,/ Ne in hir wille she chaunged for no newe."
Shakespeare makes his poem much more explicit. His Lucrece repeatedly emphasizes that only death can clear her of possible blame:

> To clear this spot by death, at least I give
> A badge of fame to slander's livery. . . .
> (ll. 1053–54)

> My blood shall wash the slander of mine ill;
> My life's foul deed, my life's fair end shall free it.
> (ii. 1207–8)

She is very careful in her explanations to her husband and relatives:

> "O, teach me how to make mine own excuse!
> Or at the least this refuge let me find;
> Though my gross blood be stain'd with this abuse,
> Immaculate and spotless is my mind;
> That was not forced; that never was inclined
>   To accessary yieldings, but still pure
>   Doth in her poison'd closet yet endure."
> (ll. 1653–59)

Her listeners acquit her of "accessary yieldings" and urge her to live, but she is quite firm:

> "No, no," quoth she, "no dame, hereafter living,
> By my excuse shall claim excuse's giving."
>
> (ll. 1714–15)

Death, in a certain sense, is a necessary expiation; the woman's suicide is the only conclusive proof that rape is actually rape.

Lucrece was a popular heroine because she met without flinching this stern necessity. In spite of the vast popularity of the Lucrece story itself, however, it was not so productive of Elizabethan analogues as were the Penelope and Susanna stories, because of Christian reservations about suicide. Elizabethans believed that a woman ought to preserve her chastity to the point of death, but they were uncertain about the relative values of lust and suicide as mortal sins. Like St. Augustine, they hesitated to condemn a woman for committing self-murder to avoid or to expiate rape, but they could not advocate it unequivocally. Suicide was quite all right for a Roman and a pagan, but not for the heroines of analogous contemporary tales.

A typical product of this dilemma is Fenton's Discourse VIII, "Julya Drowneth herselfe, for that her bodye was abused by force." Julia, a poor maid of Mantua, is wooed at great length by an attendant of the Bishop. She resists his dishonest overtures and the persuasions of his agents, until her admirer rapes her. After a long lament for her lost honor, Julia throws herself into a river. On the one hand, Fenton considers Julia a modern "pattern of pudicitye" whose "contynent lyvinge and chast disposicioun" exceed that of women of antiquity such as Lucrece, whose praise "the Romains have had alwayes in their mouthe" (II.60). On the other hand, he cannot condone "the ende of this miserable Julia; whose lyfe only deserves commendation for th' example of her vertue, and deathe worthie to be committed to oblyvyon for the signes of desperacion wherewyth it was infected" (II.91). At the conclusion of the story, Julia's body is recovered by the diligent and sympathetic Bishop, but he will "not suffer it to be buryed in the churche-yarde, or other sanctuarye, because of the desperat maner of her death" (II.92). Nonetheless, she is buried in a field with great pomp and lamentations, and a marble monument is erected in her honor. Fenton ends his tale firmly impaled on the horns of the dilemma.

This difficult problem is avoided in Painter's story, "The piteous and chaste death of one of the muleters wives of the Queene of Navarre," Tome I, novella 50. The heroine is attacked by one of her husband's servants, who enters her bedroom, Tarquin-wise, "with a naked sworde in his hande" (II.29). She struggles valiantly, twice overcoming his force. The desperate villain then thinks to subdue her strength by wounding her repeatedly with his sword, but she still continues to struggle until he has given her "xxv. mortall woundes" (II.31). At this point she commends her soul to God and falls into a coma. "After she had lost her speache and the force of her body, thys most wicked and abhominable varlet toke her by force, whiche had no more strength and power to defende her-selfe" (II.30). Thus is the woman cleared of any possible suspicion that she might willingly have acquiesced in the rape, and, at the same time, she dies to vindicate her chastity. Suicide is not in question, so her salvation is assured: "She rendred her chast body to the earth, and her soule to her Creator" (II.31). This "marter of chastitie" is buried in the church, and her funeral is honored by "all the honest dames and wives of the citie" (II.31). For us, of course, this is a hair-raising story of criminal pathology, but for Painter it is an exemplary tale with a beneficent influence; he ends by noting that "the foolish and wanton seing the honour done to that deade bodye, determined from that time forth to renue their former life, and to chaunge the same into a better" (II.31).

The story of the "muleters wife" goes to extreme lengths in removing the suspicion of lust from the ravished woman. Other modern analogues of the Lucrece story solve the problem by substituting a happy ending in which rape is avoided; this often involves the conversion of the would-be ravisher. The Lucrece pattern is thus brought closer to the Penelope and Susanna patterns. Heroines whom we may call successful Lucreces, that is, women who manage to avoid rape, are quite popular. For example, Fenton's Discourse VI tells of the "Villennie of an Abbot in seking to seduce a mayde by force, and her vertue in defending her honor against him and his companyons of traison" (I.247). The abbot, his overtures repulsed by a goldsmith's daughter, attempts to kidnap her; under a pretext of love to him, she obtains a sword from his henchmen, and then proceeds to lay about her stoutly, giving the abbot a wound in the face. Feeling her strength failing, she jumps into a river, preferring drowning to dishonor, but she is providentially rescued by passers-by. She thus escapes the fate worse than death without committing a mortal sin.

Another successful Lucrece, interesting because she defends herself, as do Fletcher's heroines, with rhetoric rather than with a sword, is Lucilla, in the third tale in Barnaby Rich, *Riche His Farewell to Military Profession* (1581).[21] This story, "Nicander and Lucilla," originally from Cinthio, tells of a girl impoverished but of gentle birth, who is not allowed to marry her Nicander because his covetous old father insists upon a large dowry. Don Hercules, son of the Duke of Ferrara, falls in love with Lucilla; she is too low in birth and fortune for him to marry, so he determines to offer a rich dowry if she will consent to his desires. He first approaches the girl's impoverished mother, who reluctantly consents to act as bawd to her own child and arranges for Don Hercules to enter Lucilla's bedroom while the girl sleeps.

The scene is intended to be erotic and clearly reminds one of the entry of the infatuated Tarquin into the bedroom of the unsuspecting Lucrece. Don Hercules, however, is no tyrant, and tries to persuade the girl rather than force her. Her rhetoric, however, is superior to his; here is a sample of her exhortation to virtue:

> if Honestie, if Justice, if Religion, have that power and force in your noble mynde, whiche in reason thei ought to have, I doe beseche you, and for that loves sake that you saie you beare me, that you will preserve and kepe unstained my honestie, and that it would please you with the sounde discourse of reason, to temper that fervent appetite which hath brought you hether, to the prejudice and breathe of my honestie and credit. In doyng where of you shall shewe your self to be, in deede that noble Prince that

21. Ed. T. M. Cranfill (Austin, Tex., 1959). In-text citations refer to page numbers in this edition.

the highnesse of your birthe and bloud doeth promise you should
be, whereas if you should force and violate me a Virgine, and a
weake maiden without defence, there could thereof ensue nought
els to me but dishonor and reproche, and withall small praise
would it be unto your excellence, when it shall be saied that you
had overcome a simple Damsel. (p. 101)

With this speech Lucilla converts Don Hercules; she is saved,
according to the author, by "the force of her own vertue" (pp. 102–
3). Don Hercules controls his sensual appetites and not only provides the girl with the promised dowry but also arranges her
marriage. "What vertue, or what continence of Alexander, or of
Scipio maie be compared to this" (p. 104), asks Rich, and offers
a page of such comparisons and praises for the young prince. The
gentlewoman is equally praiseworthy:

And thus this honeste Damsell Lucilla, by the meanes of her
Chastitie, the vertue and excelencie whereof did winne and mais-
ter the harte of that yonge Prince, muche more then the perfection
of her bodily beautie had dooen before, obtained the thyng she
moste desired and joyed in, whiche was to have Nicander to her
housebande. (p. 105)

It may be noted that a Lucrece who saves herself with words alone
comes rather close to being a Pamela.

This Pamela-like effect is very pronounced in Fletcher's *Maid in
the Mill,* a play that uses this modified Lucrece pattern. Fletcher
also uses the pattern of rape followed by suicide; this pattern appears
in his Roman play *Valentinian,* a context in which suicide is admirable. Fletcher's use of the rape pattern in *The Queen of Corinth*
is rather anomalous and will be discussed in chapter 7.

The Lucrece pattern also appears in the legend of Appius and
Virginia, which is essentially the same story. (Daphne and Syrinx
offer other analogues.) Renaissance versions of Appius and Virginia
are limited in value as exemplary tales because an even stronger
objection attaches to Virginius's murder of his daughter than applies
to Lucrece's suicide. There are many Elizabethan versions of Appius
and Virginia—plays by R. B. in 1564 and by Webster in 1624, and

George Pettie's story of "Icilius and Virginia"—but they modify the story by emphasizing the relationship between Virginia and her betrothed, Icilius. In this way the author can display exemplary chastity by portraying Virginia as remaining faithful to Icilius by spurning the lewd overtures of bawds sent to her by Appius. The sight of Virginia defending her own honor appeals more than the denouement, in which Virginia is ultimately saved from Appius's lewd designs by her father's resolve rather than by her own virtue.

A moral objection also applies to the story of Camma, another faithful woman whose life is often told by Elizabethan storytellers. The tale of Sinorix and Camma appears in Hoby's *Courtier, The Diall of Princes,* Pettie's *Petite Pallace,* and in Humfrey Gifford's *A Posie of Gilloflowers* (1580). Camma is happily married to Sinnatus and resists the dishonest overtures of Sinorix. Sinorix murders Sinnatus and arranges with Camma's relatives to marry the widow. Unwilling to wed this villain, Camma poisons him and then herself. Moralists frequently cited Camma for her wifely loyalty but were unwilling to press the exemplum too far. Pettie's version indicates why. Although Pettie commends her "constancie and chastitie" and considers her "worthy to bee compared to Lucrece, Penelope, or what woman soever that ever had any preheminence of praise for her vertue," he considers Camma in danger of damnation for her "wilfull and voluntary death."[22]

Penelope, Susanna, Lucrece—these three heroines provide models of good wives for the Elizabethan imagination. Elizabethans tend, in some degree, to see all good wives as copies of these three mirrors of modesty. These heroines also provide the basic story patterns for the representation of good wives: the Penelope pattern, defense of chastity against seduction; the Susanna pattern, defense of chastity against the slander of a lecherous villain; the Lucrece pattern, rape and suicide; and the modified Lucrece pattern, defense of chastity against a would-be rapist. Slander, seduction, rape—here are the so-called sensational situations of Fletcherian drama, the products

---

22. *Petite Pallace,* pp. 37–38. Versions of the Camma story are discussed by Douglas Bush, "The Petite Pallace of Pettie His Pleasure," *JEGP* 27 (1928) : 162.

of Fletcher's supposedly unhealthy imaginings. They come from Elizabethan exemplary literature.

It was as easy to combine as it was to modify the patterns of the three great mirrors of modesty. We have already seen how Greene combined the Susanna and Penelope motifs to portray the faithful wife of the erring playwright in *Never Too Late* and *Francesco's Fortunes*. His example shows the possibilities for storytellers in manipulating and combining the basic patterns of the three examples of chastity. Indeed, the three stories already overlap to some degree. The parallel between Lucrece's spinning during her husband's absence in Ardea and Penelope's weaving is noticed, as we have seen, in Greene's *Penelope's Web*. Tarquin's threat to ruin Lucrece's reputation by accusing her of adultery is carried out against Susanna by the Elders. Ulysses' return to Ithaca in disguise to discover Penelope's situation reminds one of Collatine viewing Lucrece unawares at her spinning. These and other plot elements are repeated in numerous stories of persecuted wives and maidens.

The Elizabethan tendency to apprehend the chaste woman in terms of exempla and archetypical situations is balanced by the corresponding tendency to apprehend the lustful woman in terms of similarly archetypical patterns. Just as Fletcher's faithful wives find their models in the famous mirrors of modesty, so his villainesses are modeled on the famous mirrors of immodesty. These wanton women were considered mirrors also, for they were exempla of the type of behavior a woman should avoid.

The Reward of Whoredom: Helen, Lais, Messalina

Writers could cite as many examples of vicious women as of virtuous ones. The great archetypes of faithless women were Helen and Cressida. "A kite of Cressid's kind" is a commonplace in sonnets and ballads for the fickle woman.[23] Helen is a more ambivalent figure, because she was not only the example par excellence of evil behavior in a wife but was also "the face that launched a thousand

---

23. See, for example, *Gorgeous Gallery*, p. 38; *The Paradise of Dainty Devices*, ed. Hyder E. Rollins (Cambridge, Mass., 1927), pp. 117-18.

ships," the highest symbol of earthly beauty. Nonetheless, many a poetaster resolutely shut his eyes to this vision of beauty and castigated Helen in verse. She is made to lament her life in the hell described in Robinson's *The Reward of Wickednesse* (1574) and by T. P. in "The reward of whoredome by the fall of Helen," which was printed in *A Gorgeous Gallery of Gallant Inventions* (1578). She is roundly denounced by Thomas Howell in "Ruine the Rewarde of Vice" (1581) and by Richard Barnfield in "Hellens Rape, or A light Lanthorne for light Ladies" (1594).[24] In her aspect as unfaithful wife, Helen is commonly paired off against Penelope, as we have seen already in Colse's *Penelope's Complaint*. Any of the English poetical miscellanies will furnish several further instances. Thomas Norton's "Against women either good or bad," for example, is a misogynistic exercise on this standard comparison:

> For one good wife Ulysses slew
> A worthy knot of gentle blood;
> For one ill wife Greece overthrew
> The town of Troy. Sith bad and good
> Work mischief, Lord, let be thy will
> To keep me free from either ill![25]

For our purposes the poem's misogyny is of course irrelevant; Norton's verse is interesting because of its assumption of Penelope as the exemplar of good women, and Helen of bad.

Although Helen and Cressida are so facilely used as exempla of lightness, their lives are not usually made patterns for fiction[26] as are the lives of Penelope, Susanna, and Lucrece. The light woman in literature may be reviled as a Helen or a Cressida, but she is seen under the figure of Lais, the irresistible courtesan. This is doubtless due to Reformation ethics, which cause a polarization in attitudes toward women. A woman is either good or she is a whore. If she is

---

24. *Howell's Devises,* ed. Walter Raleigh (Oxford, 1906), pp. 18–19; *The Poems of Richard Barnfield 1594–1598,* ed. Edward Arber, *The English Scholar's Libary* 14 (London, 1882): 38–40.

25. Ed. Norman Ault, *Elizabethan Lyrics* (London, 1925), p. 30. Also in *Tottel's Miscellany,* 1:201.

26. Spenser's tale of Hellenore is a notable exception; see the discussion of *The Faerie Queene* in chap. 5.

a professional, she is a siren-like Lais. If she is a court lady, as is the case in Fletcher's plays, the Lais figure tends to merge with the figure of Messalina, who becomes, for an age familiar with Juvenal's Sixth Satire, the archetype of the woman who uses her high position to gratify her inordinate lusts. Because Elizabethans did not, as do their modern readers, think in terms of pathology, they were fascinated with nymphomaniacs like Messalina because they saw nymphomaniacal behavior as an example of deliberate wickedness. Just as the author of *The Yorkshire Tragedy* delineates a pathological murderer in Walter Calvery but sees his protagonist's actions in moral terms, so the Elizabethans delineated the symptoms of nymphomania in literature but saw such behavior in terms of deliberate evil.

The modern example of the Messalina-like nymphomaniac who most fascinated Elizabethans was the Countess of Celant. Painter, Fenton, and Whetstone told her story,[27] and Marston adapted her life as the basis for *The Insatiate Countess*. The Countess of Celant's life was very satisfactory, for, after enjoying years of lascivious pleasure and then inciting her lovers to murder each other, she was arrested and beheaded, thus demonstrating, according to Painter, that "God which is a rightfull judge· woulde not suffer hir wickednesse stretch any further" (III.77). Painter concludes his narration of her life with obvious satisfaction:

> Thus miserably and repentantly dyed the Countesse, which in hir lyfe refused not to imbrace and follow any wickednes, no mischiefe shee accompted evill done, so the same were imployed for hir pleasure and pastime. A goodly example truely for the youth of our present time, sith the most part indifferently do launch into the gulfe of disordred lyfe, suffring themselves to be plunged in the puddles of their owne vayne conceiptes, without consideration of the mischieves that may ensue. (III.77)

When Fletcher portrays a villainess in a chastity play, she is seen as a woman like the wicked Countess of Celant. His Brunhalts, Bachas, and Megras are all Messalina figures.

---

27. Painter, Tome II, novella 24; Fenton, Discourse VII; Whetstone, *Rock of Regard,* pp. 16–35. The latter is a verse complaint in which the Countess of Celant laments her evil life and points out the moral of her fall.

Messalina and Penelope—between these two poles the Elizabethan artistic imagination moved in its portrayal of lustful and chaste women. Fletcher's Penelope-like Orianas are contrasted with his Messalina-like Brunhalts. There is another factor, however, that must be taken into account when examining the antecedents of Fletcher's chaste heroines. This is the Elizabethan attempt to portray native heroines as examples of chastity able to stand on the same footing with the archetypes of Greek, Roman, and Biblical story. The stories of native heroines, from Jane Shore to Britomart, were as useful to Fletcher as were the exempla from antiquity. Fletcher had a hand in some fifty plays, after all, several dozen of them chastity plays, and he needed as much material as he could find. The development of a pattern for the chaste English heroine not only provided him with such material, but also modified, to some degree, the conception of what a chaste woman should be and do. In the next chapter, then, we shall consider chastity literature that describes English heroines.

5

English Patterns of Pudicity

The impulse to glorify chastity led not only to the frequent retelling of the lives of Penelope, Susanna, and Lucrece but also to the popularity of stories like "The Lady of Bohemia," which were seen as modern analogues. The growing self-consciousness of the Renaissance as a new era able to measure itself against antiquity is very explicit, for example, in Fenton. He decries "the negligence we use in recording the rarietyes of our time." He himself is bold enough

> to preferr the benefitt of oure time; which, participating wyth their golden age in any respect of honest gift or qualitie, is hable to present a furniture of as many examples and authorities of vertue as we rede were founde in the politike state of Rome . . . or when one Pericles . . . bare authoritie in the florishing Acadimia of Athens. (II.58)

Moreover, he continues, we are "lyvynge under a better clymat and constellacion, enjoying more pure lawes, and aspiringe nerer th' ymage or semblaunce of dyvynitie" (II.60). As an illustration of his theory, Fenton tells of the chaste Julia, an Italian Lucrece, because she exemplifies "at this day sundry pattorns of pudycitye in the persons of all degres of women, aswel noble as of meaner condicion, exceding the vertue of such as antiquitie hath in so great veneracion" (II.60).

103

Heroines of English History and Legend

Englishmen could not, however, remain content very long merely to admire heroines from modern Italian story. The desire to make the modern age rival antiquity soon became a chauvinistic desire to find "a Britaine Lucretia, or an English Susanna."[1] With the same national consciousness that led to the belief in Brutus, a descendant of Aeneas, as founder of Britain, and of a Troynovant in London, English authors wished to glorify the examples of chastity from the history and legend of their own country. They were not very successful in the effort until the 1590s (the same decade, interestingly enough, that brought to bloom in Shakespeare's history plays the Tudor version of the Wars of the Roses). They had, of course, same slight claim to the Duchess of Savoy; Painter manifests obvious satisfaction in the fact that she was the sister of the King of England. There was also the Countess of Salisbury, who, according to legend, converted Edward III from lust.

There are several versions of this story,[2] but as Painter tells it (Tome I, novella 46), King Edward, while the Earl of Salisbury is fighting abroad, goes to the assistance of his young wife, beseiged by the Scots. Edward is conquered by her beauty, but she resists his advances and remains faithful to her absent husband. When the Earl dies, King Edward continues to woo her, but she refuses his dishonorable suit until the lovesick king persuades her father and mother to solicit their own daughter to sin. Desperate, the Countess of Salisbury presents herself to King Edward but draws a knife, announcing that she prefers death to dishonor. Edward, moved by this display of virtue, repents and makes her his lawful queen. With the exception of the concluding marriage, this story of Edward reminds one of Martius in *The Triumph of Honor,* who is deaf to all persuasions to virtue until the chaste Dorigen threatens to kill herself.

---

1. Henry Willoby, *Avisa,* Spenser Society Publications, no. 42 (Manchester, 1886), p. 2.
2. See the discussion by René Pruvost, *Matteo Bandello and Elizabethan Fiction* (Paris, 1937), pp. 31–32.

The Countess of Salisbury, being a fellow countrywoman, sends Painter into transports of praise. He links the tale as a companion-piece to his immediately preceding story of the "fayre and innocente" Duchess of Savoy, because it displays "the perfect figure of woman-hode" and "the glorious reward that chastitie conduceth to her imbracers" (I.334). Painter describes his purpose in translating this tale as being

> aswel for encouragement of Ladies to imbrace constancie, as to embolden them in the refusal of dishonest sutes, for which if they do not acquire semblable honour, as this Lady did, yet they shall not be frustrate of the due reward incidente to honour, which is fame and immortall prayse. (I.335)

He goes on to praise the Countess of Salisbury's resistance against prayers, promises, and threats, her "singuler preservation in defence of her chastitie inexpugnable," which "esclarisheth to the whole flocke of womankinde the brighte beames of wisedome, vertue, and honestie" (I.335).

At the same time that Painter praises the Countess, he displays uneasiness as to the authenticity of the story. He is careful to advise his readers that he has checked the story against the chronicles of Fabian, Polydore Virgil, and Froissart, and finds a great number of serious errors, notably that Edward III is mistaken for his son Edward, the Black Prince. "Yet the grace of the historie for all those errours is not diminished" (I.336). Painter feels uneasy also about another objection that may arise about the story. Edward was a great hero, "eternized for his victories and vertues in auncient Annales, Chronicles and Monuments, forren and domesticall" (I.336). Perhaps this story of a chaste heroine beleaguered by a lustful monarch will dishonor the illustrious race of English kings. Nevertheless, Painter is anxious to tell his tale, so he points out that kings, like "all nature's children," are "subjecte to the infirmities of their first parentes" (I.336).

This problem, however, meant that English writers were left with a series of royal mistresses—Jane Shore, Elstred, and Rosamond—as warning exempla. As the woman was to blame for a liaison of this nature, no serious stigma attached to Edward IV, Locrine, or Henry II. Moreover, with the example before them of Mary Magdalene, an adulteress who not only repented but eventually became a saint, Elizabethans found it easy to forgive an adulteress if she was repentant and if she suffered enough for her sins.

Jane Shore was the first of these repentant adulteresses to appear in Elizabethan exemplary literature. Thomas Churchyard's "Shore's Wife" was included in the 1563 edition of *The Mirror for Magistrates;* this verse complaint portrays a very repentant woman indeed, one easy to forgive and moralize over. Indeed, Churchyard's interpretation of her life makes this forgiveness the easier, since Jane is allowed to offer the excuse of an unhappy marriage, forced upon her when she was too young to resist, and to describe the severe punishment and public humiliation she endured, after Edward's death, at the hands of Richard III. Her inclusion in the *Mirror* is striking because only she among the other characters is included for a non-political failing. The nature of that failing is made clear in the moral she draws:

> Example take by me both maide and wyfe,
> Beware, take heede, fall not to follie so,
> A myrrour make of my great overthrowe:
> Defye this world, and all his wanton wayes,
> Beware by me, that spent so yll her dayes.[3]

After Jane Shore, a series of victims of lust were popularized in prose and verse.

The next was Elstred, mistress to the legendary British king Locrine; John Higgins told her story in *The First Part of the Mirror for Magistrates,* published in 1574. Elstred was a German princess who came to England with the invading army of Humber, King of the Huns. After Humber's defeat and death, the beauty of the captive princess conquered Locrine. Unfortunately, however, the King was already betrothed to Gwendoline, whom he married for fear of her father's power. He nevertheless kept Elstred as a mis-

---

3. *The Mirror for Magistrates,* ed. Lily B. Campbell (Cambridge, 1938), p. 386.

tress, hiding her for many years from the jealous queen in a special cave. After Gwendoline's father died, Locrine divorced her and married Elstred. The incensed queen gathered an army, defeated the king, and ordered Elstred and her daughter to be drowned. Higgins's language in this verse complaint clearly shows imitation of Churchyard's poem, but his moralizing differs considerably. Although Elstred complains that her fall was due to climbing above her social station and warns women lest they be abused by their own beauty, Higgins draws a further moral based on Locrine's defeat and death: "Wherefore let noble men beware of beauties grace,/ Lest so inflam'd they chaunce to fall thereby."[4] Locrine's fault, however, lies not so much in his taking a concubine as in his highhanded dismissal of his lawful queen. This was as politically inept as it was immoral, for the queen's relatives were powerful military and political allies. Amid the political questions, Elstred becomes insignificant; she was not to appear as a sentimentalized adulteress until some twenty years later.

The verse complaint embodying the repentance and sufferings of a royal mistress did not reach a respectable level of artistic achievement until Samuel Daniel's *Complaint of Rosamond* (1592), the single most influential of such verse narratives.[5] In Daniel's hands the *Mirror* tradition of exemplary tales in verse becomes a fine art. *Rosamond* is also significant for our discussion because Daniel farces out his poem with the motifs that his contemporary Greene was using to portray chastity in his prose tales. Daniel's interpretation of Rosamond's life constantly points out the moral direction of the tale as a warning exemplum. The spirit of Rosamond rises in shame from the "infernall deepes" (l. 1), complaining that she is forgotten, while

---

4. *Parts Added to the Mirror for Magistrates,* ed. Lily B. Campbell (Cambridge, 1946), p. 101.

5. See the discussion by Homer Nearing, *English Historical Poetry 1599–1641* (Philadelphia, 1945), pp. 23 ff. Cf. Tucker Brooke, *The Renaissance,* vol. 2 in *A Literary History of England,* ed. Albert C. Baugh (New York, 1948) : 403. For Shakespeare's use of *Rosamond* in his *Lucrece,* see the Variorum edition of his poems, ed. Rollins, pp. 425–26. In-text citations of *Rosamond* refer to Samuel Daniel, *The Complete Works in Prose and Verse,* 4 vols. (London, 1885), vol. 1.

> Shores wife is grac'd, and passes for a Saint;
> Her Legend justifies her foule attaint.
>
> (ll. 25–26)

Rosamond requests the same attention from her poet, for her story will "teach to others what I learnt too late" (l. 67). She begins her lament by describing her youthful happiness in the country before her preferment to court, "There where to stand, and be unconquered,/ Is to b'above the nature of our kinde" (ll. 103–4). Her beauty inflames the old king, Henry II, who "seekes all meanes to undermine" her virtue:

> Which never by assault he could recover,
> So well incamp'd in strength of chaste desires:
> My clean-arm'd thoughts repell'd an unchaste lover.
> The Crowne that could command what it requires,
> I lesser priz'd then Chastities attires.
>
> (ll. 211–15)

Rosamond stands firm until assaulted by an old she-bawd whose "smoothest speech" lasts eleven stanzas.

This speech leaves Rosamond "in a doubt," and she debates the issue with herself, reminding herself that she should choose death "ere Serpent tempt thee taste forbidden Tree" (l. 332). As in Greene's version of Susanna's life in *The Myrrour of Modestie,* the agents of lust are "serpents," and the state of sexual innocence is by implication likened to the innocence in Paradise before the fall. Rosamond is not so courageous as Susanna, however, and when she reminds herself that Henry can defame her honor if she refuses him, she is frightened into compliance. As Henry has made no such threat of slander, it seems apparent that Daniel has dragged in this argument deliberately, in order to imply a contrast between the biblical heroine and the fallen woman. Sin brings Rosamond no pleasure. Jane Shore had at least enjoyed a transient pomp and power, but Rosamond does not even enjoy Henry's lovemaking, and, as soon as she has submitted to him, instantly repents:

> Now did I finde my selfe unparadis'd

From those pure fields of my so cleane beginning. . . .

(ll. 456–57)

Moreover, Henry's age breeds jealousy, so he keeps her a virtual prisoner in a specially constructed labyrinth. Rumor of this liaison reaches the "wronged Queene," who forces poor Rosamond to take poison. Rosamond dies wretchedly and alone after a fifteen-stanza deathbed speech of repentance and despair, urging court beauties to preserve their chastity. She inveighs most bitterly against she-bawds, who are

> Serpents of guile, Devils, that doe invite
> The wanton taste of that forbidden tree,
> Whose fruit once pluckt, will shew how foule we bee.
>
> (ll. 747–49)

The poem concludes with Henry's lament over her dead body. Daniel's poem points with great emphasis to the miserable fate that awaits adulterers.

Daniel set a style by infusing the motifs of chastity literature into the verse complaint. Thomas Lodge carefully follows Daniel's pattern in his *Complaint of Elstred* (1593),[6] making another royal mistress point a moral. Lodge changes the emphasis of Elstred's life so as to make more obvious the similarities to Rosamond's. Locrine, after he marries, is given a speech persuading Elstred to remain his mistress. The cave of the *Mirror* account, where she lives in secret as Locrine's concubine, becomes a labyrinth built for her by the king. She is given a lament over Locrine's dead body that parallels Henry's lament over the corpse of Rosamond. The queen upbraids Elstred for her lasciviousness, but Elstred defends herself by declaring that her sin was "unwilling and enforced" (p. 80). Nonetheless, she is, of course, repentant and acknowledges that it was not Fortune that brought her downfall and death. Rather, "It was but justice, from the heavens inflicted/ On lustfull life, defamed and convicted" (p.

---

6. Lodge appended *Elstred* to his sonnet sequence *Phillis*, as *Rosamond* was appended to Daniel's *Delia* (Nearing, p. 24). In-text citations of *Elstred* refer to Thomas Lodge, *The Complete Works*, 4 vols. (London, 1883; repr. New York, 1963), vol. 3.

75). Lodge's *Elstred* was not the only imitation of Daniel's immensely popular poem. Also in 1593 appeared two more versions of Jane Shore's life. Antony Chute retold her life in *Bewty Dishonored,* and Churchyard augmented his earlier version of her life for inclusion in *Churchyard's Challenge,* a miscellany of his works in prose and verse.[7]

The poetic historian Michael Drayton produced in *Matilda* (1594) an English heroine whose life more closely paralleled the lives of the three preeminent examples of chastity. His verse complaint tells of a fair maid persecuted to her death by King John because she refused to become his mistress. King John, unlike Edward III, was not a popular hero[8] and therefore was more suitable for the role of lustful tyrant. Matilda, for her part, was entirely suitable for the role of heroine, because she defended her chastity to the point of death without actually committing suicide. Drayton's dedication of his poem to Lucy Harrington commends Matilda as

A mirror of so rare chastitie, as neither the fayre speeches, nor rich rewards of a king, nor death it selfe, could ever remove from her owne chast thoughts: or from that due regard which shee had of her never-stained honor.[9]

Drayton is quite careful to point out that his heroine is superior to the sentimentalized adulteresses of previous poems. Matilda begins her complaint by dedicating her story to "sacred Vestalls" (l. 16) and by invoking Queen Elizabeth as a suitable muse for her poet, "That he may write of sacred Chastitie" (l. 61). She objects that a poet has placed Rosamond "in our Sainted Legendarie" (l. 31), for

---

7. In his dedication of *Churchyard's Challenge* (London, 1593) to Lady Mount Eagle and Compton, the author explains that "because Rosimond is so excellently sette forth (the actor whereof I honour) I have somewhat beautified my Shores wife" (p. 136). Chute's version is discussed by Nearing, p. 24.

8. In spite of the efforts of Bishop Bale and John Foxe to portray John as a Protestant martyr. The literary fortunes of King John in the early Renaissance are discussed by S. F. Johnson, "The Tragic Hero in Early Elizabethan Drama," *Studies in the English Renaissance Drama,* ed. J. W. Bennet et al. (New York, 1959), pp. 157-71.

9. Michael Drayton, *Works,* ed. J. William Hebel (Oxford, 1931; repr. London, 1961), 1:210. In-text citations refer to this edition.

"all his skill cannot excuse her cryme" (l. 35). Even Shore's wife and Elstred are praised by "modern Poets"; these "looser wantons" are praised when the virtuous are neglected. There is one encouraging exception in Lucrece:

> Lucrece, of whom proude Rome hath boasted long,
> Lately reviv'd to live another age,
>
> . . . .
>
> She is remembred, all forgetting me,
> Yet I as fayre and chast, as ere was she.
> (ll. 36–37; 41–42)

This is undoubtedly a reference to Shakespeare's poem, published earlier in the same year, and Drayton's admiration is obvious. Clearly he wishes to imply by the comparison that Matilda is to be thought of as an English Lucrece.

Drayton incorporates into his poem the traditional ideas about chastity: Chastity is a gift of grace, the court is a pernicious environment, bawds are devils, and a chaste death confers a kind of sainthood. Matilda's troubles begin when rumor of her virtue and beauty reaches King John and arouses his passion. Her father foresees the danger and warns Matilda at length against "this wanton Prince" (l. 253), while praising chastity and good fame. In a contrasting movement, Matilda hears a seduction speech from the King, who flatters her beauty, appeals to her pity, and offers power, advancement for her friends, a life of ease, and protection from the Queen's jealousy. Matilda wavers, "till Grace divine from highest heaven came" (l. 446). Fortified with this heavenly succor, she leaves the court, where her chastity is "in danger every hower" (l. 461), and takes refuge with her father. To remove this protection, John accuses her father of treason; in the ensuing civil war, the king is successful and Matilda's father is banished. The grieving father laments his daughter's unprotected state, and envies the Roman Virginius (l. 596) who was able to save his child from tyranny.

The King continues to woo Matilda and continues to be frustrated. Finally, to ease his agony, he sends a poisoner, "A divell, walking in a humaine shape" (l. 730), to Dunmow abbey, where Matilda is now living as a nun. King John's devilish agent makes one last attempt to persuade her to lust and then forces her to swallow poison. She welcomes death, as John has actually done her a favor:

> Hee is the tuch by whom my gold is tryed,
> Onely by him my death is sanctified.
> (ll. 895–96)

Matilda dies a sainted martyr to chastity. Matilda's sainthood is emphasized by Drayton's description of King John's repentance, which causes him to do penance by a monthly pilgrimage to Dunmow abbey:

> And in a simple Palmers weede disguis'd,
> With deepe devotion kneele him downe to pray:
> Kissing the place, whereas my body lay.
> (ll. 1109–11)

The same idea of Matilda's sanctity is expressed, also in 1594, in Richard Barnfield's "Complaint of Chastity." Chastity herself is the speaker and singles Matilda out for praise because she chose poison rather

> Then staine that milk-white Mayden-virgin Rose,
> Which shee had kept unspotted till that time:
> And not corrupted with this earthly slime
> Her soule shall live: inclosed eternally,
> In that pure shrine of Immortality.[10]

All the English heroines reappear in Drayton's *England's Heroicall Epistles* (1597), an imitation of Ovid's *Heroides*. This work contains verse letters imagined to be written between Rosamond and Henry II, Matilda and King John, Edward the Black Prince and the Countess of Salisbury, and Edward IV and Jane Shore.[11] Matilda and the Countess of Salisbury were apparently the only chaste heroines that English history had to offer. Elizabethans had their queen, of course, as a living exemplum, but they could hardly portray her life

---

10. Barnfield, *Poems,* p. 37.
11. Drayton, vol. 2.

in fiction while she was still living. An alternative for a writer who wished to glorify English chastity further, would be to invent or find his own heroine.

This is the method used in that strange work, Henry Willobie's *Avisa* (1594). *Avisa* is a full-scale treatment of the Penelope story in several thousand lines of execrable verse, but the prefatory matter and the poem itself hint very strongly that the heroine is an English wife actually alive at the time of composition. *Avisa* is probably a *pièce à clef* embodying some now-lost literary gossip.[12] Whatever its hidden topical allusions, the poem takes the form of an elaborate glorification of a chaste English heroine. It marks an extreme point in the elaboration of speeches of seduction and of the defense of chastity, for *Avisa* is a narrative poem with the narrative links removed so that only these speeches remain. The result is a compendium of all the conventional arguments either for or against chastity; as such, the poem deserves rather lengthy quotation and summary.

The subtitle describes the poem as "the true Picture of a modest Maide, and of a chaste and constant Wife." The dedication "To all the constant Ladies and Gentlewomen of England that feare God" urges, "If mine Author have found a Britaine Lucretia, or an English Susanna, envy not at her praise (good Ladyes) but rather endeavour to deserve the like" (p. 2). This introductory material claims that Avisa is an acronym for *Amans uxor inviolata semper amanda,* or "A loving wife, that never violated her faith, is alwayes to be beloved" (p. 4). The construct is clever. The heroine's name is surely based on the Latin, "Rara avis in terris, nigroque simillima cygno,/ Foemina casta volat," quoted (p. 8) in "The Epistle to the Reader." The five wooers Avisa refuses in the poem represent the Italian, Spanish, French, German, and English styles of solicitation. As Englishmen have adopted all these modes of seduction, the survey

---

12. See G. B. Harrison's essay in his edition of *Avisa* (London, 1926). In-text citations refer to the Spenser Society edition. Other speculations about contemporary allusions in *Avisa* can be found in Leslie Hotson, *I, William Shakespeare* (London, 1937) and Tucker Brooke, "Willobie's *Avisa,*" *Essays in Honor of Albert Feuillerat,* ed. Henry M. Peyre (New Haven, 1943). Critics agree only in assuming that the work is topical; they are unable to agree on the precise nature of its topical significance.

will show "how honest maides and women in such temptations should stand upon their gard" (p. 6).

Commendatory verses signed Vigilantius Dormitanus deserve quotation at length for their expression of chauvinistic desire to display an English heroine more exalted than those women heretofore considered the chief exemplars of chastity:

> Though Collatine have dearely bought,
> To high renowne a lasting life,
> And found, that most in vaine have sought,
> To have a faire and Constant wife
>   Yet Tarquine pluckt his glistering grape,
>   And Shake-speare paints poore Lucrece rape.
>
> Though Susan shine in faithfull praise,
> As twinkling starres in Chrystall skie:
> Penelop's fame though Greekes do raise,
> Of faithfull wives to make up three:
>   To thinke the Truth, and say no lesse;
>   Our Avisa shall make a messe.
> . . . .
>
> Then Avi-Susan joyne in one,
> Let Lucres-Avis be thy name.
> This English Eagle soares alone,
> And far surmounts all others fame,
>   Where high or low, where great or small,
>   This Britan Bird outflies them all.
>   (pp. 15–16)

This introduces the reader to Canto I, in which the author declares that his muse "To vertues prayse hath past her vow" (p. 17). He has chosen a heroine superior to Penelope, and one whose "beauties warre,/ For trials passe Susanna's farre" (p. 18). Avisa's chastity is a special gift of grace (pp. 20–21) and has kept her constant in spite of England's late transformation into "Sodoms sinke" (p. 23), a situation denounced by the use of copious biblical comparisons.

The remaining seventy-three cantos are divided into five trials, or temptations, by the following suitors: a nobleman (cantos 2–13), who solicits Avisa before her marriage; a "caveileiro" (14–22), who represents the "Roysters, young Gentlemen, and lusty Captaines" (p. 45) who approach her after her marriage to an innkeeper; D. B., a Frenchman (23–33), the "close and warie sutor" who uses "a long continued course of curtesie" (p. 58); D. H., Anglo-Germanus (34–43), who is converted from lust by Avisa; and Henrico Willobego, Italo-Hispalensis (44–74).

Each of these five courtships is conducted according to the Elizabethan idea of literary decorum. The nobleman, for example, woos according to the proper character of a noble. He begins proudly, congratulating her on her good fortune in attracting him; she will have riches, fine clothes, power, and her friends will be similarly advanced. He laughs at her for being "precise" (i.e., puritanical) and points out that her betters—Queen Joan of Naples, Cleopatra, Messalina—have been "wont to play" (p. 30).[13] She is too young to perceive her good fortune; youth and beauty will soon decay. He offers secrecy and the protection of his "mightie name"; if she desires, he will find her a husband (as Fletcher's King in *The Maid's Tragedy* is to do for Evadne) to "be a chimnie for the smoke" (p. 39). When the nobleman is rebuffed, his love turns to hate and he threatens to obtain revenge by ruining her reputation. This proud, haughty approach, which turns to revenge when refused, is characteristic of nobles, kings, and of any suitor far above the social station of the maid addressed. Drayton's annotations of his *Heroicall Epistles* are illuminating on this point. His note to the letter from King John to Matilda tells us that this lover well expresses the "humors" of a king in love:

> first, jesting at the Ceremonies of the Services of those Times; then, going about by all strong and probable Arguments, to reduce her to Pleasures and Delights; next, with promises of Honour, which he thinketh to be the last and greatest Meanes, and to have greatest power in her Sexe.[14]

---

13. Cf. above, chap. 3, Breton's citation of Cleopatra as an example of constancy. Unlike Penelope, Cleopatra is an ambivalent figure, cited both for her wantonness and for her constancy to Antony. Shakespeare plays skillfully on this ambivalence in *Antony and Cleopatra*.

14. Drayton, 2:152.

The description is equally applicable to Fletcher's lustful tyrants.

Avisa's replies to the nobleman indicate the appropriate response to such lofty offers. Though she is poor, she disdains to be a whore; true happiness is built on virtue, not wealth. Avisa's answer shows that she has profited from the mistakes of others:

> Shores wife, a Princes secret friend,
> Faire Rosamond, a Kings delight:
> Yet both have found a gastly end. . . .
>   (p. 28)

She reminds the nobleman that his high station makes it incumbent upon him to set a good example. Messalina and her kind are not queens, but queanes (i.e., whores). If death is the reward of sin, can one be too precise? She refuses to listen further, for his feeling cannot be love, because he wishes to bring her soul to damnation. When he offers force, she produces a knife, threatening to kill him or herself rather than yield to his "divelish traines" (p. 41). She defies his threats of revenge, trusting, like Susanna, in the Lord.

Avisa faces a different sort of suitor in the "caveileiro," a bluff, hearty military man. He offers her "knackes" and trinkets and takes her first refusal as a fashionable affectation. Indeed, her first repulse heartens him, because those who make the most of their consciences are usually the worst offenders. Puzzled by her continued refusal, he finally offers to give over his suit if she will swear that she has never been unfaithful to her husband. When she does so swear, he departs good-naturedly. In dealing with this soldier, Avisa has much to say besides giving him an oath that she is a faithful wife. She chides him for assuming that a woman is in love with him merely because she has pleasant manners. Her house is not a stews, and she has no desire to catch "the French mans badge" (p. 48), which he has doubtless picked up from his queanes. She lectures him about the laws of God and men against adulterers; significantly, her examples—the laws of the Locrenses, the Romans, and the Arabians—are taken straight from the "Homily on Adultery."

Avisa can reply in the soldier's own martial metaphors:

Though you be loth to sound retreate,
This mount's too strong for you to get.

. . . .

No captaine did, nor never shall,
Set ladder heere to scale the wall.

(p. 55)

Her broad double entendres and her references to venereal disease
show her as knowledgeable and worldly as she is innocent, a combination of qualities that reappears in the typical Fletcherian heroine.

The next suitor, the Frenchman D. B., places himself in the flattering posture of the lover overcome with Avisa's beauty; only she can
assuage the terrible torments caused by his love for her. He offers
himself as a "secret frend," for, as he declares, all ladies nowadays
take a friend in addition to a husband. This has always been ac-
counted but a "pettie crime," for even King David and Solomon
had their concubines and were still beloved of the Lord. Avisa
dismisses the Frenchman and his torments out of hand, recommend-
ing a doctor, or, preferably, repentance. She denounces his "lewd
example": David and Solomon were punished for swerving from
God's law. Avisa has no intention of allowing a sophistical perversion of biblical precedent; she is as sure as Greene's Penelope that
love is constant only when it is based on virtue, not on appetite.

In contrast to D. B.'s French approach, D. H., the Anglo-Ger-
manic lover, begins his suit with modest blushes, professing inability
to flatter or deceive. Visiting her house one day "and finding her all
alone amongst her Maides spinning" (p. 84), he writes a letter
comparing her to Penelope at her weaving. Avisa scorns his shy
blushes as "slie conceits" (p. 77) and makes plain her love and
fidelity to her husband, who has an advantage over Ulysses in that
he is always at home. Eventually D. H. acknowledges that his
professed love was only lust, and, had she given in, he would have
considered her a whore. Her virtue, however, has converted him,
and he gives up his "lewde attempts" on her chastity, hoping she
will accept him as her "honest friend" (p. 90) if time proves him
so. The reforming power of chastity, a power we have seen already

in "Nicander and Lucilla," quickly becomes a commonplace in chastity literature.

The "Italo-Hispalensis" love of Henrico Willobego has a less conclusive ending. H. W. is young and presumably in love for the first time; he adopts the pose of the courtly lover, suffering and secret. He persists obstinately in his suit, even when Avisa counters him with biblical quotations. When she refuses to hear him any further, he writes her long letters. He takes to his bed, "refusing both foode and comfort for many dayes together" (p. 124), until his friends fear for his health and sanity. Finally, she commands him to write no more, and he unhappily gives up his assaults and is left in despair. The implication of this concluding section of the poem is clear; courtly love is not idyllic but destructive. H. W. is not unappealing; he is a young man, in love with love, and in his suit reminds one forcibly of Philautus and his hopeless suit to Camilla in *Euphues and his England* (1580).

The author of *Avisa* seems to have intended, by this combination of popular motifs, moralizing, and topical allusions, to produce a best seller. If so, he was not disappointed, for *Avisa* remained in print for forty years.[15] The poem is interesting not only because of its subject matter but also because its exclusive reliance on dialogue shows how easily such debate on chastity could be transferred to the stage.

The portrayal of these English examples of chastity introduces a slightly different note into chastity literature, and that is the rather strident self-righteousness of the chaste heroine. The copious overstatement of principle and moral is apparently the result of the sense of strain that English authors feel in their attempt to exalt "a Brytaine Lucretia or an English Susanna." The Penelopes, Susannas, and Lucreces in English dress are prigs, as we have seen in chapter 4, but they have the assurance of history that they are famous exempla. This assurance comes from that topsy-turvy anachronism which credits these heroines with intimations of their own futures, as when Greene's Penelope complacently accepts her maid's prediction that "blind Homer" will undoubtedly sing her praises as

---

15. Harrison, *Avisa,* pp. 184–85.

a chaste wife. English heroines are even greater prigs, in the effort, apparently, to claim their future praises right away. This attempt to insist upon the future means that the reader is treated to such odd spectacles as Avisa proclaiming her honest intentions for some seventy interminable cantos and a repentant adulteress like Rosamond carefully pointing out the moral lesson demonstrated by each event in her wretched history. "Chaste fury," rather an unlikable quality, becomes a part of the personality of succeeding chaste heroines, not excepting those of Fletcher.

Another feature contributed by tales of English chastity is the heavier emphasis placed upon the "sainthood" of the chaste heroine. There are a number of reasons for this. Many of these stories actually derive from saints' lives, particularly those modeled upon the Susanna pattern. The "Ladie Falslie Accused" who is saved by the miracle of the lions is surely related to the life of a saint. There are numerous virgin martyrs who are protected by kindly animals; a bear protects the virginity of St. Columba of Sens against the evil machinations of the Emperor Aurelian.[16] *Les Miracles de Notre Dame* dramatized many such stories; number XXVII, for example, deals with the history of a Roman empress falsely accused of adultery.[17] Presumably English miracle plays used materials similar to the French miracles, but this is of course impossible to prove, because this dramatic tradition was extirpated in England at the Reformation. We are not, however, concerned in this study so much with specific sources as with attitudes, and the point to notice here is that sixteenth-century Englishmen were familiar with saints' lives and their subjects; although Anglicans no longer prayed to the saints, they honored them. It was natural, then, for them to see their own chaste heroines as saints and specifically to call them such. This tendency could only be reinforced by the high value that the Reformation placed upon chastity and the great horror with which it viewed lust. If lust becomes more devilish, naturally chastity be-

---

16. Omer Englebert, *The Lives of the Saints*, trans. Christopher and Anne Fremantle (New York, 1951), p. 496. Jean Johnson, pp. 51–52, cites other examples of virgins protected by lions.

17. Grace Frank, *The Medieval French Drama* (Oxford, 1954), p. 123.

comes more angelic and saintly. Drayton's Matilda is explicitly likened to a saint, even to the point where her grave becomes a shrine to be visited by the repentant King John.

Another factor in the sanctification of chaste heroines is the desire to produce an English "Legend of Good Women" to compare with the collections of Boccaccio and particularly of Chaucer. The important change is that Chaucer's heroines were martyrs of love, while Elizabethan heroines were martyrs to chastity. When Drayton published his revised version of Matilda's life in 1605, he retitled it *The Legend of Matilda*. The impulse to impose the "Legend of Good Women" pattern is illustrated by Hugh Holland's *Pancharis,* published in 1603, but written, as the author tells us, some years earlier as an intended compliment to Queen Elizabeth.[18] The subject of Holland's poem is the marriage between Owen Tudor and Queen Katherine, widow of Henry V, the marriage that led ultimately to the Tudor dynasty. Holland never gets that far, however; only the first part of the poem is finished. The purpose of this opening section is to establish Katherine as the perfect widow and queen dowager. She is an excellent mother to the infant Henry VI and charitable to widows and orphans, but, most importantly, she is chaste. She is so modest that "Might once no minion dare to kisse her glove,/ (Much lesse her hand) or mistresse her miss-call" (p. 19). The birds in Windsor Forest carol her praises: "Long live Diana and faire Katherine!" (p. 21). She wins such fame for her exemplary behavior

> That on a time the goddesse of the wood,
> Diana, sorely longed once to see
> This abstract model of all womanhoode,
> And next her selfe the flowre of chastitie.
>
> (p. 20)

She is, in fact, specifically called a "saint" because of her rigorous chastity (p. 30), and by the mythologizing impulse her story is thus elevated to a position among the legends of good Englishwomen being constructed by a series of English poets from Daniel forward.

---

18. Ed. Collier, *Illustrations,* 2:53. In-text citations refer to this edition.

The sanctification of chaste heroines becomes part of the pattern of chastity literature. As we have seen in chapter 2, Fletcher's Casta is specifically called a saint some half dozen times in *The Triumph of Death*. Many other chaste heroines of his are described as saintly and angelic. Although thoroughly cognizant of the pattern of saints' lives, many Elizabethans because of their Protestant bias preferred to see virtue triumphant rather than virginity martyred. The Reformation taste for stories with happy endings (or for stories of retributive justice, such as the wretched end of the leprous Cressida) induces a consequently heavier emphasis upon the reforming power of chastity. Allegiance to this idea modified Lucrece into Pamela. This same process operated in English versions of other chastity stories.

Greene's Version of the Chastity Test

A very important illustration of this process is Greene's *Philomela* (1592). Greene gives his story an Italian setting, but as it shows the English modification of a story popular in other languages, it may be considered among the tales of English chastity. *Philomela* is a variation of the story of the chastity test, a motif that Fletcher uses repeatedly.

A well-known classical version of this motif is the Ovidian legend of Cephalus and Procris,[19] a husband and wife frequently cited in Elizabethan lists of famous lovers. The Ovidian legend is erotic and tells of the wooing of the goddess Aurora. The original flavor of the tale is preserved in Thomas Edwards's erotic epyllion *Cephalus and Procris* (1595). The second half of the tale, which deals with Cephalus's testing of his wife, was frequently detached and converted into a moral tale.[20] This half of the story begins when the

---

19. Citations in the text refer to book and line numbers in Ovid, *Metamorphoses*, trans. Arthur Golding (1567), ed. W. H. D. Rouse (London, 1904).

20. Pettie's prose version in his *Petite Pallace* (1576) alters the motivation to the extreme detriment of Procris's character. His Cephalus tests his wife's chastity because her character is so shallow as to make him wonder about her honesty. Pettie's version is worth mentioning because it must have given further currency to the testing motif, but his interpretation of Procris's character is an anomaly in the period. Chapman's *The Widow's Tears*

jealous goddess Aurora makes Cephalus uncertain of Procris's fidelity and precipitates him into such jealous misery that he decides to assume a disguise and make "triall of her troth" by assaulting "hir honestie with great rewards and gifts" (VII.941, 931). When Cephalus returns home to find Procris chastely mourning the absence of her husband, his heart almost misgives him; nevertheless, he continues with his plan and finds his wife honest:

> What should I make report how oft hir chast behaviour strave
> And overcame most constantly the great assaults I gave?
> .   .   .   .
> .   .   .   .   What creature having his
> Wits perfect would not be content with such a proofe as this
> Of hir most stedfast chastitie? I could not be content:
> But still to purchase to my selfe more wo I further went.
>   (VII.949–50; 953–56)

Cephalus renews his overtures, and at last Procris capitulates, whereupon her husband upbraids her fiercely. Overcome with sorrow, Procris flees from her home and husband and lives in self-imposed exile in the mountains, where she leads the life of one of Diana's nymphs. The remorseful husband begs for forgiveness, assuring her that he himself could not have held out against "such a great assault":

> When I had this submission made, and she sufficiently
> Revengde hir wronged chastitie, she then immediately
> Was reconcilde: and afterward we lived many a yeare
> In joy, and never any jarre between us did appeare.
>   (VII.975–78)

Cephalus, then, is guilty of succumbing to a base jealousy, and Procris is guilty, technically speaking, of adultery.

The many Elizabethan versions of Cephalus and Procris were eventually superseded in popularity by a very similar story, Cervantes' "El Curioso Impertinente," which became the basis for

---

(1603–1609) is an amusing combination of the stories of Cephalus and Procris and the Widow of Ephesus.

numerous Jacobean and Restoration plays. Cervantes tells the story of the husband who was too curious for his own good in chapters 32–35 of *Don Quixote* and again in one of his exemplary novels. *Don Quixote* was published in 1612 in Shelton's translation, and was perhaps available earlier in manuscript form. At any rate, the story was published in Paris in 1608 with the Spanish and French versions on opposite pages and was thus available to the many Elizabethans who could read French.[21] In this story, Cervantes describes Anselmo's desire to test the virtue of his wife, Camilla. For Anselmo, virtue is not virtue until it has been put to the test. He asks Lotario, his closest friend, to tempt Camilla; Lotario is appalled but consents, reluctantly, after a long debate between the two men. Lotario actually behaves virtuously to Camilla but reports to Anselmo what he wishes to hear—that his wife has resisted illicit overtures. Anselmo is angry when he discovers this deception and insists that Lotario fulfill his promise. At this point, Lotario actually does fall in love with Camilla and succeeds in seducing her. Lotario and Camilla engage in many intrigues and counter-intrigues to deceive Anselmo, but their infidelity is eventually discovered by the husband, and, after a great deal of complicated action, all three of the principals meet unhappy deaths. Anselmo commits suicide after writing a note acknowledging that these unhappy events were the result of his own curiosity and that he was the author of his own dishonor.

This plot pattern was very popular among Jacobean playwrights. *The Second Maiden's Tragedy*, for example, follows Cervantes' story in great detail. The plot is made the vehicle for the expression of that increasingly ambivalent feeling about jealousy, discussed in chapter 3, which is noticeable in the Jacobean period. In both the Cephalus and Procris story and the tale by Cervantes, the husband is at fault for being unnecessarily jealous, and yet subsequent events seem to vindicate him somehow, even though the results are unhappy. On the whole, however, audiences preferred to be reassured rather than disillusioned about female chastity. The Cervantes version of

21. A. S. W. Rosenbach, "The Curious-Impertinent in English Dramatic Literature before Shelton's Translation of *Don Quixote*," *MLN* (1902) : 358.

the chastity test, in which the wife succumbs to temptation, is used only once by Fletcher, in an unsuccessful play called *The Coxcomb*.[22] In all his other versions of the chastity test, a motif that he used repeatedly, Fletcher followed the pattern of *Philomela,* in which the tested heroine remains chaste.

Greene's *Philomela* contains a medley of motifs from the Susanna, Penelope, and Lucrece stories, and from Greek romances such as Heliodorus's *Ethiopian History,* in which the long-suffering heroine Chariclea successfully passes a chastity test by standing unharmed on a burning brazier.[23] The husband in Greene's tale, "Il Conte Phillippo Medico" of Venice, is not, as is Cervantes' Anselmo, afflicted merely with a fatal curiosity. Rather, he suffers from a jealousy that is clearly pathological and that leads him to behave as wickedly as the Elders who slandered Susanna. Although his wife, Philomela, has been an example of chastity throughout their marriage, Phillippo tells his friend Lutefio that he can "never bee merrie at his hart" until he has "made an assured proofe of hir chastitie" (XI.121). The virtuous Lutefio is reluctant to act the part of seducer, but he finally agrees "to make experience of hir honestie."

Lutefio begins his feigned assaults by confiding to Philomela that he loves the wife of a dear friend. She responds with a five-page lecture against lust; some of her arguments are paraphrased from the official "Homily against Adultery" (cf. above, chap. 3):

> Barbarous nations punishe it with death: meere Atheistes in Religion avoid it by instinct of nature . . . and wilt thou that art a Christian than crucifie Christ anew, by making the harbour of thy soule the habitation of Satan? (XI.130)

The report of Philomela's harangue against adultery does not satisfy Phillippo. He persuades Lutefio to write a long letter of seduction. Philomela is indignant and writes a stinging retort; she is charitable enough, however, to put the best construction she can on his actions;

---

22. Even in this play Fletcher goes to great lengths to justify the heroine. See the discussion in chap. 8.

23. For Greene's use of the Greek romances, see S. L. Wolff, *The Greek Romances in Elizabethan Prose Fiction* (New York, 1912).

"I judge the best & hope that I imagin truth, thou dooest it but to trye me" (XI.147–48). After reading her letter, Lutefio refuses to have anything further to do with his friend's mad testing of his wife. He upbraids the jealous husband for being "so sottish with Cephalus to betray thy wives honour" (XI.150). Lutefio then goes straight to the virtuous Philomela to apologize, though he conceals Phillippo's foolishness. He assures her that his letter was merely a chastity test, designed "but to make triall howe you liked Phillippo, to whome I owe such faith that it would greeve me he should have a wife false" (XI.153). It is important to notice that Philomela finds this stratagem unexceptionable ("if to trie me, thou shalt finde the more favour") and pardons Lutefio instantly.

When Philomela becomes pregnant, Phillippo pays two of his servants to swear falsely that they caught Lutefio and Philomela in the act of adultery. The supposed culprits are tried with shameful publicity before the Duke of Venice; Phillippo is granted a divorce. The sorrowing Philomela in her "martirdome" (XI.175) assumes the name Abstemia and takes ship for Palermo. She has provided herself with a poisoned ring in case anyone should attempt to ravish her. Her fears are not baseless, for the ship's captain has already decided to play Tarquin to her Lucrece. Fortunately, however, he overhears her chaste meditations and is converted: "His love was so qualed with the rarenes of her qualities, that he rather indevoured to honor her as a saint, then to love her as a paramour" (XI.179).

Meanwhile, the two perjured witnesses repent and confess, and Phillippo, exiled, sets out to search for the missing Philomela. All the principals arrive in due course in Palermo. Phillippo, now as full of despair as he was before of wrath and jealousy, tries to end his life by confessing to the recent unsolved murder of the son of the Duke of Palermo. Philomela, the model of a miraculously forgiving wife, appears at this trial and confesses to the murder herself in order to save her despairing husband's life. In true romance style, the supposedly murdered prince appears himself, and the trial is ended in universal forgiveness. Phillippo is so overcome by Philomela's saintly behavior that he dies of grief and joy. Palermo's son offers his hand to this paragon of womanhood, but, faithful to her Phillippo even after death, Philomela declines his offer and ends her days in Venice as a widow. Which "constant chastety made her so famous, that in her lyfe shee was honored as the Paragon of vertue," and, Greene assures his readers, her fame is "holden canonized until this day in Venice" (II.204). Philomela is no Procris or Camilla; she is constant to the end and reaps a deserved canonization.[24]

Fletcher uses this pattern for the chastity test in numerous plays, among them *The Knight of Malta, The Faithful Shepherdess, Women Pleased, The Little French Lawyer,* and *The Custom of the Country.*

The chastity test needs further discussion because of the critics' misapprehensions about this convention. While the test always appears to the heroine as a simple threat to her chastity, the motives of the tester may vary. The pathologically jealous husband, like Cephalus, or the pathologically curious one, like Anselmo, may be a very unattractive figure. A surrogate tester like Lutefio has only the highest motives. Lutefio wishes to disprove Phillippo's fear; he wishes the heroine to remain chaste rather than to fall. He is the opposite of the would-be seducer, who wishes the lady to succumb. In Fletcher generally, as in Greene, the tester acts from the highest motives and wishes to prove the lady chaste; he wishes, to use a phrase from chapter 3, to catch the lady in the act of chastity. A chastity test, then, is the sign of a hero rather than of a villain. All too often, however, critics read a scene containing a chastity test as though it were a genuine attempt at seduction. These critics then castigate Fletcher for creating heroes who act like blackguards. We have seen an example of this in the discussion in chapter 2 of Montague, the hero of *The Honest Man's Fortune.* Another hero who has been similarly maligned is Miranda, who is the tester in two chastity tests in *The Knight of Malta* (see below, chap. 7).

In *Philomela,* however, we have a key to a correct understanding of the premises underlying the plot pattern of the chastity test.

---

24. Robert Davenport's play *The City Nightcap* (1624) follows *Philomela* in detail until the conclusion, when yet another chastity test is given to the long-suffering heroine.

Phillippo's jealousy is unmotivated and even barbarous, but such behavior, when repented of, is to be forgiven by the good wife. Lutefio demonstrates his virtue in his reluctance even to feign the role of a seducer, but none of the characters, least of all Philomela, regard the chastity test as an unforgivable insult to a woman. Rather, Philomela honors Lutefio for his concern over the chastity of his friend's wife, and she welcomes the opportunity to demonstrate her virtue. As in Cervantes, virtue is not virtue until it is tested. The wife who passes the chastity test tends to merge with the Penelope and Susanna archetypes in that she has resisted adultery and thus disproved the false suspicions of her honesty.

Similarly, in *The Honest Man's Fortune* the Duke of Orleans is a victim of unreasonable jealousy and behaves brutally to his wife, but he easily receives forgiveness as soon as he repents. The test of the Lady's chastity by the honest Montague is a sign that he is an admirable character, and the Lady welcomes the opportunity to demonstrate her fidelity to her husband. The Lady of Orleans is like Susanna insofar as she is the woman falsely accused of adultery, and she is like Penelope insofar as she resists the temptation to commit adultery. In her speech defending her honor against the suspicions of her husband, she asserts herself "so honest, that I care not if the chast Penelope/Were now alive to hear me" (X.216). Similarly, we have seen Oriana vindicated of slander by a chastity test in *The Woman Hater*. After Oriana passes the test, the Duke asks her to forgive his suspicions and extols her as an exemplum, as a woman "borne to teach men vertue" (V.iv.77). Fletcher's characteristic use of the chastity test, then, follows the precedent set by Greene.

Greene in many ways created the model for the chaste heroine. He was eminently skillful in blending together the great archetypes of exemplary female behavior. The narrative in *Philomela,* for example, falls into four parts: Philomela resists seduction, like Penelope; she is falsely accused of adultery, like Susanna; she converts a would-be ravisher, like a Christian Lucrece; and she forgives her husband's atrocious behavior, like Patient Griselda. This archetypical richness is surpassed in Spenser's portrayal of English virtue.

Spenser

Books III and IV of Spenser's *Faerie Queene,* the Legends of
Chastity and Friendship, are the finest expression of the Reformation
glorification of chastity. Spenser's romance contains all the important motifs of Elizabethan chastity literature. Chastity is for Spenser
one of the "twelve private morall vertues"[25] necessary to a gentleman, and its position in Book III, immediately following the books
of holiness and temperance, raises it to an exalted position among
the religious and philosophical virtues. This elevation is deliberate.
Spenser begins his introductory cantos to Book III by declaring,
"It falls me here to write of Chastity,/ That fairest vertue, farre
above the rest. . . ." Moreover, chastity is given this prominence in
a major literary work, one immediately recognized as such by contemporary readers.

Chastity is appropriately embodied in a woman, Britomart, but,
equally appropriately, in a woman who is also a knight, as chastity
is a virtue necessary to both sexes. Spenser's virgin-knight is an
image for several basic assumptions. Most importantly, chastity is
imaged as an active and militant rather than a passive and long-
suffering quality. Britomart's rescue of Amoret from Busirane is a
positive act. Moreover, chastity has mystical powers. These powers
are embodied in Britomart's enchanted lance, which strikes down the
allurements of riches in the figure of Marinell,[26] the guardian knights
of Malecasta, and even her own beloved Artegall when he is disguised as a "Salvage Knight" unmoved by the charm of womanhood.
The magic lance is not Spenser's only indication of the mystical powers
of chastity. We are told that Argante, the lustful giantess, can only
be overcome by a chaste virgin. Her equally lustful twin brother,
Ollyphant, runs away when he sees Britomart and Sir Satyrane
approach:

---

25. From Spenser's letter to Raleigh, *The Poetical Works of Edmund
Spenser,* ed. J. C. Smith and E. de Selincourt (London, 1912), p. 407. In-
text citations refer to this edition.
26. William Nelson, *The Poetry of Edmund Spenser* (New York, 1963),
p. 227.

> It was not Satyrane, whom he did feare,
>> But Britomart the flowre of chastity;
>> For he the powre of chast hands might not beare,
>> But alwayes did their dread encounter fly.
>>> (III.xi.6)

Similarly, Greedy Lust flees back to his lair when he sees the virgin-huntress Belphoebe.

As the personification of militant and mystical chastity, Britomart has the paradoxical quality of both attracting and repelling lust:

> For she was full of amiable grace,
>> And manly terrour mixed therewithall,
>> That as the one stird up affections bace,
>> So th'other did mens rash desires apall. . . .
>>> (III.i.46)[27]

It is this power to allure that allows the heroine a chance to prove that she is chaste, for a woman must be wooed before she can resist. An Avisa must defend herself with words, but Britomart has a magic lance, and, when she attracts the misguided overtures of Malecasta, she defends herself with her stout right arm. Furthermore, because Britomart is apprehended by the other characters as a knight, she never has to defend herself against unwelcome masculine attention. In spite of Britomart's love for Artegall, she functions in the plot as a man rather than as a damsel in distress. That function is reserved for Florimell and Amoret—heroines of whose adventures Britomart is, so to speak, the guardian spirit.

---

27. Willobie gives Avisa similar powers; Diana bestows upon that heroine a "double grace":

> A face, and eye, that should intise:
> A smile, that should deceive the wise.

> A sober tongue that should allure,
> And draw great numbers to the fielde;
> A flinty heart, that should endure,
> All fierce assaults and never yeeld,
>> And seeming oft as though she would;
>> Yet fardest off when that she should. (p. 20)

These two heroines are alike in that their distress is continual. Florimell flees from a lustful forester, Arthur, a witch's son, a hyena-like monster that feeds on women's flesh, and a lustful fisherman; she then falls into the hands of Proteus, who tries to seduce her. Amoret is stolen away during her wedding feast by the wicked Busirane, who keeps her in torment for seven months because she refuses to gratify his lust; she is falsely accused of adultery with Britomart; she is captured by the monster Greedy Lust. In terms of both allegory and fable, beauty and womanhood are continually in danger of slander, seduction, and rape. This is true of all the chastity literature we have looked at and is certainly true of Fletcher's heroines, whose constant distress is one source of the alleged prurience of his plays. As we have seen, however, in Greene, this continual distress is the result of blending together the three archetypical threats to chastity in the adventures of one heroine, so as to make her that much the more exemplary than any one of her three great predecessors.

In dealing with these conventionalized situations, Spenser uses the traditional characters and themes found in other chastity literature. Chastity is the special gift of the gods (Belphoebe is reared by Diana), and God protects the chaste with providential assistance in times of distress. For example, when Florimell is about to be raped by the old fisherman, her cries for help are not at first heard.

> But sith that none of all her knights is nye,
> See how the heavens of voluntary grace,
> And soveraine favour towards chastity,
> Doe succour send to her distressed cace:
> So much high God doth innocence embrace.
> (III.viii.29)

Succor then arrives in the person of the sea god Proteus. Unfortunately, Proteus himself is overcome by Florimell's beauty and tries to seduce her with "daily" temptations and "fained kindness," using his talents for transformation to take on shapes that he thinks will attract her. He behaves like the conventional suitor of high degree; when Florimell scorns his suit,

> With harder meanes he cast her to subdew,
> And with sharp threates her often did assaile,
> So thinking for to make her stubborne courage quaile.
>
> (III.viii.40)

Finally he takes revenge by imprisoning her for seven months in a deep dungeon. Florimell's firm endurance of this trial of chastity makes her worthy of sainthood:

> Most vertuous virgin, glory be thy meed,
> And crowne of heavenly praise with Saints above. . . .
>
> (III.viii.42)

The author goes on to say that, inferior as his verses are to angelic carols, he is doing his best to praise Florimell's "goodly chastitee" so that every honorable dame may imitate her deeds.

This expressed intention of teaching by good example extends also to teaching by bad example. When Spenser begins his tale of the wanton Hellenore, a "second Hellene," and her seduction by Paridell, a descendent of the Trojan Paris, he explains his purpose in terms conventional in the Renaissance:

> But never let th'ensample of the bad
>   Offend the good: for good by paragone
>   Of evill, may more notably be rad,
>   As white seemes fairer, macht with blacke attone;
>   Ne all are shamed by the fault of one. . . .
>
> (III.ix.2)

In proof of this last point, Britomart is present at the banquet during which Paridell begins his seduction of Hellenore but is not "shamed by the fault of one."

Spenser uses another kind of contrast for didactic purposes, the contrast between the golden age and "nowadays" that is common in Fletcher; we have noticed it already in *The Triumph of Honor*. In Book IV, The Legend of Friendship, Arthur is escorting Amoret and Aemylia through the woods and they are forced to take refuge in the poor cottage of Slander, who accuses the fair damsels of being whores. But Arthur, the perfect prince, has nothing but honorable intentions toward his fair charges, for this was in the antique age when the world lived "In simple truth and blamelesse chastitie" and "Held vertue for it selfe in soveraine awe" (IV.viii.30). Spenser is ironically careful to warn his readers that Arthur's behavior should not be misconstrued,

> Sith now of dayes such temperance is rare
> And hard to finde, that heat of youthfull spright
> For ought will from his greedie pleasure spare. . . .
>
> (IV.viii.29)

Again, it can be seen that a device that has earned Fletcher a reputation as a cynic turns out to be a familiar didactic method of admonishing the degenerate modern world.[28]

In discussing Spenser's contribution to Elizabethan chastity literature, I should mention one other section of *The Faerie Queene,* The Legend of Holiness. Book I is of course the story of St. George, of the Red Cross Knight and his service to the English church. Insofar as Book I is concerned with Una, however, it is a variation on the plot of the lady falsely accused of adultery. Una and Red Cross are traveling in perfect amity together until they meet the hypocritical Archimago. This wicked magician disguises an evil spirit in the shape of Una and sends her to seduce the sleeping knight. Red Cross is both dismayed and enraged at this shamelessness, but controls himself until Archimago, again using disguised spirits, makes Red Cross think he has taken Una in the act of adultery with a page. The distraught knight abandons his lady and is snared by the false charms of Duessa.

Spenser then takes up the narration of the adventures of the abandoned Una with the observation that

> Nought is there under heav'ns wide hollownesse,
> That moves more deare compassion of mind,
> Then beautie brought t'unworthy wretchednesse
> Through envies snares or fortunes freakes unkind. . . .
>
> (I.iii.1)

---

28. Antecedents of the "nowadays" attitude are discussed by Peter, *Complaint and Satire,* pp. 68–69.

Una, "the flowre of faith and chastity" (I.iii.23), wanders through the woods alone and meets a fierce lion. Instead of attacking her, the lion fawns on her and kisses her feet. The affection of lions for chaste maids and wives provides providential vindication and support for the lady falsely accused, just as in Painter. Una is then abducted by the pagan knight Sansloy, who kills her lion and carries her into a wild forest where he attempts to rape her. Her cries for help attract a crowd of fauns and satyrs, whose uncouth appearance frightens Sansloy away. These usually lustful creatures are so struck by Una's beauty that they treat her with great courtesy and obedience, even worshiping her as the "Goddesse of the wood" (I.vi.16).

Spenser uses the conventional motifs of chastity literature to give the Protestant ideals of marriage and chaste affection a new dignity of expression. Only Spenser among Elizabethan authors manages to present chaste heroines who are not priggish. Florimell and Amoret are attractive idealizations of chaste womanhood; the militant aspect of their chastity is separated from their personalities and allegorized in the figure of the knightly Britomart. By using allegory, Spenser avoids the mistakes of other writers, who produced self-righteous prigs. It is to be credited to Fletcher's good taste that his first play, which is also his first chastity play, *The Faithful Shepherdess,* tries to glorify chaste womanhood by attempting to capture Spenser's atmosphere of faery. To this play we shall now turn.

6
The Faithful Shepherdess

The Faithful Shepherdess (1608–1609),[1] Fletcher's first play, has always been highly praised for its fine lyric qualities and has always been a favorite anthology piece. That its subject is ideal chastity has never been contested, though many critics have objected to the moral quality of the play. The plot materials used to portray chastity are wholly conventional and are combined from a number of different sources.

Because of the title of *The Faithful Shepherdess* and Fletcher's letter to the readers of the published edition of the play, critical opinion has been unanimous in deciding that Fletcher's first play was the product of his desire to emulate in English Guarini's *Il Pastor Fido*. Fletcher adapted his Italian model by substituting a faithful shepherdess for Guarini's faithful shepherd. This was to have significant consequences for the theme of his play. Guarini's theme is the transforming power of love.[2] His hero Mirtillo is faithful in the sense that he perseveres in his love for Amarillis even when he has no hope of obtaining her and ultimately offers to sacrifice his life that she may live. In pursuit of thematic unity, Guarini

---

1. Ed. W. W. Greg, Variorum edition of *The Works of Francis Beaumont and John Fletcher,* gen. ed. A. H. Bullen, 4 vols. (London, 1904–12), vol. 3.

2. See the discussion by W. F. Staton and W. E. Simeone in *A Critical Edition of Sir Richard Fanshawe's 1647 Translation of Giovanni Battista Guarini's Il Pastor Fido* (Oxford, 1964), p. xiii.

has all his characters discuss, at some time in the play, the power of love. When Fletcher inverted the basic idea to create a faithful shepherdess, the theme necessarily altered, for the word *faithful* when applied to a woman implies not only constancy but also chastity. Accordingly, Fletcher's heroines, Amoret and Clorin, display chastity as well as loyalty. The theme becomes the transforming power of chastity; all of the characters in his play therefore discuss, not love, but chastity. The only part of Guarini's play that helps Fletcher to embody this theme is the episode in which Guarini's heroine, Amarillis, is falsely accused of adultery because of the machinations of the jealous Corsica. Accordingly, in *The Faithful Shepherdess,* Fletcher's heroine, Amoret, is falsely accused of wanton behavior because of the machinations of the jealous Amarillis.

Looking for material to portray a chaste heroine, Fletcher quite naturally turned to Spenser as the most successful poet of chastity in English. His Clorin is clearly modeled upon Spenser's Una, who is worshiped by the usually lustful satyrs as the Goddess of the Wood.[3] Fletcher's satyr refers to Clorin as "my goddess in the wood" (III.i.203). Fletcher used another episode from Spenser for the portrayal of Clorin, the section of Book VI in which Timias and Serena are cured of the slanderous wound of the Blatant Beast by the hermit of the woods. The hermit tells his patients that the only cure for such a wound is amendment of life:

> Abstaine from pleasure, and restraine your will,
> Subdue desire, and bridle loose delight,
> Use scanted diet, and forbeare your fill,
> Shun secresie, and talke in open sight:
> So shall you soone repaire your present evill plight.
> (VI.vi.14)

Similarly, Clorin cures the wound of Alexis, a wound received in

---

3. See Ward, *History,* 2:664: "The relation between the Satyr and Clorin may have been suggested by passages in the *Faerie Queene;* while a notable if more general resemblance has been pointed out between the transformation of Amarillis into Amoret and the Spenserian false Una and false Florimell."

the pursuit of illicit love, by advising that he reform his wanton desires into a chaste affection:

> Shepherd, thou canst not possibly take rest,
> Till thou has laid aside all heats, desires,
> Provoking thoughts that stir up lusty fires,
> Commerce with wanton eyes, strong blood, and will
> To execute; these must be purged until
> The vein grow whiter; then repent, and pray. . . .
>
> (IV.ii.107–12)

Fletcher also borrowed from Spenser the technique of portraying chastity by means of allegory. It is a familiar observation that Fletcher created the characters in his play to represent points on a spectrum—from pure lust, in the person of the Sullen Shepherd, to pure love, in the person of Clorin, with Perigot and Amoret at midpoint, representing an ideal of chaste affection. This allegorical construct resembles Spenser's separation of various aspects of beauty, love, and chastity into the characters of Florimell, Amoret, and Britomart. Because Fletcher imitates Una's adventures in Clorin's influence over the satyr, the satyr cannot be used for the lustful villain, as he is in Italian pastoral. This explains why Fletcher transfers this role to the Sullen Shepherd, a transference that has puzzled critics who have seen *The Faithful Shepherdess* only as an imitation of Guarini.[4]

In order to glorify chastity, Fletcher gives that virtue mystical and magical powers, just as Spenser does. Britomart's magic lance is not suitable, however, to a pastoral setting, and Fletcher locates the mystical and magical powers of virginity in its owner. Clorin, amazed at the obeisance done her by the rough satyr, explains this homage as done to her purity:

> Yet I have heard—my mother told it me,
> And now I do believe it—if I keep
> My virgin flower uncropt, pure, chaste, and fair,
> No goblin, wood-god, fairy, elf, or fiend,

---

4. W. W. Greg, *Pastoral Poetry and Pastoral Drama* (London, 1906), p. 268.

Satyr, or other power than haunts these groves,
Shall hurt my body, or by vain illusion
Draw me to wander after idle fires. . . .

(I.i.111–17)

We not only hear of the magical power of virginity to protect its owner, we also see this power dramatized, as, for example, when the River God is able to cure Amoret's first wound instantaneously because she is "an unpolluted maid" (III.i.388).

Because of this imitation of *The Faerie Queene,* the Guarini pastoral setting of flocks and pipes passes, after Act I, into a magical Spenserian forest peopled by river gods and furnished with magic wells. The atmosphere is no longer that of the pastoral world but is that of fairyland, a world of enchantment. Just as Spenser's Archimago convinces Red Cross of Una's wantonness by means of magical disguises, so Amarillis convinces Perigot of Amoret's wantonness by means of magical illusion. This atmosphere of faery, more than any other quality of *The Faithful Shepherdess,* shows how far Fletcher diverges from his Italian model. Fletcher calls attention to his Spenserian borrowings by imitating some of the lyrics in Spenser's *Shepherd's Calendar* in a song sung by his own shepherds.[5] This "happy lay" was taught by "honest Dorus," he that "was the soul and god of melody" (V.v.213–15). The compliment to Spenser is apt. Fletcher also imitated one of Shakespeare's most popular plays, *A Midsummer Night's Dream.*[6] *The Faithful Shepherdess* is cast, like Shakespeare's play, in the form of a nocturnal, with pairs of lovers wandering at cross-purposes through an enchanted woods by night.

The result of this synthesis of sources is a moonlit lyric pastoral with interwoven plots dealing with Clorin, with Cloe, and with Amoret and Perigot. Clorin embodies ideal constancy. Her shepherd lover has died before the play begins, and she vows in I.i to remain faithful to him even after death; she decides to live in seclusion in

---

5. Greg points out the verbal similarities in the notes to his edition, Variorum, 3:109.

6. The resemblance has been noticed often; see, for example, Greg, *Pastoral Poetry,* p. 269.

a forest bower, where she will use herbal arts to relieve all mortal diseases: "These I can cure, such secret virtue lies/ In herbs applied by a virgin's hand" (I.i.39–40). Clorin's constancy wins her fame as "the Virgin of the Grove" (I.iii.61) and inspires love in the shepherd Thenot, who declares:

> Only I live t' admire a chastity,
> That neither pleasing age, smooth tongue, or gold,
> Could ever break upon. . . .
>
> (I.iii.48–50)

Thenot worships Clorin as "the best of all/ Her sex" (II.ii.49–50) and the "soul of virtue," "blest for ever" (II.ii.162–63). When he declares his love to her, she denounces the "sacrilegious foul disgrace" (II.ii.101) that he does to her dead lover. Thenot explains that it is precisely her loyalty that he admires. He is in perpetual misery, with his "affection, set/ On that which I should loathe, if I could get" (IV.v.19–20).

This "lover's pain," which no herb can allay, Clorin cures "by wit" (IV.v.9–10). She affects wantonness, pretending that she has abandoned her fidelity in order to offer herself to Thenot. Thenot is horrified, urging her to return to her vow: "Think but how blest/ A constant woman is above the rest!" (IV.v.45–46). When she persists, Thenot forsakes the woods. Clorin rejoices in her success: "'Tis done:—great Pan, I give thee thanks for it!—/ What art could not have cured is cured by wit" (IV.v.77–78). Clorin's pretended wantonness has a larger therapeutic effect on Thenot than merely curing his hopeless passion for her. His original adoration of her sprang from his misogyny; he believed all women inconstant and was amazed at the report of Clorin's life.[7] When Clorin dis-

---

7. Greg, *Pastoral Poetry,* p. 274, condemns the "profound cynicism, all the more terrible because apparently unconscious, with which the author is content to dismiss Thenot, cured of his altruistic devotion by the shattering at one blow of all that he held most sacred in woman." This is surely to miss the point. Thenot's so-called altruistic devotion arose originally from his misogyny; this is made quite clear in his plea to Clorin:
> Why dost thou wound
> His heart with malice against women more,
> That hated all the sex but thee before?
> (IV.v.48–50)

illusions him, he resolves not to look for perfection hereafter in a woman, but to choose a sweetheart as other men do. Clorin's pretense of wantonness in no way injures her character; she continues to practice healing and to reap fame as a living saint, as "holy Clorin" (V.iv.15).

In marked contrast to Clorin is the wanton shepherdess, Cloe. She longs for a lover and laments the "cold and dull chastity" (I.iii.8) of shepherds nowadays (an amusing inversion of "nowadays" satire). Cloe first approaches Daphnis, the "modest shepherd" (I.iii.89), and makes an assignation with him for that night in the forest. When he promises that her chastity will be safe with him, she repents her poor choice and appoints a meeting with the lusty Alexis, who is more to her taste. Both shepherds appear at the appointed meeting place. There Daphnis overhears Alexis searching for Cloe that he may quench his "burning lust" (II.iv.36). Daphnis, in contrast to the jealousy Perigot is to display later under somewhat similar circumstances, refuses to think ill of Cloe because of Alexis's words. Daphnis reflects that this may be but an "illusion":

> Sure, such fancies oft have been
> Sent to abuse true love, and yet are seen
> Daring to blind the virtuous thought with error. . . .
> (II.iv.41–43)

He is resolved that Cloe is still true, and, when he meets his sweetheart, assures her, "Only to your chastity/ I am devoted ever" (II.iv.78–79). Cloe is disgusted by such "idle shamefastness" (II. iv.106) and, to get rid of him, tells him to wait for her in a hollow oak tree.

Cloe quickly finds Alexis, who is as eager as she for "stol'n delight" (III.i.143). They are prevented from their pleasures by the lustful Sullen Shepherd, who wounds Alexis; the attacker and Cloe both flee at the sudden appearance of the satyr. The trusty

---

He has earlier made the assumption that "appetite" is the "great god of women" (II.ii.146). Cf. IV.v.37–39. The villain of the piece, the Sullen Shepherd, is also a misogynist; see his comment on Amoret in III.i.356–57. Thenot resembles Gondarino in *The Woman Hater;* his fantastical love torments hardly deserve the sympathy extended to them by Greg.

satyr is making his nightly rounds, watching over mortals; among his other duties, he watches to see "if any be/ Forcing of a chastity" (III.i.184–85), in which case he will summon the fairies to "pinch him to the bone,/ Till his lustful thoughts be gone" (III.i.190–91). The satyr rescues Alexis and takes him to Clorin to be healed. When Cloe returns and finds Alexis gone, she decides, as a last resort, to join Daphnis in the oak tree.

Meanwhile, Perigot and Amoret meet in the same woods to repeat their troth-plight vows by the magic well. These two lovers represent the mean of chaste affection between the opposite poles of Cloe's wantonness and Clorin's fidelity to the dead. It needs to be emphasized that Perigot and Amoret are betrothed (see III.i.441) and therefore, in Elizabethan eyes, virtually married, for in the ensuing action Perigot reacts as husband as well as lover. The unfortunate adventures that befall these sweethearts are the work of the jealous Amarillis, who wants Perigot for herself. She intends to break his match with Amoret and enlists the aid of the Sullen Shepherd by promising to gratify his lusts. Her confederate is quick with invention: "I'll slander Amoret,/ And say, she seems but chaste" (II.iii. 35–36). Indeed, he has already promised knacks and toys to the boy Hobbinal if he will say that he caught Amoret and the Sullen Shepherd at their "private sport" (II.iii.47). This use of a young innocent recalls the ruse of the false and lustful steward in Painter's story of "A Ladie Falslie Accused."

Amarillis has a more subtle plan by which Perigot can be made to think Amoret unchaste. With the help of her accomplice, she uses magic to transform herself into the exact likeness of Amoret. She then joins Perigot and attempts to seduce him. This attempt to destroy Amoret's reputation by means of a magically created double strongly resembles the episode in *The Faerie Queene* in which the spirit magically disguised as Una is sent by Archimago to seduce the Red Cross Knight. It also recalls the episode in which Florimell's reputation is jeopardized by the loose behavior of her magically created double, the snowy Florimell. Perigot, who had earlier professed himself to Amoret as "the true admirer of thy chastity" (I.ii.

129), is horrified at the "wanton tricks" (III.i.292) of the feigned Amoret and denounces her as a "serpent" (III.i.302). He is so disillusioned that he attempts to kill himself; dissuaded from self-murder, he then pursues the feigned Amoret with his sword. In the ensuing confusion he wounds the real Amoret, declaring, "Death is the best reward that's due to lust" (III.i.345). Though brutal, Perigot's behavior is conventional. As we have seen, death is the fate determined on by the husband (and Perigot is troth-plight husband) in stories of the lady falsely accused; moreover, in real life the "Homily on Adultery" praised ancient civilizations that, without a knowledge of true religion and guided by mere decency, assigned the death penalty to adulterers. Perigot's fault, as indicated by the context, is not that he thinks lust should be punished by death; rather, it is his failure to trust Amoret. This is surely the point of the parallel set up with Daphnis, who makes the opposite mistake when he refuses to believe "illusion" and trusts the false Cloe.

As in the case of Florimell's worst distress, succor arrives for Amoret in the person of a water deity. Fletcher's God of the River, however, is better behaved than Spenser's Proteus. The God of the River falls in love with Amoret as Proteus does with Florimell, but, instead of threatening the distressed maiden, the River God woos her to live with him and be his love. When she refuses, telling him of her betrothal to another, he cures her wound and immediately sets her free. The forgiving Amoret then sets out to find her unkind Perigot. Perigot, newly aware of the deception practiced against him, takes her for the disguised Amarillis and denounces her hypocrisy. Amoret mistakes his meaning, thinking he is accusing her of unchaste behavior, and defends her chastity and constancy:

> I am that maid,
> That yet untainted Amoret, that play'd
> The careless prodigal, and gave away
> My soul to this young man that now dares say
> I am a stranger, not the same, more wild;
> And thus with much belief I was beguiled:

> I am that maid, that have delay'd, denied,
> And almost scorn'd the loves of all that tried
> To win me, but this swain. . . .
>
> (IV.iv.134–42)

Her seemingly false words provoke Perigot beyond endurance, and, still taking her to be Amarillis, he wounds her again with his sword.

Amoret is again rescued, this time by the ever-vigilant satyr, who takes her to Clorin's bower, where Fletcher gathers all the characters together for the concluding act. Amoret mistakenly fears that the satyr intends to ravish her; in this extremity, she trusts to the power of virginity: "I am a maid; let that name fight for me" (V.ii.18). The satyr reassures her, and Clorin has a remedy for her wound, an herb that will heal if applied "with spotless hand on spotless breast" (V.ii.35). Everyone is astonished when the herb does not work. When Amoret protests that she is chaste, Clorin realizes that "Some uncleanness nigh doth lurk" (V.ii.47). A search discovers Cloe and Daphnis nearby in the hollow oak. Clorin purges the infected air with holy water, and, to protect her patients from evil influences, tests the chastity of all newcomers with a magic taper. The test of chastity by means of fire is similar to the test of chastity by means of the burning brazier in Heliodorus's *Ethiopian History*.

The other culprits are brought in by the Priest of Pan, who has rescued Amarillis from an attempted rape by the Sullen Shepherd. The experience so frightened Amarillis that she prayed Pan to transform her into a reed in imitation of the chaste Syrinx. When rescued by the Priest, Amarillis vows never again to be wanton, and demonstrates her sincerity when she easily passes the test of chastity by flame. The unrepentant Sullen Shepherd is banished, but Cloe, like Amarillis, reforms and is plighted to Alexis. The last straggler is Perigot, who has come to Clorin to be purified. Because he has wounded a maiden, his hand, "with chaste blood stained" (V.iv.20), cannot be cleansed. This stain remains irremovable until the astonished Perigot is forgiven by the Amoret he thought dead. The play concludes with Clorin admonishing every shepherdess to be an exemplum, to be faithful to her lover and to live

> As such a one that ever strives to give
> A blessed memory to after-time;
> Be famous for your good, not for your crime.
> (V.v.161–63)

They must pray that the god will send them "New desires, and tempers new,/ That ye may be ever true!" (V.v.210–11).

Thus with exhortation, precept, and example, Fletcher's *Faithful Shepherdess* attempts to inculcate and glorify chastity. Clorin, like Britomart, becomes the guardian spirit, so to speak, of the love adventures of the other characters, whom she cures, reforms, or punishes, as the case requires. Amoret, like Spenser's Amoret and Florimell, endures all three of the conventional threats to chastity: She is falsely accused, by means of magical illusion, of wanton behavior; she resists the seductive speeches of the God of the River; she resists what she thinks is an attempt by the satyr to ravish her. After all these trials, she, like Greene's Philomela, can forgive the man whose initial lack of faith in her was the cause of all her woes. Finally, chastity is tested as well as tried; Daphnis, Cloe, Amarillis, and the Priest of Pan all undergo the test of chastity by the taper's magic flame. The use of these conventionalized situations leaves no doubt that Fletcher's play intends to inculcate and glorify chastity.

Nonetheless, critics have doubted not only Fletcher's success, but even his intention. Lamb's statement is the original of such objections:

> Nothing short of infatuation could have driven Fletcher upon mixing up with this blessedness such an ugly deformity as Cloe: the wanton shepherdess! Coarse words do but wound the ears; but a character of lewdness affronts the mind. Female lewdness at once shocks nature and morality. If Cloe was meant to set off Clorin by contrast, Fletcher should have known that such weeds by juxta-position do not set off but kill sweet flowers.[8]

The juxtaposition of bad and good examples, a didactic device common in the Renaissance, was offensive to Lamb's Victorian sensibilities, which caused him to disapprove of the portrayal of evil women. It would be easy to laugh at Lamb's Victorianism, were it

8. *Specimens*, 2:36.

not that his moral objection, in a slightly disguised form, has become embedded in criticism of *The Faithful Shepherdess* and has led to some rather odd conclusions.

W. W. Greg in *Pastoral Poetry and Pastoral Drama* takes Lamb's argument a step further. Condemning Cloe as "a yahoo" and "a study in erotic pathology," he spells out in detail how the play, to borrow Lamb's phrase, kills sweet flowers. He then draws the conclusion that the ideal of chastity that Fletcher "sought to honor was one with which he was himself wholly out of sympathy":

> In this antagonism between Fletcher's own sympathies and the ideal he set before him seems to me to lie the key to the enigma of his play. Only one other rational solution is possible, namely that he intended the whole as an elaborate satire on all ideas of chastity whatever.[9]

Now, since Greg is Victorian in his sensibilities, it is interesting to find that Clifford Leech, who takes a modern psychoanalytical approach to the plays, draws, in different language, much the same conclusion. Leech feels that Fletcher approaches his material in *The Faithful Shepherdess* with "a certain wryness, a controlled humor"; the villains are comic, and chastity itself "is not kept free from absurdity."[10] Greg and Leech, each for different reasons, both see the play as in some way a parody of the ideals of chastity. The basic similarity of these two opposite points of view illustrates the paradoxical nature of Beaumont and Fletcher criticism. Victorian critics, because they come from a culture that has carried the Reformation ideals of chastity to such an extreme that lust cannot even be mentioned, object to the presentation of the extremes of lust and chastity as "immoral." The twentieth century, because it no longer sees chastity as a virtue, repeats the same criticisms in different terms and calls the Fletcherian "obsession" with extremes of lust and chastity either "ironic" or "unhealthy." This explains why nineteenth-century criticisms of Beaumont and Fletcher tend to be re-

---

9. Greg, *Pastoral Poetry,* p. 274.
10. Leech, *The John Fletcher Plays,* pp. 40, 44.

peated at the present time. Neither point of view coincides with the view of the Elizabethans, who thought both good and bad examples were moral and instructive. What the sixteenth century thought moral is "immoral" to Victorians and "unhealthy" to moderns.

In the case of this particular play, however, the dissatisfaction that both nineteenth- and twentieth-century critics feel about *The Faithful Shepherdess* was matched by the dissatisfaction felt by Fletcher's contemporaries. The play was a failure when first performed. Only its lyric beauty has elevated *The Faithful Shepherdess* to its present position as one of Fletcher's major plays. The dissatisfaction of the original audience suggests that the basic problem of *The Faithful Shepherdess* is not moral but aesthetic. All the major critics of the play have had aesthetic as well as moral objections to it, but they have been unable to separate them into the two categories. If that separation can be made now, it should illuminate what I take to be the fundamental aesthetic problem of any play that attempts to glorify chastity.

We can clear the ground for a discussion of the artistic failure of *The Faithful Shepherdess* by pointing out that Fletcher's own suggestion as to the reason for the failure of the play is undoubtedly not a complete explanation. In his letter "To the Reader" in the first quarto edition (1609–10), Fletcher asserts that his audience ignorantly expected a pastoral tragicomedy to be "a play of country hired shepherds in gray cloaks, with curtailed dogs in strings, sometimes laughing together, and sometimes killing one another. . . ."[11] While there may be some truth in this statement, the letter is informed throughout with the pique of a young playwright who feels that his talents have not been appreciated and who therefore scorns his audience. Quite naturally, Beaumont loyally supports his friend and in his commendatory verses to the play goes even further than Fletcher in scorning the audience; Beaumont suggests that publication cannot harm the reputation of the play because

> Your censurers must have the quality

---

11. Variorum, 3:18.

Of reading, which I am afraid is more
Than half your shrewdest judges had before.[12]

These tart quips notwithstanding, playgoers in 1608 were used to
fairly sophisticated fare and might have been brought to accept this
new form of pastoral had it been well handled.

The other commendatory verses in the quarto edition give more
useful clues. George Chapman's verses commiserate with Fletcher
over the fate of his pastoral "being Both a Poem and a Play":

A poem and a play too! why, 'tis like
A scholar that's a poet; their names strike
Their pestilence inward, when they take the air,
And kill outright. . . .[13]

Chapman scorns "the vulgar" for their failure to appreciate a dramatic poem, but the fact is that the verse of *The Faithful Shepherdess* is lyric rather than dramatic. This is not to object to the
interlarded lyrics or to the use of couplets, but rather to notice that
the bulk of the verse is unsuited to dramatic utterance. This lyric
quality means that the play reads more as though it were a closet
drama than a stage piece—one reason, perhaps, why the poem has
been so suitable for anthologizing. Fletcher must have realized the
artistic problems of his verse medium, for he abandoned his lyrics,
except for occasional songs, and turned to that loose, conversational
form of blank verse which is the sign of his work in the collaborations.

Guarini's play, however, which Fletcher's in some ways resembles, was popular, and it is even more lyric than Fletcher's, verging
at times on opera and ballet. Taking into account the difference in
Guarini's audience and the Italian taste for lyric entertainments, we
still notice that Guarini's play is better than Fletcher's for the
simple reason that *Il Pastor Fido* has a better plot. The "soul" of
this play is an intricate double plot with a powerful fifth-act recognition scene based on *Oedipus*. The plot is very well made, and the
characters respond to the pressure of events and develop quite plau-

---

12. Variorum, 3:12.
13. Variorum, 3:13.

sibly, so that boy gets girl and girl gets boy. By contrast, *The Faithful Shepherdess,* as Greg has repeatedly pointed out, has almost no plot at all. There are complications in abundance, but no real plot in the true sense of the word.[14] The logic of events is the logic of allegory. Although there is some thematic development,[15] there is no forward movement in the events. The fifth-act finale, for the most part, only restores the equilibrium of the conditions of the first act.

This lack of plot is the basic flaw in the play, and plot development is the basic problem in constructing any play about chastity. The primary difficulty that faced Fletcher was the difficulty of dramatizing in art a virtue that in life is essentially passive. Normally, as Coleridge pointed out, virginity or chastity is a state of being, a state of not acting.[16] Elizabethans, however, saw the moral life as a conscious struggle and therefore wished to represent chastity as an active virtue. This inevitably involves certain absurdities. Chastity, by virtue of its own nature, cannot be tempted and cannot fall without ceasing to be chastity. Shakespeare was the only Elizabethan playwright to solve this problem successfully. In *Othello* he places the struggle between faith in purity and lustful imaginings within Othello's mind, thus allowing Desdemona to be touched by lewdness from the outside only. This solution, however, is *sui generis.* Chastity literature revolves around the chastity of woman, and for a woman there can be no internal struggle with lust, for, once a woman admits lustful imaginings, she is no longer chaste.

The solution to this problem that Fletcher attempted in his first play was the solution of Spenser—allegory. The state of being chaste is personified in Clorin and Amoret and the state of being unchaste in Cloe and Amarillis. What was successful in allegorical narrative poetry, however, was not successful in drama. The allegorical nature of the characters means that there can be no real dramatic conflict between characters and no real development of character. A Mankind figure in a morality play may fall to sin and then repent, but chastity, because of its own nature, can never fall.

---

14. Greg, *Pastoral Poetry,* p. 268; he repeats his objections in a stronger form in his introduction to the Variorum edition of the play, 3:7.
15. See the discussion by Wallis, *Fletcher,* p. 188.
16. Coleridge, p. 657. Quoted in chap. 1.

Clorin, Amoret, and Daphnis are the same in Act V as in Act I. Alexis and Cloe apparently "reform," but their reformation is not a matter of change in character but of change in circumstances. In Act I Cloe is wanton because she wants a husband (I.iii.152–53), and Alexis loves her; in Act V Alexis still loves Cloe and she is no longer wanton because she is betrothed to him (V.v.19–20). Betrothal legitimizes their feelings without changing them. Fletcher also copies Spenser in representing the mystical, spiritual power of chastity by means of magical trappings—the test of chastity by fire, the stain of maiden blood that cannot be washed off, the power of a virgin to heal all illnesses. The magic that makes a point in Spenser's leisurely allegory, destroys dramatic tension on stage. Because of the overwhelming power of virginity and chastity, threats to these virtues can never be more than nominal, and therefore suspense and surprise are impossible.

The principle of contrast that Fletcher adapts from Spenser, the definition of chastity by juxtaposition with its opposite, is so poorly handled by Fletcher in this play that it fails of its intended effect. As A. W. Ward pointed out long ago, the contrast in the play between love and lust is only superficial.[17] Amarillis acts from jealousy rather than lust, and the lust of Cloe and the Sullen Shepherd is comical. Ben Jonson's commendatory verses to *The Faithful Shepherdess* are illuminating here. He claims that the play failed because it was too moral for the auditors. They damned the play because "it had not to do/With vices, which they look'd for and came to." Jonson professes to Fletcher that he is "glad thy innocence was thy guilt."[18] The fact is that Fletcher's play takes chastity seriously, but not lust. As we have seen in previous chapters, Elizabethans expected lust to be vilified in proportion as chastity is glorified. A lecher is a villain. The villains in Fletcher's play, however, are all rather amusing; indeed, they impress one as a group of naughty adolescents (this is especially true of Cloe) rather than as wicked villains. Spenser also has "salvage foresters" who, like the Sullen Shepherd, try to ravish distressed damsels rather as a matter of

17. Ward, 2:665.
18. Variorum, 3:13.

principle, but the reader is kept unaware of their comic possibilities by Spenser's poetry and melody and by his control of his allegory. While Fletcher showed good taste in the attempt to imitate Spenser, he did not show equally good judgment about his medium or about his own ability to imitate "the soul and god of melody." Despite Fletcher's considerable talents as a lyric poet, when he attempts to re-create on stage those characters who in Spenser are aesthetically distanced and given a certain dignity by virtue of the allegory, he creates instead characters who are, in the last analysis, ludicrous.

After the failure of *The Faithful Shepherdess* Fletcher abandoned the attempt to re-create *The Faerie Queene* on the stage, although he continued, as we shall see in succeeding chapters, to borrow incidental bits of ornament and situation from Spenser. Fletcher did not abandon, however, the use of the principle of contrast to inculcate chastity. Rather, he reverted to the stronger contrasts employed by his earlier predecessors in chastity literature, writers like Greene, Fenton, and Painter. Instead of portraying varying shades and degrees of lust and love, as in *The Faithful Shepherdess*, Fletcher portrayed the extremes, saintly chastity and villainous lust. The struggle between chastity and lust becomes a struggle between heroine and villain; the result is melodrama.

Moreover, Fletcher uses not only the melodramatic plots of his predecessors, but also their techniques. Fletcher's plays are marked by the same subordination of plot to rhetoric that is, as C. S. Lewis points out, the dominant characteristic of fiction in the latter half of the sixteenth century.[19] Chaste heroines defend an essentially passive virtue with words rather than deeds. Rhetorically elaborate speeches of seduction and of the defense of chastity become the emotional center of Fletcher's chastity plays. It is the content of these plays, the fact that the chaste heroine can make a counter-attack against a lustful villain only in words, that determines the rhetorical quality of these plays. It is not surprising, then, that recent studies by critics such as Mizener and Waith have evaluated the plays on the basis of the Fletcherian rhetoric.

---

19. Lewis, *Sixteenth Century*, p. 418.

A tale or play of attempted seduction allows for all kinds of persuasion and refusal. These speeches fall into conventional categories; among these are the villain's debate between lust and chastity, the seduction speech, the defense of chastity, the heroine's rebuke to the bawd, the eulogy of chastity, and the lament of the ravished heroine. Such speeches form the substance of the play that glorifies chastity.

Although Fletcher misjudged his medium and failed artistically in his first effort to portray chastity, he did not err in his judgment as to what themes and situations his audience wished to see represented. After the initial failure with Spenserian material in *The Faithful Shepherdess,* Fletcher used more conventional situations to create a series of popular chastity plays. To these plays we shall now turn.

7

Typical Chastity Plays

Fletcherian chastity plays use the typical patterns found in the stories in verse and prose that extol chastity; they portray Lucrece figures, they contrast women good and bad, and they portray the woman falsely accused of adultery. Fletcher uses three variations of the Lucrece story. *Valentinian* follows the traditional pattern, in which the heroine dies after having been raped; *The Queen of Corinth,* a collaboration with Field and Massinger, gives an anomalous inversion of this pattern; and *The Maid in the Mill,* a collaboration with Rowley, uses the modified Lucrece pattern, in which the heroine avoids rape by her own efforts.

Rape, as presented in *Valentinian* (1610–1614),[1] is the extreme trial of chastity. The heroine, Lucina, like Lucrece, is a Roman matron whose chastity can be overcome only by force. The extraordinary fullness and unity of the treatment of Lucina and her ravisher in the first three acts make the last two acts seem, by contrast, more incoherent than they in fact are. The concuding acts shift from the rape pattern to a revenge action.

The opening scene is expository; the heroine is described by four noblemen who pander for the Roman emperor Valentinian, who indicate the quality of Lucina's chastity by describing the great temptations she has already scorned. The scene has, in addition, a

---

1. Ed. Robert Grant Martin, Variorum 4.

rather interesting secondary effect. The panders recount to each other their spurned offers with such rhetorical fullness that the audience itself becomes the recipient of the persuasions. The total effect of the scene implies the question: Would you have refused such offers? The competition among the panders presents the temptations in climactic order, the climactic temptation being a threat— the emperor might use force. Rape was the ultimate temptation because, as we have seen earlier, it was supposed that a woman might prefer to be forced, as that would seem to save her honor. The mention of force has brought from Lucina the only display of emotion the panders have yet described:

> She pointed to a Lucrece that hung by,
> And with an angry look, that from her eyes
> Shot vestal fire against me, she departed.
>   (I.i.91–93)

The panders are frankly appalled that anyone should be so old-fashioned as to resist such offers. Lucina remained as "cold as crystal," so cold that the panders think "she is no woman,/ At least, as women go now" (I.i.44–45). Lucina seems to them "the holiest thing," a "temple," a "phoenix" who can only be taken "in her ashes" (I.i.78–81). The panders hope that the she-bawds will have better luck, as they will persuade by example as well as theory.

Accordingly, in I.ii, which dramatizes what has been described in the first scene, Lucina is besieged by two old beldams, who ply her hard with reasons drawn from their own experience. Their persuasions allow Lucina to make two set speeches in defense of chastity. She denounces them as "devils" (I.ii.41). Even in age their faces show that they were once beautiful and pure maidens; will they now "turn mortal devils?" (I.ii.117). Like Amoret, she uses her honor as a religious talisman: "I charge ye, in the name of chastity,/ Tempt me no more!" (I.ii.43–44). The she-bawds hint at rape, and again the action turns outward to question the audience:

> A ravish'd kiss from anger,

·   ·   ·   ·   ·   ·   ·   ·   ·   ·   ·   ·

Stuck with such pleasing dangers, gods, I ask ye,
Which of ye all could hold from?
(I.ii.135–38)

Lucina makes it clear that her "life shall make it certain" (I.ii.159) that she will never stoop to whoredom.

Lucina's Collatine is the great soldier Maximus, whose dearest friend, Aecius, should be his Lucius Junius Brutus. Aecius, however, is one of Fletcher's obsessively loyal generals. He is utterly opposed to political disobedience, even had he "both the blessings of the Bruti,/ And both their instigations" (I.iii.81–82). The implication is clearly that Lucina can expect neither protection nor retribution from Aecius. Aecius's loyalty, however, gives for a moment some glimmer of hope for the besieged wife. At the end of the act, Valentinian is so moved by Aecius's honesty that he feels he could repent all his sins, were it not for the great beauty of Lucina: "But she is such a pleasure, being good,/ That, though I were a god, she'd fire my blood" (I.iii.245–46). Valentinian's short speech here is the conventional debate of the tyrant between lust and reason. Thus the entire first act is relentless in its focus on the danger to Lucina's chastity. The tension of this act is heightened, rather than dispelled, by Valentinian's brief stirrings of conscience at the close of the act. Chastity is in danger, but not yet lost.

Act II duplicates Act I in method and structure. All the scenes are focused upon the ever-increasing peril to Lucina. Aecius cashiers a captain for daring to voice legitimate grievances against the emperor, thus dramatizing what has already been described, namely, that Lucina can expect no uprising against the tyrant. Valentinian wins Maximus's ring at dice and uses it to lure Lucina to court. Scenes iv–vi portray the technique of court seduction conventional on stage during the period. The victim enters the court fearfully, and her fears are increased by being met by known panders. The air is perfumed and rich jewels are "laid in the way she passes" (II.iv.9); light love songs are heard. Lucina's attendant maids are cut off in the anteroom. As she timorously looks for her husband, Lucina is again subjected to the suggestions of the panders. Again, and with ominous foreshadowing, she makes her position clear. Rather than become Valentinian's whore, she insists, "I'll rather find my grave" (II.v.71) and, "The gods shall kill me first" (II.v.89).

When Valentinian finally enters, Lucina kneels and begs for her chastity in a speech of some power:

> Look upon me,
> And, if ye be so cruel to abuse me,
> Think how the gods will take it! Does this beauty
> Afflict your soul? I'll hide it from you ever;
> Nay, more, I will become so leprous,
> That ye shall curse me from ye. My dear lord
> Has serv'd ye ever truly, fought your battles,
>
> . . . .
> Let not my virtue be the wedge to break him!
> I do not think ye are lascivious;
> These wanton men belie ye: you are Caesar,
> Which is, the father of the empire's honour.
> Ye are too near the nature of the gods,
> To wrong the weakest of all creatures, women.[2]
>> (II.vi.14–20; 29–34)

The heroine's kneeling plea for her chastity is conventional; compare the "heaved-up hands appeal" of Shakespeare's Lucrece:

> My husband is thy friend; for his sake spare me:
> Thyself art mighty; for thine own sake leave me:
> Myself a weakling; do not then ensnare me. . . .
>> (ll. 582–84)

Valentinian announces to the audience in an aside that he "dare not do it here" in the open court, but to Lucina he says that all has been but a chastity test: "I did but try your temper" (II.vi.36). Again the ambivalence of the end of the act arouses the momentary hope that chastity may yet be saved.

The similar endings of the first two acts are designed to make the reversal of Act III all the more startling. The third act opens

---

2. According to the commendatory verses of Thomas Stanley, printed in the First Folio, Fletcher's Lucina drew from the tearful audience "streams of melting sorrow." Glover and Waller, 1:xxvii.

with the words " 'Tis done." This is followed, as convention demands, by the lament of the ravished heroine. Lucina's lament is given greater dramatic point than that of Shakespeare's Lucrece because it is addressed to the ravisher himself:

> Lucina.   As long as there is motion in my body,
>   And life to give me words, I'll cry for justice!
> Valentinian.   Justice shall never hear ye; I am justice.
> (III.i.32–34)

Lucina then begs for death, threatening that the gods will punish "The sacrilegious razing of this temple" (III.i.39). She lays a curse upon him: "The sins of Tarquin be remember'd in thee!" (III.i.91).

Lucina is left with that sense of guilt typical of the ravished woman: "For I am now no wife for Maximus,/ No company for women that are virtuous" (III.i.74–75). Maximus assumes, rightly, that she intends suicide. Aecius has the conventional arguments against this: "Compell'd and forc'd with violence/ To what ye have done, the deed is none of yours" (III.i.221–22). The loyal Aecius has another, more novel reason why Lucina should not commit suicide. If she would live but a year, her life might be the means to "draw from that wild man a sweet repentance" (III.i.211). Maximus has the conventional arguments on the opposing side. The wrong is not just his or hers, but is "tied to after issues" (III.i.237) in their descendants. Furthermore, if she lives, posterity may doubt whether she was truly chaste:

> Must they not ask how often she was ravish'd,
> And make a doubt she lov'd that more than wedlock?
> Therefore she must not live.
> (III.i.244–46)

Lucina leaves the stage with the assurances of Aecius and her husband that her death will "stand to eternity" (III.i.275) as an exemplum. She dies immediately, though not by her own hand, but from "grief and disgrace" (IV.i.1). Thus she is prevented, even in a Roman context, from actually striking the blow herself, like Lucrece. Valentinian is outraged at her death; earlier he had believed his panders when they promised "to make her love her wrongs,/ And dote upon her rape" (IV.i.7–8). The only women left to him are the court stales, whom he denounces as Messalinas and as whores like Lais (IV.i.54).

Meanwhile, Maximus moves from wronged hero to ambitious revenging villain as the subject of the play moves from rape to revenge. The final part of the Lucrece pattern, the overthrow of the lustful tyrant, is so expanded and amplified by Fletcher that the play, as has often been noticed, breaks into two halves. By Act V, Maximus's schemes have so corrupted him that he seizes the imperial throne for himself. To make his new position secure, he decides to marry Eudoxia, the widowed empress. To woo her, he claims to have planned everything for the sake of her love; he even asserts that he connived at the rape of his own wife. Eudoxia then brings the revenge action full circle by poisoning Maximus at his coronation.

Fletcher here departs from his source in Procopius's *De Bello Vandalico*. According to the historian, Eudoxia sends to the king of the Vandals for help. The Vandals invade Rome, and Maximus, while attempting to escape, is stoned to death by the Romans.[3] Fletcher alters Eudoxia's revenge in such a way as to recall the popular story of Sinorix and Camma (see above, chap. 4). When Sinorix murdered Camma's husband in order to be able to marry her, Camma murdered the villain on her wedding day. For this deed she was frequently extolled as an exemplum of wifely loyalty. Whether or not Fletcher had this story specifically in mind is impossible to say. It is possible, however, that the resemblance might suggest itself to at least some members of the audience. At any rate, the play closes with the soldiers honoring Eudoxia as a "saint" (V.viii. 115), much as Camma was honored.

Valentinian, then, uses the standard motifs of chastity literature to mold the history of Lucina's rape to the Lucrece pattern. The central debate in III.i. about Lucina's suicide turns on the idea that rape implies a kind of guilt for the ravished woman and that only her death can expiate this guilt. The treatment of rape in *The Queen*

---

3. Variorum 4:211.

of Corinth (1616–c. 1618)[4] is in marked contrast to the conventional treatment of this subject in *Valentinian*. In this later play the arguments for the continued life of the ravished woman—that she is morally innocent and that she may, by continuing to live, bring her ravisher to repentance—are allowed to triumph. The lady who is raped neither dies of grief nor kills herself in order to prove that she did not consent; instead, she marries the ravisher, and he is forgiven.[5]

Because the villain is forgiven, the play has either been condemned as being morally oblique[6] or taken as a rhetorical exercise debating the dilemma proposed in this Senecan *controversia:*

A woman who has been raped may choose whether her seducer shall be executed or shall marry her without a dowry.

In one night a man raped two women; one chooses his death, the other chooses to be married.[7]

Neither of these attitudes is entirely adequate. *The Queen of Corinth* uses the problem posed by the *controversia,* but rape, as such, is not the subject of the play.

The actual subject is the contrast between the good man, exemplified by Euphanes, and the bad, represented by Crates, his older brother. Crates, like Oliver in *As You Like It,* has denied proper support to his younger brother. Euphanes, enabled to travel by the free gift of the rich and virtuous Beliza, has distinguished himself and has, as the play opens, just returned to Corinth. Preferred to

---

4. Glover and Waller, vol. 6. As the Glover and Waller edition of the plays is a reprint of the Second Folio, there are no line numbers, and scene divisions are erratic. For the convenience of the reader, in-text citations of this edition give act and scene numbers and, after a semicolon, the page number in the volume cited.

5. This situation, objectionable to Fletcher's critics, is a frequent motif in New Comedy and appears also in folklore (Jean Johnson, p. 26). Fletcher could expect a large part of his audience to be familiar with the similar situation in Terence's *Hecyra.* Cf. *The Spanish Gypsy* (1623) by Middleton, Rowley, and Ford.

6. Ristine, p. 117; G. C. Macaulay, "Beaumont and Fletcher," *Cambridge History of English Literature* (Cambridge, 1910), 6:146.

7. Waith, *Pattern of Tragicomedy,* p. 89; discussed further, pp. 136–37 and 204–5.

royal attention by Beliza, he soon becomes the favorite of the Queen. Euphanes uses the power of his new position with modesty and justice, showing a "passive fortitude" (III.i;41) in the face of the insults of the bitterly envious Crates. When a reconciliation between the brothers is effected late in the play, Crates loses his envious humour and becomes a virtuous man determined to right the past wrongs he has done.

And Crates' deeds have been grievous. At the opening of the play he assisted Prince Theanor to rape Merione. Theanor had long wooed and expected to marry Merione, but his mother, the Queen, broke off the match and gave her to Agenor, Prince of Argos, to cement a peace treaty between these two countries. On the eve of Merione's wedding, Theanor, disguised in a vizard, ravishes her in the Temple of Vesta, and leaves her drugged on her own doorstep, where she is found by the Queen and all the wedding guests. This sensational episode has usurped all the attention of critics. But it is only an episode. Merione appears very little on stage except for a scene of passionate lamentations after the rape. Thereafter she lives as a "recluse Nun" (II.iii;25) and hardly speaks. The emphasis falls not on the plight of the woman, as is the case in the plays of chastity, but on the actions of the men.

The plot is taken up with the miracles of liberality and self-sacrifice performed by the good men—Euphanes, Agenor, Leonidas, and Cronon—while the evil men—Crates and Theanor—both of whom are victims of envy, plot to remove Euphanes from the Queen's favor. The hostility between Euphanes and Crates is emphasized as the dominant theme by a subplot dealing with Onas, who, like Euphanes, has been sent by Beliza to travel but who comes home as great a simpleton as before. An uncle is attempting to cheat Onas out of his estate, as Crates attempts to cheat Euphanes out of his. That the substance of the play is the adventures of Euphanes has not been noticed because critics have been unable to see anything in the play but the rape.

The climax of the play, the trial of Theanor for rape, is also the greatest of Euphanes' good deeds for the Queen and Corinth; it is he who engineers the stratagem that brings Theanor to repentance and, ultimately, to forgiveness. He devises his plan when the repentant Crates tells him the identity of Merione's ravisher and of Theanor's intention to rape Beliza. Euphanes persuades Merione to disguise herself as Beliza and to allow herself to be raped a second time. This ruse is only a more extreme version of the familiar Jacobean bed trick, and it has the same beneficent effects as the bed tricks in *All's Well That Ends Well* and *Measure for Measure*.[8] Now the Senecan dilemma comes into play. Beliza, pretending to have been raped, demands the death sentence for the ravisher; Merione, who still loves Theanor, begs that he be allowed to marry her. The Prince himself, now deeply repentant, breaks the deadlock by offering to marry Merione and then to be beheaded for Beliza. As soon as the marriage ceremony is performed, Euphanes and Crates reveal their virtuous stratagem to reclaim the heir of Corinth from his evil ways, and they receive the thanks of the Queen.

Although rape is the topic for debate in the trial scene, the resemblance of the scene to the conclusion of *Measure for Measure* emphasizes that the real issue at stake is not chastity, but rather justice versus mercy. The formal debate is framed by almost allegorical pleas to the presiding Queen from the two ladies. At the opening of the trial:

> Beliza. I was ravish'd,
> And will have justice.
> Merione. I was ravish'd too,
> I kneel for mercy.
> (V.iv;73)

And at the conclusion:

> Merione. Mercy, O mercy Madam!
> Beliza. Great Queen, justice!
> (V.iv;75)

Merione has only one long speech at the trial, and in that speech she drops the issue of rape and renews a plea for leniency:

---

8. See the chapters on these plays in Robert G. Hunter, *Shakespeare and the Comedy of Forgiveness* (New York, 1965).

> Let this Court be then the image of Joves throne,
> Upon which grace and mercy still attend,
> To intercede between him and his Justice. . . .
>
> (V.iv ;74)

(Her plea alludes to the debate of the four daughters of God for an erring soul, a frequent motif in the morality plays.) *Measure for Measure* is even more specifically suggested by the adaptation of the names Merione and Beliza from Mariana and Isabella.[9] Fletcher's intention here seems clear. Since he frequently reworked Shakespearian plays by making the issues more extreme,[10] the question Fletcher poses in *The Queen of Corinth* might be stated this way: Isabella and Mariana can forgive Angelo for seduction by means of threats; can Merione and Beliza forgive Theanor for rape? The greater the offence, the greater the mercy extended. In both plays a trick of disguise allows the villain to be forgiven, since consummation is effected only with his betrothed.

The emphasis upon Euphanes as the hero and upon an extension of the *Measure for Measure* dilemma makes rape very much a secondary issue in *The Queen of Corinth*. The rape is devised as a test not of chastity but of mercy. Nonetheless, it is easy to see why critics have seen the play's primary theme as being rape. The opening scenes give as much emphasis to the projected marriage and the rape of Merione as to the quarrel between Euphanes and Crates. This kind of misleading exposition to secure a spectacular opening act is not uncommon in Fletcher's plays. A familiar example is the spectacular opening scene of *The Two Noble Kinsmen,* in which the Three Queens interrupt Theseus's marriage to Hippolyta; the play's primary subject, however, is the relationships of Palamon, Arcite, and Emily.

An examination of Fletcher's treatment of rape in *The Queen of Corinth* shows how carefully he has subordinated the rape episode to the general design of the play. In order to prepare for the forgiveness of Theanor's crime, Fletcher very carefully maintains sympathy for

---

9. D. H. McKeithan, *The Debt to Shakespeare in the Beaumont and Fletcher Plays* (Austin, Tex., 1938), p. 157.
10. *Ibid.,* passim.

the young prince. His mother, the Queen, has long encouraged his suit to Merione, but, because the Queen has been reared in Sparta, her emotions are rigidly controlled, and she expects to control the emotions of the young with the same rigidity:

> She has not only forc'd him with rough threats
> To leave his Mistriss, but compell'd him . . .
> . . . .
> To wait upon his Rival.
>
> (I.i;3)

Merione herself objects to the political marriage with Agenor, declaring that it is hardly "Within my power to make a second gift/ Of my poor self" (I.ii;6). Theanor plans the rape to break the marriage between Merione and Agenor (V.iv;77); sexual consummation of the betrothal between Theanor and Merione would be equivalent to a civil marriage ceremony.[11] Even so, Theanor has to be encouraged in his plan by the spiteful Crates, for he has doubts about using this means to break the match:

> And yet the desperate cure that we must practice
> Is in it self so foul, and full of danger,
> That I stand doubtful whether 'twere more manly
> To dye not seeking help. . . .
>
> (I.i;3-4)

Except for this brief speech, the plans for the rape are kept decisively offstage. There is no kneeling plea of the maiden for her chastity and no threatening speech from the ravisher.

Merione's lament for her wronged chastity, which opens Act II, is brilliant but brief. Conventionally, she curses the gods and denounces her ravisher, who has "sacrilegiously robb'd this fair Temple" (II.i;18).[12] She of course accuses Theanor's confederates of being

---

11. Betrothal itself conferred marital rights if the formal betrothal vows were made in the present tense. In the case of consummation after betrothals made either in the present or the future tense "and without any marriage ceremony, the offenders laid themselves open to punishment by the church, but their union was recognized as a valid marriage by both church and state." Powell, pp. 3-4.

12. Cf. *Valentinian* III.i.39, quoted above.

"the Devils own servants" (II.i;18). At this point in the lament, Merione should, according to convention, plead with her ravisher for death. Instead, she pleads for marriage: "You have had your foul will; make it yet fair with marriage;/ Open your self and take me, wed me now" (II.i;18). This plea prepares for the conclusion of the play. Merione's attitude is not, however, to be taken as a sign of moral weakness. Crates assures the prince that she will hide her dishonor: "She must and will conceal it; nay, forget it,/ The woman is no Lucrece" (II.iii;20). This is not the case, however; Merione immediately decries the villainy that has been done to her, even though she feels the usual guilt of the ravished maiden:

> Let no good thing come near me, virtue flie me;
> You that have honest noble names despise me,
> For I am nothing now but a main pestilence. . . .
>   (II.iii;23)

Normally, at this point, the ravished maid should declare her resolve to die, in spite of all persuasions that she live. Fletcher, however, very carefully truncates debate on this subject. Merione announces that she will "live a poor recluse Nun" until she dies or "till Heaven shall . . . send me comfort" (II.ii;25). This can only mean that she still has hope that her ravisher will reveal himself and marry her. From this point on, Merione is carefully kept offstage until she is needed for the concluding trial scene.

Heaven sends "comfort" to Merione, as we have seen, through the good offices of Euphanes. She herself is a passive figure in the plot. In her sufferings she displays the same "passive fortitude" that distinguishes Euphanes' behavior toward Crates. The Spartan-bred Queen of Corinth herself is the chief exemplar of passive fortitude in the play, hence the title. She shows self-discipline in giving up the daughter-in-law she wishes in order to make a treaty advantageous to her country, in subduing her affection for Euphanes, and, later, in trying and condemning her own son with impartial justice. Fletcher has modified the conventional rape pattern to make Merione's intention to suffer her wrongs with patience illustrate the larger theme of his play. Merione is a Christianized Lucrece in that she does not contemplate suicide as a remedy for rape.

The Maid in the Mill (1623)[13] shows another kind of Christianized Lucrece, one who converts her would-be ravisher by her own virtue and wit. That part of *The Maid in the Mill* which concerns us is based on Painter's story of Duke Alexander de Medici of Florence.[14] One of the Duke's courtiers abducts a miller's daughter, ravishes her, and keeps her prisoner. The miller's daughter, according to Painter, is "a Paragon and mirror of chaste life and modesty" (II.410), who

> Voluntaryly woulde have killed her selfe lyke a Lucrece, if the feare of God, and dreadfull losse of Body and Soule, had not turned hir mynde, and also hoped in God that the Ravysher should repayre the fault whych he committed. . . . (II.418)

In order to make her ravisher the more willing to marry her, the girl, who is "sage," begins "subtilely to dissemble and fayne to take Pleasure" in her captivity, which is actually "more bitter than any Aloes" (II.418). Meanwhile, the miller appeals to the Duke for redress; Alexander commands the ravisher to marry the girl and gives her a handsome dowry.

Fletcher relocates the story in Spain; the just ruler is now named King Philippo.[15] The lustful gentleman is the rich Count Otrante, and the miller's daughter is called Florimell. Count Otrante abducts her and secures her in his country estate, where he alternately threatens her with rape and attempts to seduce her. Fletcher probably chose the name Florimell to remind his audience of Spenser's Florimell, who was also imprisoned by a tyrannical lover of high degree, Proteus. Spenser's Proteus is notable as a would-be seducer

---

13. Glover and Waller, vol. 7.

14. R. Warwick Bond, "On Six Plays in *Beaumont and Fletcher, 1679,*" *RES* 11 (1935):258.

15. The change in setting was probably made in order to take advantage of the current interest in the Spanish marriage proposed for Prince Charles. Another Philippo, Phillip III, was currently King of Spain. It was in 1623 that Charles and Buckingham made their romantic (if ill-advised) visit to Spain. See Willson, pp. 429ff.

because he changes shapes in the attempt alternately to please and then to intimidate Florimell. Similarly, Otrante is distinguished by the number and variety of his ruses to undermine the virtue of his prisoner. Florimell is as resourceful in the defense of her chastity as Otrante is in his threats; her last resource, like that of Painter's heroine, is to "fayne to take Pleasure" in that which is bitter as gall to her.

Otrante explains to Florimell that he intends to have her, by force if necessary. In defense of her chastity, Florimell at first attempts to reason with him. When he persists, her defiance evokes the legend of Philomel:

> My body you may force, but my will never;
> And be sure I do not live if you do force me,
> Or have no tongue to tell your beastly Story. . . .
> (III.ii;40)

More subtle than Tereus, Otrante attempts a ruse to subdue Florimell. He commands his men to put her out of doors and to heap scorn on her. This they do, accusing her of being such a common and unwholesome whore that the count has turned her off for fear of catching the pox. When Florimell has been reduced to tears, Otrante reenters and makes the would-be ravisher's traditional threat of slander:

> Yield now, or you are undone: your good name's perish'd
> Not all the world can buy your reputation;
> 'Tis sunk for ever else, these peoples tongues will poison ye
> (III.ii;44)

To drive the warning home, he gives her a sample of his power by commanding his men to make a (protean) change in their behavior by treating her as a saint.

Florimell learns from this charade quite another lesson than the count intended. When next she confronts her would-be ravisher, she pretends to be the common and unwholesome whore she was accused of being. Her "counterfeited staiedness" (V.ii;62), she claims, was an attempt to catch him; that way he would never have known who gave him the pox. She chatters on in this vein, interrupting her wanton discourse from time to time with off-color songs that pick up the sexual connotations of "mill" and "stones" already established earlier in the play.[16] Here, for a sample, is her opening stanza:

> Now having leisure, and a happy wind,
> Thou mayst at pleasure cause the stones to grind,
> Sayls spread, and grist here ready to be ground,
> Fie, stand not idlely, but let the Mill go round.
>
> (V.ii;61)

The audience is reassured that this is pretense by her aside: "Pardon me Modesty,/This desperate way must help; or I am miserable" (V.ii;64). Florimell resembles Avisa in using broad double entendres and her knowledge of syphilis to repel a would-be seducer. Her pretense of wantonness has the desired effect on Otrante. He is aghast and loses his appetite for her entirely:

> I do confess I freeze now,
> I am another thing all over me:
> It is my part to wooe, not to be courted. . . .
>
> (V.ii;62)

At this point, however, Florimell's nerve fails; she turns and weeps. Baffled by her behavior, the count decides, "She is either a damn'd divel, or an Angel" (V.ii;65).

Fortunately, at this moment King Phillipo arrives, Florimell is rescued, and Otrante repents. She explains to Otrante that her pretense of whoredom was to prevent his raping her:

---

16. The mill is given a sexual connotation the first time it is mentioned in the play; the clown, in an argument with Franio, the miller, says, "I will see your Mill gelded, and his Stones fry'd in steaks" (II.i;15). Franio uses similar language when he complains of Count Otrante to King Phillipo:
> The Lord wants a water-Mill, and means to grind with her
> Would I had his stones to set, I would fit him for it.
>
> (III.i;37)
When Otrante's servants heap scorn upon Florimell, accusing her of being a whore, they mock, "Is your Mill broken that you stand so useless?" (III.ii;43).

> My Lord, I am no whore, for all I faigned it,
> And faign'd it cunningly, and made ye loath me:
> 'Twas time to out-do you: I had been rob'd else. . . .
>
> (V.ii;66)

The count offers to make the miller's daughter any amends within
his power. Like Pamela, she takes her would-be ravisher as husband.
She claims him not as a reward for her own virtue, however, but as
a reward for preserving his honor:

> I do ask you, and I deserve ye,
> I have kept ye from a crying sin would damn ye
> To Men and Time. . . .
>
> (V.ii;67)

Thus, by virtue and by wit, Florimell averts rape and dishonor. Her
ruse to avoid being ravished is the most extreme case of pretended
wantonness in the canon. It gives brilliant theatrical possibilities to
her role, allowing the performer to play the parts of both "Angel"
and "Devil."

These two aspects of the female character are separated in a group
of Fletcherian plays that pit the saintly heroine against a wicked
villainess rather than against a lustful villain. The contrast between
women good and bad supplies the emotional force in *Thierry and
Theodoret, The Double Marriage,* and, in a different way, in *The
Maid's Tragedy.*

In *Thierry and Theodoret* (1607–1621)[17] a collaboration by
Beaumont, Fletcher, and Massinger, the opposite extremes of lust
and chastity are represented by Brunhalt, a Messalina figure, and
Ordella, the "Saint of her Sex" (V.i;68). The play suggests an
inversion of the plot of *King Lear;* Brunhalt, the wicked queen-
dowager, torments and murders her two good sons, Thierry and
Theodoret, in order to continue unchecked in her lustful life.[18]
Brunhalt's behavior also suggests the story of the Lady of Chabrye,
whose life was described by Bandello and retold by Fenton (Discourse IX). The widowed Lady of Chabrye also murdered her two

---

17. Glover and Waller, vol. 10.
18. McKeithan discusses the similarities to *Lear,* pp. 142ff.

sons in order to protect her licentious life. Brunhalt's villainies are psychologically improbable in the extreme, but, as lust was considered the root of all evil, no wickedness done by an unchaste woman would surprise a Jacobean audience.

In the opening scene we find her being upbraided for her "loose and lazie pleasures" by her eldest son, Theodoret, Duke of Austracia. He denounces his mother for keeping as servants

> Bawds, Leachers, Letches, female fornications,
> And children in their rudiments to vices,
> Old men to shew examples. . . .
>
> (I.i;4)[19]

Theodoret urges his mother to behave "from example" of ladies who have been good as well as great; her duty as a member of royalty is to set a good example. As it is now, ballads are written about her lust. God sees her concealed sins, which are so great that Theodoret can no longer call her mother. He orders her to spend the remainder of her days repenting in a strict convent. Brunhalt replies with a long, though of course false, defense of her honor. A false defense of chastity is a counter-attack against the accuser rather than a

---

19. The syntax of this passage is compressed, appropriately, to indicate Theodoret's near hysteria. The sense is clearer when compared with the similar passage in Jonson's *Sejanus* describing the Emperor Tiberius's retreat at Capri:

> He hath his slaughter-house, at Capreae;
> Where he doth study murder, as an art:
> And they are dearest in his grace, that can
> Devise the deepest tortures. Thither, too,
> He hath his boys, and beauteous girls ta'en up,
> Out of our noblest houses, the best formed,
> Best nurtured, and most modest: what's their good
> Serves to provoke his bad. Some are allured,
> Some threatened; others (by their friends detained)
> Are ravished hence, like captives, and, in sight
> Of their most grieved parents, dealt away
> Unto his spintries, sellaries, and slaves,
> Masters of strange, and new-commented lusts,
> For which wise nature hath not left a name.
>
> (IV.iv.388–401)

From the edition of *Sejanus* by W. F. Bolton (London, 1966). Brunhalt is in many ways a female Tiberius.

statement of belief in the absolute standards of chastity. Brunhalt charges Theodoret with listening to base informers rather than observing the reverence due a mother; her "known credit" is her own best witness.

This scene closely resembles the key scene in Fenton's version of the "Lady of Chabrye," in which "The eldeste sonne chargeth his mother with incestuose life" (II.109). Like Theodoret, the eldest son reminds his mother that the person of high position is "bounde in doble sort to a wonderful care of integretie in lyving in himselfe, so as hys authoritie and effectes of upright conversacion may serve (as a lyne) to lead the meaner sort" (II.109). He also orders his mother to reform; otherwise the world will make "open exclamation" against her "lascivius order of lyfe" (II.110). The son promises personally to murder her lover, just as Theodoret promises personally to punish Brunhalt's lewd minions. The Lady of Chabrye, like Brunhalt, counter-attacks by accusing her son of being "credulus in every reapport" (II.111) against his own mother.

Such scenes are common in Elizabethan fiction; frequently a son, husband, father, brother, or interested friend will lecture a fallen woman and attempt to bring her to repentance. The dissuasion-from-lechery speech is much like the defense-of-chastity speech in its urging of reasons for continence. The most famous of such scenes in the drama is, of course, Hamlet's closet interview with Gertrude. Gertrude is no Messalina, and she is touched by Hamlet's speech, but both the Lady of Chabrye and Brunhalt are impervious to persuasions to repentance.

Brunhalt flees secretly from Austracia to the court of her younger son, Thierry, King of France. She incites Thierry to lead an army against Theodoret to revenge her "slandered" honor, and her mortification is intense when the two brothers are reconciled. She seizes the first opportunity to murder Theodoret. Meanwhile, her influence in the French court is threatened by Thierry's marriage to the chaste and virtuous Ordella. Brunhalt's machinations against her rival set up the two key scenes in the play—III.i, the trial of Ordella's continence, and IV.i, the trial of Ordella's wifely loyalty.

Brunhalt arranges for Thierry to take a potion that will render

him impotent on his wedding night. His inability will completely
alienate Ordella:

> If she have any part of woman in her,
> She'll or fly out, or at least give occasion
> Of such a breach which nere can be made up. . . .
> (II.i;19)

This plan, and the expectation expressed of Ordella's reaction, prepare for a trial of Ordella's chastity. The new queen's goodness
foils Brunhalt's schemes completely. Act III opens with Thierry in
despair at his impotence on the bridal night. He cannot believe
Ordella's calm acceptance of the situation and wonders

> did upbraided nature make this pair
> To shew she had not quite forgot her first
> Justly prais'd Workmanship, the first chast couple. . . .
> (III.i;31)

Thus is Ordella compared to the unfallen Eve. Though her "pulse
beats," Ordella asserts that the greatest blessing she sought in marriage was her husband's "virtue and his calm society." When the
incredulous king is finally able to believe that his bride can bind
herself to the pleasures only of eye and ear, her "surer sence made
useless," he is almost hysterical with admiration: "Oh, who would
know a wife, that might have such a friend?" (III.i;32). Thierry's
impotence is not gratuitous sensationalism; rather, it is a test of
Ordella's chastity. The high point of the scene for a Jacobean audience would surely be Ordella's affirmation of content with continence. The resolve to lead a continent life in wedlock is common in
stories of saints' lives. Accordingly, Ordella is praised as a saint.
Thierry declares that "virgins of our age" will convert her "example
to a miracle" (III.i;34).

Unable this way to break Thierry's marriage, Brunhalt now works
on his fear of leaving the kingdom without an heir. She bribes a
famous astronomer to tell the king that he will have many heirs if
he slays the first woman that leaves Diana's temple on the following
morning. Brunhalt then arranges for Ordella to be that woman.

Thierry does not recognize his wife because she is veiled, and he asks her to sacrifice her life for France. In this, the most important scene of the play, Ordella vows herself willing to die that Thierry may live in his posterity. For this resolve she is praised as the greatest exemplum of honor, "such examples as the former ages/ Were but dim shadows of" (IV.i;45). She will be "sainted" (IV.i; 47). Ordella is content to create spiritual children only:

> . . . he that reads me
> When I am ashes, is my Son in wishes,
> And those chaste dames that keep my memory,
> Singing my yearly requiems, are my Daughters.
> (IV.i;46)

When Thierry unveils his wife, he is appalled and will not make the necessary sacrifice, for "There is an Angel keeps that Paradice" (IV.i;47) in Ordella's face. He rushes heartbroken from the stage. When Ordella hears of the astronomer's prediction, she immediately offers to commit suicide but is dissuaded from self-murder by the virtuous counselor Martel, who begs her:

> rob not us
> And those that shall hereafter seek example,
> Of such inestimable worthies in a woman.
> (IV.i;48)

In order to gain time to unmask Brunhalt, Martel persuades Ordella to go into retirement while he reports that she has committed suicide.

Martel returns to court and delivers a eulogy of the supposedly dead queen. His praise stresses the ideal nature of her character as one in whom

> All was, that Athens, Rome, or warlike Sparta,
> Have registered for good in their best Women:
> But nothing of their ill. . . .
> (IV.i;53)

As an exemplum, Ordella in this movement of the play suggests Alcestis, whose wifely loyalty, expressed in her willingness to die that her husband might live, was frequently extolled in moral literature. Martel, by preventing Ordella's suicide, takes the place of Hercules rescuing Alcestis from death. Later in the play, Martel returns the supposedly dead Ordella to Thierry, as Hercules restored the supposedly dead Alcestis to her husband, Admetus. Martel, like Hercules urging Admetus to take a woman into his home, urges Thierry to marry again.[20]

Unfortunately, Ordella and Thierry are not happily reunited as are Alcestis and Admetus. Brunhalt, fearful that Thierry will marry again, poisons her younger son. Her plots become so complicated that she overreaches herself; all her villainies are discovered, and she chokes herself for spite. The other characters denounce her as a "monster" (V.i;66), a "plague" (I.ii;10), and a "Tygress" (I. ii;7). Ordella, who dies out of sympathy for her dying husband, is hailed as the "perfect woman" (V.i;69), "blest and happiest woman" (V.i;69), and an "Angel" (V.i;68).

A similar contrast between women good and bad is the purpose of *The Double Marriage* (1619–1623).[21] This collaboration by Fletcher and Massinger is interesting because it synthesizes and modifies material from a number of sources in order to achieve this contrast between feminine virtue and villainy. The historical background and the characters' names are taken from Phillippe de Comines,[22] but, as Waith has demonstrated, the plot is a combination of two Senecan *controversiae*, "The Daughter of the Pirate Chief" and "The Woman Tortured by the Tyrant because of her Husband":

A youth, captured by pirates, wrote his father for a ransom; no ransom was sent. The daughter of the pirate chief forced the youth to promise he would marry her if he were freed; he promised. She left her father and followed the young man. He returned to his father and married her. An orphan heiress appears; the father

---

20. Compare the use of the Alcestis myth in the conclusion of *Much Ado About Nothing* and in *The Knight of Malta* (discussed below). The conclusion of *The Winter's Tale*, in which the statue of Hermione comes to life, has much the same effect.
21. Glover and Waller, vol. 6.
22. Bond, *RES*, p. 258. Discussed further by E. M. Waith, "The sources of *The Double Marriage* by Fletcher and Massinger," *MLN* 64 (1949):509.

orders his son to marry her, abandoning the daughter of the pirate chief. When he refuses, his father disinherits him.

A woman, tortured by a tyrant to make her confess what she knew of her husband's tyrannicidal plot, continued to deny everything. Her husband later killed the tyrant. He then sent her away on the grounds of barrenness, since in five years she had had no children. She brings action for ingratitude.[23]

Virolet, the hero of the play, is, as Waith points out, the son in the first and the husband in the second *controversia*. As such, we would expect to see him torn between duty to father and gratitude to the pirate's daughter, between duty to his wife and the desire to have children. This is not the case, and for several reasons. Most important is the change wrought in the plot by making the heroine, Juliana, stand in the place of both the tortured wife and the rebuffed heiress. She becomes a Patient Griselda figure, and interest tends to focus on the contrast between her virtuous sufferings and the villainies of the pirate's daughter.

Fletcher alters the plot further so as to make it center emotionally in the dilemma of the woman. The opening scene, as has often been remarked, is obviously modeled upon the confrontation between Brutus and Portia in Shakespeare's *Julius Caesar*.[24] The noble Virolet has joined in a conspiracy to overthrow the tyrannical King Ferrand, and, at the passionate insistence of his virtuous wife, Juliana, makes her his confidante. The suggestions of *Julius Caesar* in this scene are so many that it will arouse in the audience a strong expectation that Juliana will behave like Shakespeare's Portia and, through nervousness and curiosity, teeter on the edge of revealing her husband's plans. Fletcher's Juliana, however, outdoes the Roman matron, frequently cited as an exemplum of constancy and fortitude; not only does she remain steadfast, she suffers on the rack without re-

---

23. Waith, *Pattern of Tragicomedy*, pp. 89–90.
24. See McKeithan, pp. 167ff. McKeithan omits to notice one of the most interesting Shakespearean parallels in the scene. Fletcher creates a boy, Lucio, modeled on Brutus's boy, Lucius, to illustrate the hero's thoughtfulness of others in times of great public stress.

vealing to the wrathful tyrant the whereabouts of her husband. Indeed, she is as steadfast under torture as the early Christian martyrs, and the language of the play calls attention to this similarity: " 'Tis a miracle,/ She tires th' executioners" (I.i;335).

Defeated by her fortitude, Ferrand tries another plan to rid himself of Virolet. He offers the conspirators their lives if they will rescue his nephew from his arch-enemy, the pirate Duke of Sesse. They agree, and Virolet is made captain of the expedition. Virolet is one of those Fletcherian heroes who are fated and impotent in all their attempts at positive action. Accordingly, we next see him taken prisoner by the pirates. Sesse's Amazonian daughter, Martia, falls in love with him and offers him his freedom if he will marry her. Surprisingly, Virolet assents with only this token struggle:

> I love you;
> But how to recompence your love with marriage?
> Alas, I have a wife.
>
> (II.i;351)

Though we understand that Virolet's wife and father are being held as hostages for his successful return, the suddenness of his decision is astonishing. If Fletcher's first purpose were debate for its own sake, as Waith suggests, we should expect here a full-blown debate from Virolet. The emphasis, however, is not on the hero's plight; it is reserved for the scene in which Virolet announces to Juliana that he has divorced her. Thus the interest is not focused on the plight of the husband forced to virtual bigamy, but rather on the plight of the cast-off wife.

Juliana bears her divorce with a patience that surpasses that of Griselda. As a wealthy, high-born lady who has undergone torture to save her husband's life, she has conferred obligations upon him that could not have been dreamed of by the poor peasant Griselda, raised to high estate solely by the whim of her husband, Walter. As in the case of Ordella, Fletcher is working in the direction of creating an exemplum of womanly behavior that exceeds the precedents of ancient story. Juliana, obedient as Griselda, does not bring an action against Virolet for ingratitude, as does the abandoned wife in the *controversia,* but instead patiently gives up her husband to her rival. This is undoubtedly the key scene in the play. Juliana here displays obedience, as she had earlier demonstrated fortitude in the torture scene. Virolet praises her lavishly as a saintly exemplum:

> Sweeter in thy obedience than a Sacrifice;
> And in thy mind a Saint, that even yet living,
> Producest miracles . . . .
> . . . .
> The fortitude of all their sex, is Fable
> Compar'd to thine; and they that fill'd up glory,
> And admiration, in the age behind us,
> Out of their celebrated urns, are started,
> To stare upon the greatness of thy spirit;
> Wondring what new Martyr heaven has begot,
> To fill the times with truth, and ease their stories. . . .
>
> (III.i;367)

Juliana lives up to these praises by declaring Virolet obliged to Martia for his life, giving up her dowry, and commending his new wife.

The remainder of the play contrasts Juliana's virtuous behavior when she is cast aside by her husband, and Martia's villainies in the same circumstances. Virolet, having fulfilled the letter of his promise to Martia by marrying her, refuses to consummate the marriage, and Martia vows revenge. She becomes the concubine of Ferrand, her husband's most loathed enemy; as Virolet's legal wife, she will thus make him a notorious cuckold. Juliana's behavior provides a marked contrast. She spurns Martia's impudent suggestion that she join with her in revenge against Virolet. Further, she not only refuses the lustful advances of Ferrand's wicked agent, Ronvere, she also refuses the embraces of Virolet, the man she loves passionately, who is morally, though not legally, her husband. Fletcher, with great ingenuity, arranges for Juliana to be with Virolet at the moment Martia comes to threaten him with revenge. The pirate's daughter storms at him: "Take back your love, your vow, I give it freely;/ I poorly scorn it" (IV.i;384). Virolet is overjoyed. He feels free of all obligation to Martia, and, though she kill him the next day, he tells Juliana:

Yet have I time once more to meet my wishes,
Once more to embrace my best, my noblest, truest;
And time that's warranted.

                    (IV.i;385)

Juliana, however, recalls him to his religious obligation:

Good Sir, forbear it:
Though I confess, equal with your desires
My wishes rise, as covetous of your love,
And to as warm alarums spur my will to:
Yet pardon me, the Seal oth'Church dividing us,
And hanging like a threatning flame between us,
We must not meet, I dare not.

                    (IV.i;385)

The scene is incredibly ingenious in presenting the only possible temptation to the chastity of such an exemplary lady as Juliana.

This ingenuity is typical of Fletcher. So also is his manipulation of source material to make such a situation possible. There is not the slightest indication of a trial of chastity in either of the *controversiae* used for the plot. Fletcher evidently intended to show that a woman who could display extraordinary fortitude under torture would be as extraordinarily chaste. Juliana's chastity is re-emphasized in the last act when the grieving father of Virolet eulogizes his daughter-in-law at length:

Look on this,
This face, that in a savage would move pitty,
The wonder of her Sex, and having said
'Tis Juliana, Eloquence will want words
To set out her deservings. . . .

                    (V.i;402)

Immediately we see the contrasting behavior of another father. The pirate Duke of Sesse threatens his daughter Martia with death as a reward for whoredom. He, too, finds that he wants words "to set out her deservings":

Thou, I want a name,

By which to stile thee: All articulate sounds
That do express the mischief of vile woman,
That are, or have been, or shall be, are weak
To speak thee to the height.

                                        (V.i;405)

By this time the ineffectual Virolet has been forgotten, and the crowning of a successor to Ferrand is perfunctory. The emotional force of the conclusion is centered in these parallel speeches, of eulogy for the good woman, of scorn for the bad.

In *The Double Marriage* the nominal hero, Virolet, is secondary in importance to the good and bad women who control his fate. The inverse is true in Beaumont and Fletcher's *The Maid's Tragedy* (c. 1608–1611).[25] As is usually the case in those collaborations in which Beaumont had the dominant hand, the emphasis falls upon the role of the man rather than upon the plight of the woman. *The Maid's Tragedy* centers in the plight of the inexperienced Amintor when he finds himself married to the king's whore and in Amintor's friendship with Melantius. The play is only marginally a chastity play. Insofar as *The Maid's Tragedy* is concerned with chastity, it sets up a conventional opposition between the good woman, Aspatia, and the bad though finally redeemed woman, Evadne.[26]

Evadne, the royal mistress who marries Amintor to cover her affair with the king, is one of Beaumont and Fletcher's most brilliant creations. Because there are a number of fine analyses of the famous wedding-night confrontation between Evadne and Amintor, this study will note only the conventional portrayal of her repentance and its consequences. In IV.i her brother, Melantius, forces from her the name of her lover and insists on her repentance. As we have seen in the discussion of *Thierry and Theodoret,* this type of scene is a staple in the fiction and drama of chastity. Melantius, as dissuader from lechery, insists that the people "in every place" (IV.i.44)

---

25. Ed. Robert K. Turner, *Dramatic Works,* vol. 2.
26. There is perhaps a literary joke in this choice of names. Aspatia was the mistress of Pericles, and Evadne was the widow of Capaneus, one of the Seven Against Thebes, who threw herself on her husband's funeral pyre. Beaumont and Fletcher reverse these familiar names to make Evadne the royal mistress and Aspatia the faithful wife who chooses self-immolation.

speak of Evadne's lusts, and he disclaims the name of brother. Evadne in turn declares that such informers are "base" (IV.i.45) and retaliates with threats. Melantius, however, forces her to repent, and after this she begins to point the moral of her fall at every turn in the action, exactly in the manner of Daniel's Rosamond. She is "miserable" (IV.i.112):

> Gods where have I beene all this time, how friended,
> That I should lose my selfe thus desperately,
> And none for pittie shew me how I wandred?
> There is not in the compasse of the light
> A more unhappy creature, sure I am monstrous. . . .
>   (IV.i.177–81)

To expiate her sins, she promises to kill the "devill King" (IV.i.261), calling on the "spirits of abused Ladies" (IV.i.168) for help in this enterprise. She urges the king to repent "if the devill/ Your lust will give you leave" (V.i.59–60). In the murder scene she again points the moral of her story:

>   Let no woman dare
> From this houre be disloyall, if her heart be flesh;
> If she have bloud and can feare. . . .
>   (V.i.16–18)

Evadne is set up as a warning exemplum, though the bloody nature of her penance and the emotional pyrotechnics of the wedding-night scene are the center of interest for a modern audience.[27]

In marked contrast to Evadne is Aspatia, constant in her love to Amintor even after he breaks his troth-plight marriage with her to marry Evadne at the king's behest. (As in *The Queen of Corinth,* sympathy is retained for the hero by having the betrothal broken off by royal command.) The contrast between the two women is nicely pointed by the structure of the play. Immediately following the wedding-night scene in which Evadne reveals her adulterous

---

27. Swinburne is the only critic, so far as I am aware, who has commented on this aspect of Evadne's character. In *Studies in Prose and Poetry,* p. 65, he calls her "the murderess-Magdalen."

liaison, the next scene shows Aspatia at her needlework among her maids. This tableau gives us the traditional pose of the faithful wife, reminding us of Lucrece spinning among her maids and Penelope working on the great web. Aspatia calls attention to herself as a type of the forsaken woman by speaking of Oenone, abandoned by Paris, and Dido, abandoned by Aeneas (II.ii.30–35). In addition, the maids are engaged in a piece of needlework depicting Ariadne forsaken by Theseus. Aspatia urges them to model the picture of Ariadne on herself: "Doe it by me,/ Doe it againe, by me the lost Aspatia" (II.ii.63–64). The scene is typical of the Renaissance tendency to see characters in terms of archetypes. As Evadne is a type of Rosamond, of the repentant adulteress, so Aspatia is a type of Ariadne.

This would suggest that Amintor is to be seen in some sense as a Theseus figure. The Elizabethans placed Theseus along with Paris, Aeneas, and Jason in the lists of faithless men. Theseus was punished in kind for his faithlessness to Ariadne when Phaedra, one of the archetypes of the evil woman, broke faith with him by attempting to seduce Hippolytus. So Amintor in punished in kind by the faithlessness of Evadne. Although there is no real cause-and-effect relationship, Amintor feels that his marriage to a whore is a punishment for his treatment of Aspatia. Twice in asides he calls attention to his marriage as a retribution:

> This tis to breake a troth. . . .
> (III.i.283)

> The faithlesse sin I made
> To faire Aspatia, is not yet reveng'd,
> It followes me. . . .
> (III.i.218–20)

The play, then, uses the figures of the good and bad women to concentrate on the situation of the man.

The hero is also the center of interest in the two other major tragicomedies in which Beaumont is the dominant author, *A King and No King* and *Philaster*. These plays deal with incest and with false accusations of faithlessness, but as Arbaces and Philaster are the major figures, the plays are anomalous as chastity plays, which usually deal with the plight of the woman.

A King and No King (1611)[28] intersects with this study in the central complication of Acts III–V, King Arbaces' temptation to commit incest with his sister, Panthea. Disaster is averted when it is discovered that Arbaces is not the king and Panthea is not his sister. For most critics, the happy ending, in which Arbaces and Panthea find that they are free to marry, is a moral and aesthetic perversion.[29] Arbaces, according to the usual argument, has not had to repent of his desire for his supposed sister and instead is saved by a clever twist of the plot. It is far from certain that the Elizabethans saw this denouement as perverse. It is altogether more likely that their attention was absorbed by Arbaces' heroic, if somewhat hysterical, efforts in Acts III and IV to overcome his supposedly unlawful desires. The basis of this hypothesis is the striking choice of the name Panthea for the heroine. This name would certainly have aroused strong preconceptions in the audience about the plot. The story of Cyrus and Panthea was a familiar one in the Renaissance, and in chastity literature Cyrus is frequently cited as an example of continence in men and Panthea of chastity and loyalty in women. In an excellent discussion of the sources of *A King and No King*, Robert K. Turner shows that many of the names are taken from Xenophon's *Cyropaedia*. In one episode of this work, Turner points out, Araspes falls violently in love with the beautiful Panthea.[30] This is quite true, but Araspes' love for Panthea is not the point of the story; the point is that Cyrus does not fall in love with Panthea.

Painter, for example, retells this episode in Tome I, novella 11 of *The Palace of Pleasure*. Panthea, wife of Abradatas, is taken captive by King Cyrus and committed to the custody of the young Araspes.

---

28. Ed. Robert K. Turner in the Regents Renaissance Drama Series (Lincoln, Neb., 1963). Also ed. George Walton Williams, *Dramatic Works*, vol. 2.
29. Most recently and most forcefully stated by Turner in the introduction to his edition of the play, pp. xxv–vi.
30. Turner, p. xiv.

Because of her great beauty, Araspes picks her out to be Cyrus's concubine. Cyrus refuses to see the lady, telling Araspes, "If I should go to see her, hearing you make this reporte of her beautie . . . I am afraide, lest she would sone alure me to go many times to behold her" (I.59–60). Araspes scoffs at the king's resolve, for he thinks love is a voluntary emotion, and visits the lady again. He promptly falls in love with her, while Cyrus remains heart-whole and untempted. It was not Araspes' love but Cyrus's refusal to see a beauty that might lead him into error that impressed the Elizabethan mind; because of this forbearance, he was extolled as an exemplum of continence. Similar stories were told of Alexander and Scipio as examples of masculine continence. Fenton comments on these stories as follows:

> The great Alexander, albeit he was more given to sensualitie then stoode wyth the honor of so worthie a prince, yet forbeare he to do wronge to the chastetie of the mother and wife of the great monarke Daryus; albeit, they being his prisoners, their honor and life were also at his disposicion. Onely he had not suche credit in his owne continencie as the Romaine Scipio; for that he durste not once come where they were for feare their bewtie wold force him to a forgetfulnes of noble vertue, where th' Affrican hadde alwaies conversacion and conference with the Spanish lady in his tent.
> (II.31)

Scipio was more continent that Alexander or Cyrus, because he could see his beautiful captive and not fall to sin; nevertheless, because they refused temptation, Cyrus and Alexander were worthy of estimation. This story of Alexander in Herodotus speaks also of a Gobryus as Darius's father-in-law and a Mardonius as Darius's brother-in-law. The names Mardonius and Gobrias appear also in *A King and No King*.[31]

It is probable, then, that Beaumont and Fletcher had in mind these anecdotes about Cyrus and Alexander when they wrote *A King and No King*. In that case, the central fact of Arbaces' passion for his supposed sister would not be so much his temptation as his resolve to keep her locked away out of his sight in order to prevent himself

31. *Ibid.,* p. xv.

from sinning. Critics of the play condemn Arbaces' passion but never mention his attempt to overcome it or the pangs of remorse he suffers; by this omission, they blacken his character unduly. The original audience might have taken a rather different view; to desire beauty is natural, but to avoid the sight of beauty in order to avoid desire is, as in the case of Cyrus and Alexander, a commendable action. This is not to argue that the boastful and arrogant Arbaces is to be seen as an exemplary figure, but it is to suggest that a more balanced view of his character would mean a more balanced view of the play, or at least a view closer to that of the original audience.

In *Philaster* (1608–1610)[32] all the pseudo-political intrigues designed to return the hero to his rightful throne turn on the plot of the lady falsely accused of adultery. The court wanton, Megra, accuses Princess Arethusa of fornication with her page, Bellario. As is conventional in stories of the lady falsely accused, Philaster, who loves Arethusa, tries to kill the erring woman. Arethusa's reputation is saved when Bellario is revealed as a woman. This plot device had already been used by Spenser in Book IV of *The Faerie Queene*. In Canto I of the Legend of Friendship, Ate accuses Amoret of fornication with Britomart, a woman disguised as a knight. Amoret's husband, Scudamour, is overcome with grief; he takes lodgings at the House of Care, where he suffers the torments of jealousy. Similarly, Philaster's jealousy is the important emotional fact in *Philaster*. Though there are many accusations and counter-accusations of lust, Arethusa is not given a set speech in defense of her chastity. *Philaster* is not a chastity play as such.

Two other plays that use the motif of the woman falsely accused of adultery are *The Lovers' Progress* and *The Knight of Malta*. *The Lovers' Progress* (1623; revised 1634 by Massinger)[33] is cleverly plotted to allow the audience to participate emotionally in the trial of chastity, which is the focal point of the play.

Sympathy and admiration are, from the opening of the play, carefully elicited for the lovers who are to be tried, the noble Lisander and the chaste Calista. Calista, before the play opens, has been

---

32. Ed. P. A. Daniel, Variorum 1.
33. Glover and Waller, vol. 5.

wooed by two dear friends, Lisander and Cleander. She has married
Cleander and proven herself a faithful and loving wife, one who

> Is not alone contented in her self
> To seem, and be good, but desires to make
> All such as have dependance on her, like her. . . .
>
> (I.i;76)

In spite of her proven virtue, the temptations to show kindness to her
former suitor are overwhelming. Her husband and her maid sing
Lisander's praises to her continually. Moreover, Lisander saves the
lives of her father and brother and is himself wounded in these
efforts. Therefore, when he begs a private interview with Calista
to receive her thanks, it is impossible for her to refuse.

Both Calista and Lisander come to their clandestine meeting with
the best intentions, but their love for each other immediately displays
itself. At this point the audience is in the same plight as the lovers;
while it wishes them to enjoy happiness together, the basic premises
of the play—the lofty friendship of Lisander and Cleander, the
noble chasteness of Calista—mean that only death and tragedy can
ensue if they give in to their love. Therefore the audience must
struggle alongside the characters to keep the meeting honest. To
make the struggle more difficult, the scene is deliberately erotic. As it
begins, Lisander vows he comes

> but to behold those eyes again,
> And pay some Vows I have to sacred Beauty,
> And so pass by. . . .
>
> (III.i;105)

Calista is aware, however, that his present calm is but a "foyl" and
that his love will "break out" (III.i;105). So she gives him a "sov-
eraign medicine" to help them both, which is a "sentence":

> She is married, and she is chaste; how sweet that sounds!
> How it perfumes all air 'tis spoken in!
> O dear Lisander! would you break this union?
>
> (III.i;105–6)

Lisander then asks that he be allowed to kiss her hand, and Calista grants this, for "Such comforts Maids may grant with modesty" (III.i;106). The touch of her hand causes Lisander to rail against "Tyrant Custom" and "Coward Honour" and to beg a kiss, which she grants of "noble pity" (III.i;106). Their reassurances to each other as they kiss show their weakening resolve:

> Lisander. I am wondrous honest.
> Calista. I dare try.
> (III.i;106)

After the kiss Calista recovers herself and urges temperate talk, but Lisander is passionate in his suit to her:

> We are no gods, to be always tyed to strictness,
> 'Tis a presumption to shew too like 'em;
>
> . . . .
> I have found a way, let's slip into this errour
> As Innocents, that know not what we did. . . .
> (III.i;107)

Calista resists with gentle firmness, until Lisander's own better nature halts his amorous fancies:

> What have I said? what blasphemy to honour?
> O my base thoughts! pray ye take this and shoot me.
> [Offering his pistol.]
> (III.i;107–8)

Thus they both win the fight against temptation. However oblique this scene may seem to us, there is no doubt that the audience is meant to agree with Lisander's praise of Calista as "Honour of woman-kind, a heavenly blessing" (III.i;109). She has on principle preserved her chastity in spite of double temptation; she has not only been wooed with fire and passion, she has been wooed by the man her heart affects.

Now that Calista has been proven by a private trial of her virtue, we are to sympathize with her when her honor, like Susanna's, must undergo a public trial. This comes about through the malice of her maid Clarinda, who attempts to blackmail her mistress. In return for keeping silent about the secret meeting with Lisander, Clarinda wants permission for her own lovers to have a free run of the house that Calista has managed so strictly and chastely. Calista is outraged:

> O my precious honour,
> Into what box of evils have I lock'd thee!
> Yet rather than be thus outbrav'd, and by
> My drudg, my footstool, one that sued to be so;
> Perish both life, and honour. Devil thus
> I dare thy worst, defie thee, spit at thee,
> And in my vertuous rage, thus trample on thee;
> Awe me thy Mistress, whore, to be thy baud?
>
>   (III.i;120)

This speech, coming as it does immediately after Calista's meeting with Lisander, will seem hypocritical unless we remember that we are now to regard Calista as a woman who has successfully passed the ultimate test of her honor and who therefore has the right to be strict. Nonetheless, we can wish that Calista's "vertuous rage" were not so like the "chaste fury" of the righteous heroines of Elizabethan fiction. After this outburst, Clarinda's lover kills Cleander and the maid accuses Calista of adultery and murder.

This plot is an interesting variation of the Susanna motif. Calista is accused, not because she refuses to gratify the desires of a man, but because she restrains the lusts of a woman. Like Susanna, she is providentially cleared. Clarinda is trapped into damaging admissions by the Daniel-like king, the murderer confesses, and Clarinda is led off to the death she sought for her mistress. Lisander is commanded to marry Calista after a year's mourning.

There are a number of peculiar things about this plot that can be alleged as due to "moral obliquity," even when recognition has been given to the Jacobean view of chastity. Most peculiar is that Calista is to be understood as loving Cleander and Lisander equally but honorably. This is, after all, the world of lofty sentiment, where lovers love each other because of their virtues; if two men are equally virtuous, they are to be equally beloved. To make this neoplatonic premise the more credible, the subplot deals at length with a triangle of lovers who are in the same predicament. Their triangular love is taken for granted by all the characters in the play; this context makes Calista's plight seem less unusual. Moreover, the subplot is seen not from the point of view of the woman's plight, as is the main plot, but from the point of view of the rival lovers, who engage in a contest of generosity to see which shall give the maid to the other. This emphasis takes the weight off the credibility of the lady's position in such a triangle. Credible or not, Calista's position is made to seem the more honorable by being juxtaposed with the sordid affairs of the maid, Clarinda, who is involved in a dishonorable triangle. Seen, then, in a context in which all the female characters are involved in love triangles, Calista's behavior stands out as exemplary.

The thematic connections between the three plots do not solve all the problems of a very peculiar play, but some, at least, may be due to the fact that Massinger revised the play for a revival eleven years after it was originally written. However much of the original intention may have been lost in the alterations, the central scene, which tries the nobility of Lisander and the chastity of Calista, apparently remains intact as Fletcher wrote it—an ingenious and successful test of the audience as well as of the characters.[34]

A somewhat similar device is used in *The Knight of Malta* (1616–1619),[35] a collaboration by Fletcher, Field, and Massinger. *The Knight of Malta* has the additional interest of displaying quite clearly the morality play structure of the chastity play. The hero, "admired Miranda" (V.ii;157), a probationary knight, is "Malta's better Angel" (V.ii;160), while Mountferrat, the experienced knight, is "her evil" one (V.ii;160). The evil knight is "the woolf to honor" (IV.ii;145); with his "venemous tooth" he infects the "chast life" (IV.ii;146) of Oriana, sister of the Grand Master of Malta.

The plot turns upon the oath of chastity of the Knights of Malta.

---

34. According to Hoy (1957), 9:151, Massinger revised most of Act I and all of Acts IV and V. Act III, which portrays the central trial of Lysander and Calista, contains only incidental revisions by Massinger in the opening and concluding scenes.
35. Glover and Waller, vol. 7.

Mountferrat, overcome by the beauty of Oriana, has repudiated his vow of continence. Oriana threatens to expose him to the Order if he persists in his suit. Mountferrat determines on revenge, and, symbolically, the Maltese cross falls from his robe. Meanwhile, the knights have formally convened to induct into full membership old Gomera and young Miranda. Miranda excuses himself as "yet/ Unworthy, and uncapable of such honor" and begs time to "rectifie" himself "for that high seat" (I.iii;88). The play is actually organized around this "rectifying" of Miranda, but this central theme is greatly obscured by the multiplicity of actions and characters in the exposition. Further, the audience is cued to expect a conventional love story as it realizes at this point that Miranda has refused membership because he loves Oriana. She is also being courted by old Gomera, but, as an ideal young maid, she expresses no preference. More convincingly than the perplexed heroines of *The Lovers' Progress,* she praises them both. Gomera, like Miranda, refuses membership in the order; he frankly declares his love for Oriana and wins the consent of her brother. It is at this moment that Mountferrat "discovers" the "most beautious Treachery" of Oriana (I.iii;91). Gomera, in an instantaneous act of faith, accuses Mountferrat of slander and challenges him to trial by combat.

In this combat, Miranda fights disguised in Mountferrat's armor. He impersonates the villain in order to throw the fight to the old Gomera. His motives, however, are left quite ambiguous at this point in the action; the audience cannot be sure of his virtuous intentions until after the successful outcome of the trial by combat. This use of ambiguity is repeated later in the play to throw emphasis upon Miranda. After Oriana is vindicated, both combatants claim her, Gomera because he fought for her honor, Miranda because he made the fight sure. The choice of Gomera runs counter to the audience's sympathies (see II.v;115).

Thus, at the end of two hectic acts (the plot is overcrowded, even for Fletcher) Miranda is left broken-hearted but with no further emotional ties to prevent his self-perfection for the Order, a mistress "Whose honor, Ermin-like, can never suffer,/ Spot, or black soil" (II.v;115). The action of the first two acts is complete in itself, and the play could end here with the investiture of Miranda. The choice between Oriana and his religious vows has, however, been imposed from without. Three more acts are required to show Miranda's knightly virtues emerging from within.

This "rectifying" begins with an extraordinarily odd chastity test. Miranda resolves to make trial of the beauteous Turkish captive Luscinda, in order to convert her to Christianity. The encounter is prepared for in such a way as to leave Miranda's actual feelings about Luscinda highly ambiguous; he is given a series of asides which indicate a sudden infatuation with her beauty:

> Come hither young one.
> Beshrew my heart: a handsome wench: come nearer,
> A very handsome one: do you not grieve, Sweet. . . .
> (III.iv;130)

By the time he exclaims, "By heaven, she fires me" (III.iv;131), it appears that Miranda, like Mountferrat, has fallen from grace and launched a full-scale seduction. Luscinda, however, is both canny and capable in bringing him back to grace. She points out the "wonder" of Miranda's being a virgin himself; instead of defending her own honor, she lectures him about his own chastity:

> Can ye deliver that unvalued treasure?
> Would ye forsake, to seek your own dishonor,
> What gone, no age recovers, nor repentance. . . .
> (III.iv;132–33)

She dramatically seizes the Cross of Malta from his probationary gown and turns it upon him. His response, "Forgive me heaven, she says true" (III.iv;133), is oddly juxtaposed with "I hope she will be Christian" (III.iv;133), the only line in the sequence that indicates Miranda's good intentions. This very peculiar scene ends with his admission:

> I did dissemble with ye,
> And but to try your faith, I fashion'd all this:
> Yet something you provokt me. . . .
> (III.iv;134)

And later in the play he confesses "a temptation near perform'd/ With this fair Virgin" (V.ii;159).

The oddness of this scene is due to the fact that it is intended to be a test of Miranda's chastity as much as of Luscinda's. He must be proven superior to Mountferrat in his ability to live by the vows of the Knights of Malta. The playwrights are in some difficulties in testing the hero's chastity, as the roles of the man and the woman are never reversed in a chastity test. The tester of chastity pretends to wish to seduce a lady in order to allow her to prove her innocence. A woman never pretends to seduce a man in order to allow him to prove his innocence. When a female character affects wantonness, she does so in order either to reform or repel a lustful seducer. The conventions of pretended wantonness and of the chastity test are complementary but not interchangeable. As a result, the authors of *The Knight of Malta* are forced into the rather ambiguous expedient of having the hero seem to succumb momentarily to his own pretense. A more decisive test of the hero's chastity comes in a similar encounter with Oriana.

Oriana, following her old custom of praising Gomera and Miranda equally, rouses her husband to jealous accusations against her chastity. These slanders cause her to sink into a faint resembling death, and she is buried in the church, from which she is rescued by Miranda. There now occurs another peculiar chastity test. This time the audience is cued in advance by Miranda's aside that he intends to try Oriana's constancy: "Hold but this test, so rich an ore was never/ Tryed by the hand of man, on the vast earth" (V.i;152). He begins by reminding Oriana of Gomera's unjust jealousy, his own earlier defense of her honor, and his saving of her life. Soon the ambiguity of his earlier encounter with Luscinda repeats itself, and with appropriately greater intensity. Miranda himself seems deeply moved:

> Oh what a tongue is here! whil'st she doth teach
> My heart to hate my fond unlawful love,
> She talks me more in love, with love to her. . . .
> (V.i;153)

There is no attempt to reconcile such outbursts with the interspersed asides that remind the audience that Miranda is only pretending. Once again the authors are in the difficult position of testing the hero as well as the heroine, and proving him superior in chastity to the villain. Miranda's asides clearly emphasize this purpose; for example, he cautions himself:

> Lord of thy self now, Soldier, and ever:
> I would not for Aleppo, this frail Bark,
> This bark of flesh, no better steers-man had
> Than has Mountferrat's. . . .
>
> (V.i;153)

At last both Miranda and Oriana emerge victoriously chaste; they decide that together they will beget "A great example to mens continence" (V.i;154).

He considers her a "miracle" but resolves to "try her to the very block" (V.i;154). He again pretends to be a Mountferrat; he pretends to be furious and threatens "a witty, and a fell revenge" (V.i;154) that will cause all men to think her false. Actually he takes her to court and, like Hercules returning Alcestis from the dead, presents her veiled as a gift to Gomera, who, like Admetus, is unwilling to take her, as this will violate his vow to live a life of penance for his unjust accusations against Oriana. This act of restoration completes Miranda's purification. In the spectacular grand finale the wicked Mountferrat is formally and ceremonially degraded from the Order while the angelic Miranda is formally initiated as a Knight of Malta. The play concludes with a double ceremony of expulsion and apotheosis; lust is expelled and chastity triumphs.

The theme of chastity triumphant is obscured in *The Knight of Malta,* as it is in several of the Fletcherian plays, by an overabundance of incident. The usual opinion finds the plot "rambling,"[36] with the result that the function of the two chastity tests has not been recognized; usually these tests have been considered out of

---

36. Alexander Dyce, *The Works of Beaumont and Fletcher,* 2 vols. (Boston, 1854), 1:30.

character for Miranda and therefore meretricious.[37] Apparently no one has noticed that the contrast between Miranda and Mountferrat is functional in terms of theme. This critical difficulty is entirely understandable. The play is so crowded that its structure is not immediately apparent, and it comes very close to being an artistic failure. As has been remarked, Fletcher was often unskillful in constructing plots, one reason, perhaps, why he depended on collaborators. A number of Fletcherian plays that deal with chastity fail because of the overcrowding or poor planning of the plot. These plays are considered in the following chapter.

---

37. See, for example, Waith, p. 137.

8

Less Successful Plays

Many of Fletcher's better plays have been ignored while chastity plays that are artistic failures receive a disproportionate amount of attention. This has come about because the failure of these plays has been attributed to Fletcher's supposed lack of moral perception rather than to his deficiencies as an artist. Critics then use these plays as "evidence" to buttress their preconceptions about Fletcher's "depravity."

This is very noticeable in the case of *Cupid's Revenge* (c. 1607–1612),[1] an early collaboration with Beaumont. Much has been written about this tragedy, partly because of Beaumont's presence, partly because of its use of materials from the *Arcadia*.[2] The play has been supposed an attempt to make up for the poor reception of *The Faithful Shepherdess*. According to this theory, the opportunistic young playwrights, not finding the ensign of Diana lucrative, moved to the banner of Cupid and wrote a play ridiculing chastity.[3] A reading of Act I seems to bear out this theory. The heroine, Hidaspes, persuades her doting father, Duke Leontius, to extirpate "a vaine and fruitlesse Superstition" (I.i.48), the worship of Cupid, and to destroy his "loose naked statues" (I.i.71). An angry Cupid

---

1. Ed. Fredson Bowers, *Dramatic Works,* vol. 2.
2. Discussed in detail by James E. Savage, "Beaumont and Fletcher's *Philaster* and Sidney's *Arcadia,*" *ELH* 14 (1947): 194–206.
3. Appleton, pp. 19–22.

descends and vows revenge. His first victim is Hidaspes herself, who falls in love with "the most deformed fellow i'the Land" (I.iv.15), Zoylus, the court dwarf. The angry duke has the dwarf put to death, hoping thereby to cure his daughter's infatuation. Instead, Hidaspes dies of a broken heart. The courtiers draw the proper conclusion: "This comes of Chastitie" (I.v.78). This entire sequence, far from being tragic, is a comic presentation of a rather comic theme. Hidaspes' love of the dwarf would have seemed comical to Jacobean taste, and is so presented in the play, Zoylus himself being the court buffoon.

At the close of this act we hear that Hidaspes' brother, Prince Leucippus, has absented himself from court, and the audience is thereby led to expect the discomfiture of the second offender against the blind god. Leucippus had seconded his sister's request that Cupid's images be destroyed, because this religion filled the land with "lustfull sinnes" (I.i.82). Audience expectation is further increased by a second appearance of revengeful Cupid. Instead, something quite different happens next. The tone switches from comic to serious, Hidaspes is dismissed from the stage with indecent haste, the other characters forget entirely about the blasphemy against Cupid, and Leucippus takes the center of the stage for four acts entirely disjunct in tone and import from the preceding playlet about Hidaspes. The prince is presented sympathetically as an honorable though credulous young hero. His adventures are delineated compactly in four acts that form a play complete in themselves, a play dealing with a favorite Fletcherian theme, the noble behavior of a high-minded young man when opposed by a revengeful and bloodthirsty whore. Here is an early treatment of a theme to be repeated in *The Double Marriage* and *Thierry and Theodoret*.

Leucippus, as Act II opens, has an affair with Bacha, and is inexperienced enough to believe her protestations that he is the first to despoil her honor. Actually she is a practiced whore, and she artfully maneuvers the young prince into making a promise never to reveal their liaison. His promise is immediately put to the test when Duke Leontius comes to Bacha's house to surprise and shame his son.

Leucippus is placed in the position of having to defend Bacha's
chastity when she simulates virtuous indignation:

> If the Prince your sonne,
> Whom you accuse me with, know how to speake
> Dishonour of me, if he doe not doe it,
> The plagues of hell light on him, may he never
> Governe this Kingdome. . . .
>
> (II.ii.117–21)

Leucippus responds with similarly inflated rhetoric, praising Bacha
above Lucrece:

> she is by heaven
> Of the most strict and blamelesse chastitie
> That ever woman was: (good gods forgive me)
> Had Tarquin met with her, she had beene kild
> With a Slave by her ere she had agreed:
> I lye with her! wou'd I might perish then.
>
> (II.ii.156–61)

Leucippus's false oath rebounds upon him; he does perish, and he
never governs his kingdom.

Leucippus's fall comes about because he is so persuasive in this
unworthy speech that his father is moved to make Bacha his duchess.
The prince's downfall, then, comes because he does not denounce
lust, not because of a stiff-necked chastity that is to be punished by
Cupid. If one is still judging the play in terms of the initial premise
of "Cupid's revenge," the confusion would be the worse compounded
at Leucippus's next appearance, when he refuses the incestuous
advances of his new stepmother. The new duchess is by now a self-
conscious villainess who takes her minions openly and thirsts for
blood vengeance against the virtuous prince. The prince is presented
throughout as a young man whose initial folly is followed by the
most exemplary behavior in the most trying circumstances. These
attitudes are consistently maintained, as Bacha systematically turns
Leontius's love of his son into hate, drives Leucippus into self-
imposed exile, and commits suicide after mortally stabbing her

stepson. What has actually happened is that the encounter between Bacha and Leucippus has been converted into a full-scale trial of chastity in which a young man, repentant for an earlier error, refuses to sin again. Thus the play has become another variation of *The Faithful Shepherdess,* in spite of the elaborately false exposition of Cupid's revenge.

Nonetheless, the authors make resolute efforts to hold the two parts of the play together. For example, Cupid, in his second descent at the beginning of Act II as a prologue to the Leucippus action, announces that the young prince is

> shot through with a shaft
> That will not rankle long, yet sharpe enough
> To sowe a world of helpelesse miserie. . . .
> (II.i.1–3)

As the authors realize, however, it will be difficult for the audience to relish the overthrow of the character to be idealized as the hero, so an attempt is made to shift the blame to Duke Leontius; as Cupid explains:

> . . . it is all the fault
> Of thy ould Father, who believes his Age
> Is colde enough to quench my burning Darts. . . .
> (II.i.6–8)

The "explanation" only makes for further confusion, for Duke Leontius is presented not as a villain but as a comic January doting on an unworthy May. He has, like the other characters, forgotten all about the supposed offense to Cupid, and dies undeceived about Bacha's true nature and thus unaware of his punishment by Cupid. Again, before the deaths at the end of Act V, Cupid descends once more to announce that the time of his revenge draws near. And Leucippus, almost with his dying breath, gives this order to the succeeding duke: "I pray you let/ The broken Image of Cupid be reedified,/ I know all this is done by him" (V.iv.215–17). This is an artistic excrescence, for the only felt sense of retribution in the play is directed against Bacha.

No amount of analysis can make a completely coherent play out of such a poorly planned work. Nonetheless, once the one-act playlet about Hidaspes and the masque-like trappings of Cupid's appearance are sheared away, the last four acts can be seen more clearly as a self-contained chastity play. If Beaumont and Fletcher's original intention was to make *Cupid's Revenge* an antithesis to *The Faithful Shepherdess,* they found themselves unable to present illicit love as anything but dishonorable. Leucippus's mistake is his failure to denounce lust. The misleading exposition, a dramatic trick successful in other plays, is not satisfactory in this play because it cannot be reintegrated with the conclusion and general theme of the play, as in *The Queen of Corinth.* The theme of chastity in Leucippus's adventures prevents such a reintegration.

This same inability to make an artistic success out of an uncongenial subject is evident in another early collaboration, *The Coxcomb* (1608–1610),[4] a play clearly related to versions of the chastity test, such as Cervantes' "El Curioso Impertinente," in which the husband, through his own foolishness, brings about his own dishonor. The wife commits adultery with her husband's best friend. This theme, like the theme of Cupid's revenge, is antipathetic to Fletcher's tendency to glorify chastity and results in another artistic failure. Fletcher tries to rationalize the wife's behavior by making the husband such a fool that the audience wishes to see him cuckolded. He then moralizes about the wife's fall, thus spoiling what could have been a successful city comedy.

Antonio, the coxcomb of the title, has a beautiful and clever wife, Maria. The discovery that his friend, Mercury, loves Maria, brings to bloom a grand and extravagant conceit in Antonio: he will aid his friend to seduce his wife, thereby immortalizing their friendship. This will gain them everlasting glory as another Damon and Pythias or Pylades and Orestes. To carry out his plan, Antonio, like Cephalus, disguises himself in order to corrupt his wife. Maria penetrates his disguise and resolves to revenge herself for this insult by letting him have his own way. She takes Mercury as a lover and considers herself "the honestest woman without blushing,/ That ever lay with

---

4. Ed. Irby B. Cauthen, Jr., *Dramatic Works,* vol. 1.

another man" (IV.viii.59–60). So far, this is an unobjectionable comic plot; Fletcher has turned a normally unhappy story into a comedy of cuckoldry. Antonio's attempt to have his wife seduced is almost beside the point; it is merely the most extravagant manifestation of his extravagant humour of friendship and is clearly intended to represent the ultimate idiocy of a natural fool. At this point, however, the tone of the main plot is spoiled because Fletcher intrudes a kind of moralizing inappropriate to this type of cuckolding comedy. Mercury is like Perigot and Philaster in being devoted to chastity, and his affair with Maria makes him loathe her. She now seems to him but a "customer" (IV.viii.29). His lengthy moralizing over her behavior puts all the preceding action in an unpleasant light and undercuts the humor of the situation.

The main plot of Maria's revenge on Antonio is juxtaposed with Beaumont's sentimental subplot of chastity in distress. It is a curious critical vagary that this subplot has been praised as pure and sublime, while the frank foolishness of the main plot has been condemned as obscene.[5] This is the result of the a priori assumption that, since Beaumont wrote the subplot, it must be more refined than the main plot written by the prurient Fletcher. This attitude is incredible when one looks at the play itself, for the secondary plot shows chastity helpless.

The heroine of this action, Viola, responds quite differently from Maria when she is ill-treated by her sweetheart. Viola agrees to a midnight elopement with Richardo, and her chastity is in continual danger once she leaves the protection of her father's walls. A great deal of emphasis is placed upon the naïve helplessness of the virgin in distress; unlike Maria, Viola is never in control of her situation. Richardo misses the assignation because he gets drunk. When he finally staggers to the meeting place, he mistakes Viola for a whore, offers to have her then and there, and fights over her with his drinking companions before he is hauled off by the constabulary. Still at the mercy of darkness, Viola is mistaken for a gentlewoman whore and nearly raped by desperate thieves. She is rescued by a country gentle-

---

5. Ward, 2:683; Macaulay, p. 90.

man, who then attempts himself to seduce her. Instead of defending chastity, Viola appeals to her would-be seducer with sentiment:

> pray you leave me here
> Just as you found me, a poor innocent,
> And Heaven will blesse you for it.
> (III.iii.93–95)

Finally she is abandoned in the fields, and the audience is left in expectation of a new series of near-rapes and seductions.

Viola's adventures, however, now take a ludicrous turn as she meets two milkmaids, who get her a position in the service of Mercury's mother. From this point the emphasis is upon the clumsy mistakes the gentlewoman makes when she turns her hand to domestic chores. Her chastity is saved by accident rather than by her principles. Meanwhile, Richardo's remorse on the sober morning after and his frantic pursuit of Viola read like a temperance tract. Viola easily forgives his lapse, and the lovers live happily ever after.

Despite critical complaints to the contrary,[6] the two plots are clearly related. Richardo, like Antonio, is a coxcomb. The one, out of an extravagant intoxication of friendship, exposes his wife to the overtures of his friend. The other, because of a deplorable lapse in sobriety, exposes his sweetheart to the drunken advances of his companions. Both are emotionally extravagant. Richardo is nearly mad with remorse (II.iv;IV.ii;V.ii), while Antonio is "almost mad with the apprehension" of gaining an everlasting name for friendship (III.ii.73). Nevertheless, the juxtaposition of the two plots is not entirely happy. Viola's sentimental helplessness looks weak when set beside Maria's capable mastery and lighthearted enjoyment of her own compromising situation. Viola's virtue is passive, and, however appealing nineteenth-century critics found this quality in her,[7] it may have been one reason the play was a failure when first performed. Audiences had been trained by the conventions of chastity literature to prefer heroic to passive chastity. The main plot fails for

---

6. See, for example, Ward, 2:683.
7. Macaulay, p. 90; Raymond M. Alden ed., *The Knight of the Burning Pestle and A King and No King* (Boston, 1910), p. xlii.

a similar reason. Because of the traditions of chastity literature, the Antonio-Maria action sets up expectations other than those that are satisfied. Because of the resemblance to familiar stories of chastity tests, particularly in the husband's assumption of a disguise to corrupt his own wife, the expectation is aroused that Maria will convert Antonio from his foolishness by displaying an exemplary chastity. The thwarting of this expectation and the intrusion of inappropriate moralizing about a cuckolding that the audience has previously been made to sympathize with make the play disappointing.

Another early collaboration by Beaumont and Fletcher, *The Captain* (1609–1612),[8] similarly fails to satisfy the expectations it arouses in the audience. The difficulty in this play arises in the portrayal of the wanton widow Lelia. Her character is constructed on the same premise that underlies the behavior of villainesses like Brunhalt, namely, that once a woman falls to lust she is capable of any crime. As Brunhalt's lusts lead her to murder her two sons, so Lelia's depravity leads her to attempt to seduce her own father, whom she does not recognize. When he reveals his identity, she argues for incest. This seduction scene (IV.iv) is, as every critic agrees, shocking. It is intended to be so, for it displays the depths to which lust may lead a woman.

Lelia is brought to repentance by her father and the honest Angelo, who suggests means similar to those Theodoret suggests to Brunhalt; Angelo advises that Lelia be conveyed to a private house

> where let her heare of nought
> But death and damning, which she hath deserv'd,
> Till she be truly, justly sorrowful. . . .
>   (IV.iv.257–59)

The problem with the play arises at this point and is a structural and artistic problem. Lelia's repentance takes place offstage. As we have seen, scenes of dissuasion from lechery were popular and frequent in fiction and drama, but these scenes always include the erring woman's speech of defiance or of repentance. The omission of Lelia's

---

8. Ed. L. A. Beaurline, *Dramatic Works,* vol. 1.

speech of conversion disappoints the expectations aroused by this very conventional situation. When Lelia reappears in V.v, she is understood to be repentant and reformed. A fool and slanderer is gulled into marrying her. This marriage legalizes Lelia's position in society, thus setting a seal of approval, so to speak, on her reformation. This is the so-called happy ending that outrages critics.

Most critics find Lelia's behavior to her father so atrocious that only her death and damnation would be acceptable to them.[9] Elizabethans, however, were quite willing, even pleased, to see a whore repent and reform, as happens not only in the tales considered in chapter 5 but also in a play popular a few years previously, Dekker and Middleton's *Honest Whore,* Part I (1604). The real problem is that Lelia's repentance is not made dramatically viable. But, however *The Captain* fails to satisfy in dramatic terms, its moral emphasis is clear-cut. Lelia is presented throughout as a warning exemplum,[10] and as such suggests Mirrha and her incestuous lust for her father, a passion that was consummated by a bed trick and that produced the child Adonis. The story of Mirrha, familiar from the *Metamorphoses,* was the subject of several contemporary verse narratives, by W. Barksted in 1607 and by H. A. in 1613.[11] Perhaps Lelia is intended as a variant on Mirrha.

The role of Lelia, like the role of Florimell, provides an actor with the chance to portray both the good and the bad woman, because Lelia is a consummate hypocrite who feigns to be unjustly slandered in order to play upon the sympathy of her admirers. As a professional gold-digger, she is a full portrait of the Lais figure and is specifically described as a siren (III.i.59). In spite of her charms, even the infatuated Julio lectures her upon the deformity of her life; in this and in several ways, the play suggests a reworking of material used

---

9. Felix Schelling, *Elizabethan Drama 1558–1642* (Boston, 1908), 2:183–84; *Cambridge History,* 6:145.

10. I disagree with Waith, pp. 107-9, who feels that Lelia is seen simultaneously as both a romantic and a satiric character. *The Captain* is like Elizabethan moral literature in emphasizing the allurements of a courtesan in order to warn of the danger she presents.

11. Bush, p. 315.

not only in *The Honest Whore* but also in Marston's *Dutch Courtesan* (1603–1604).[12]

Fletcher continues to have problems with plotting later in his career, as, for example, in the subplot of *Women Pleas'd* (1619–1623).[13] This subplot has been frequently and justly criticized as poorly thought out and disorganized in intention.[14] The plot may be summarized as follows: The young and beautiful Isabella is married to the miserly old Lopez, who is not only jealous but also denies her proper food and clothing. Addresses are paid to Isabella by Captain Bartello and by a young merchant named Rugio, whom the audience has already met as Claudio, friend of the hero of the main plot. Before either of these courtships passes beyond mere compliment, Isabella borrows several tricks from the *Decameron* to make her husband's jealousy look ridiculous in public and to expose Bartello's lust to his own wife. Lopez is so pleased at her exposure of Bartello that he forswears jealousy and stinginess and even gives the control of Isabella's personal fortune into her own hands. She in turn is completely satisfied with him as a husband now that he has reformed his outrageous behavior, and she offers to let him eavesdrop while she repels the advances of the young Rugio.

Up to this point the subplot is gay and theatrical. It is a middle-class analogue of the main plot, which retells Chaucer's *Wife of Bath's Tale*. Both plots demonstrate the moral of that tale, that women are most pleased when they obtain their own will. The subplot is spoiled, however, when at the end Rugio reveals himself as Isabella's brother, a relationship of which the audience has had no hint whatsoever. Claudio-Rugio explains that he has been testing his sister's chastity by wooing her in disguise. This explanation is unsatisfactory because passages earlier in the play seem to contradict it entirely. For example, during their first meeting, Claudio-Rugio woos Isabella with such asides as "A most delicate sweet one" and "I hope she loves me" (II.vi;260). There are other inconsistencies in the plot when considered in light of Claudio's ultimate explana-

---

12. Appleton, p. 50, discusses the resemblance of *The Captain* to *The Dutch Courtesan*.
13. Glover and Waller, vol. 7.
14. See, for example, Waith, pp. 155-57.

tion. Isabella has fully intended to have an affair with Rugio and twice makes assignations for that purpose. In II.vi their rendezvous is interrupted by the arrival of Bartello, and the motive for Isabella's first trick on him is to protect Rugio. Isabella's second elaborate trick (III.iv), this time at the expense of Lopez, begins as a subterfuge to conceal another assignation with Rugio, and again Bartello is used as a butt. Only at this point, when Isabella begins to get the upper hand over her miserly husband, does she perceive that it will be more to her advantage to rule in her household than to take a young lover. Therefore the explanation of a chastity test is thematically an excrescence, because the subplot does not demonstrate Isabella's chastity but rather her tractability when she gets her own way. The chastity-test motif actually obscures the relationship of subplot to main plot.

On the other hand, this much can be said for the resolution of the Isabella-Lopez plot. It allows Claudio to join in the general harmony at the end of the comedy rather than being driven from the stage in disgrace as a would-be adulterer. This is desirable not only to preserve the comic tone of the whole play but also because Claudio appears as a rather sympathetic and amusing character in the main plot in Act I. Some of the confusion here may be due to a later revision.[15] As the play stands, the familiar device of the chastity test is used to resolve the contradictions of poor plotting.

As in the subplot of *Women Pleas'd,* the discussion of chastity in the main plot of Fletcher and Massinger's *The Little French Lawyer* (1619–1623)[16] obscures the actual theme of the play, which is not chastity but vainglory. The theme is further obscured because the main plot is so crowded with incident. One can best approach *The Little French Lawyer* by a consideration of the subplot, which gives the play its title. This subplot deals with the amusing adventures of the lawyer La-Writ when he discovers to his astonishment that he is a swordsman. Immediately he abandons his profession and begins to

15. There is other evidence that the play is a revision besides the confusions of the subplot. See G. E. Bentley, *The Jacobean and Caroline Stage* (Oxford, 1941–1968), 3:432.
16. Ed. Cyril Brett, Variorum 4.

pick quarrels with any and all comers, even perfect strangers. Eventually he is gulled and left without a doublet one cold morning on the field of honor. This literally cools his ardor for fighting, and a thorough cudgeling for his impudence quenches it altogether. Dueling is inappropriate to La-Writ's social station and his real temperament (which is cowardly), and his vainglorious lust for fighting is beaten out of him without reflecting upon the institution of dueling itself.

Similarly, in the main plot, the heroine, Lamira, is vainglorious about her chastity, and her pride is humbled without undermining respect for chastity itself. At the opening of the play Lamira has some reason to take pride in her chastity. She has obeyed her father's wishes and given up a handsome young suitor named Dinant to marry the rich old Champernel. Dinant has no intention of giving up his suit to Lamira because of this marriage, but she has no intention of falling to adultery. Thus far her intentions are commendable. As the play progresses, however, she uses her chastity to torment and tease both her husband (III.i) and Dinant (I.iii;III.iii–v). Lamira has an exaggerated opinion of her power over Dinant (see, for example, III.i.71–75) and of her duty to punish him for loving her (see III.i.123–28). During the first three acts Lamira uses her beauty and chastity to humiliate Dinant with a series of practical jokes. After enticing him into a compromising situation, she then turns upon him self-righteously with lengthy defenses of her chastity that are inappropriate to the situation. The speeches themselves are conventional and unexceptionable, so much so that they evoke a stock response from the reader. In a performance, Lamira's farcical vaingloriousness would be amusing because the speeches are so contrary to the context; they are addressed to the gulled Dinant instead of to a lustful villain.

Dinant, after he has been repeatedly tricked, realizes that Lamira is a "proud poppet" (III.v.38) and launches a counter-attack in Acts IV and V. He devises a practical joke designed to humble Lamira by making her think that her chastity is in real danger. Dinant arranges for friends disguised as brigands to capture her in

the woods and to threaten her with rape. He then arrives on the
scene to taunt her by professing pleasure in the sight of her

> boasted honour,
> As you believ'd, compass'd with walls of brass,
> To guard it sure, subject to be o'erthrown
> With the least blast of lust.
>
> (IV.vii.42–45)

Lamira submits to this reproof, which is seconded by her cousin
Annabella, who is in the same plight because of her tricking of
Dinant's friend Cleremont. According to Annabella, the lustful
threats of the supposed brigands are "a punishment, upon our own
prides/ Most justly laid" (V.i.23–24). However, as soon as Lamira
thinks herself out of danger, she again takes a high-handed manner
with Dinant. Exasperated, he threatens to rape her in order, as he
explains, to

> break that stubborn disobedient will,
> That hath so long held out; that boasted honour,
> I will make equal with a common whore's;
> The spring of chastity, that fed your pride,
> And grew into a river of vain glory,
> I will defile. . . .
>
> (V.i.243–48)

At this threat, Lamira confesses her "gross fault" (V.i.259) and
declares herself deserving of any punishment. Dinant is satisfied that
her pride is humbled sufficiently and spares her honor.

In spite of all the talk of honor, *The Little French Lawyer* is not
really a chastity play, for Lamira's chastity is never really at issue.
Actually, neither chastity nor dueling is seriously discussed in the
play; main plot and subplot are analogous in their exposure of false
pride. Both La-Writ and Lamira are overbearing when they are in
safety and timid when faced with actual danger. Nonetheless, Lamira
uses so many of the clichés of the chaste heroine that critics have
been misled into taking her own view of her situation and conse-

quently condemning the play as morally oblique. A good actress could easily make clear the enormously comic qualities of Lamira's character and keep the tone of the whole play at the appropriately farcical level. The play suffers from being read rather than seen, for, although Lamira's language runs counter to the action, her speeches in defense of her chastity are easy to respond to without awareness of their context. The play also suffers from an over-abundance of incident, which conceals the basic thematic unity of the play.

The Little French Lawyer, like all the plays discussed in this chapter, is inept rather than immoral. Considering Fletcher's prodigious output, it is only surprising that he did not produce more failures than he did. Certainly he created many more successes than failures when dealing with the subject of chastity, and it was in four plays written near the end of his career that Fletcher was most successful in portraying chastity triumphant. To these, the best of the chastity plays, we shall turn in the next chapter.

9

The Major Chastity Plays

The best of the Fletcherian chastity plays are *The Loyal Subject,
The Custom of the Country, A Wife for a Month,* and *The Humorous Lieutenant.* But critical misconceptions about their subject matter have caused them to be underestimated.

The first of these, *The Loyal Subject* (1618),[1] deals in its main plot with the loyalty of the old general, Archas, in the face of the undeserved disgrace heaped upon him by the young Duke of Moscovia. The subplot concerning Archas's children equates his daughters' chastity to his own fidelity. The parallel between exemplary loyalty and exemplary chastity is emphasized in both language and structure.

As the play opens, the young duke's envious hostility toward Archas is encouraged by the evil counselor Boroskie. In response to this pressure, Archas retires; Boroskie is appointed general in his place. Immediately the Tartars approach the very gates of Moscow, and the cowardly Boroskie feigns illness. Moreover, the soldiers refuse to fight unless Archas leads them. The old general comes from retirement to lead the troops against the Tartars, for his loyalty, in spite of harsh treatment, has never wavered. Meanwhile, young Archas, disguised as Alinda, has been preferred to Princess Olympia's service. Immediately a relationship parallel to that of the main plot is set up by the emphasis placed upon Alinda's loyalty to the princess.

---

1. Ed. John Masefield, Variorum 3.

During the Tartar invasion all the ladies-in-waiting desert the princess except Alinda. The favors she receives from the princess and the duke arouse the envy of the maid, Petesca, who functions as evil counselor in the second plot, mirroring Boroskie in the main plot.

Archas wins a brilliant victory, but the duke, at Boroskie's instigation, receives him coldly as a test of his humility. With Archas in retirement, Boroskie suggests, the duke can buy the soldiers' loyalty. Archas accepts his disgrace with humility, but the soldiers scorn to accept pay without honor. Boroskie interprets this to the duke as an indication that Archas is keeping them in pay to alienate their loyalty, and he unjustly charges that Archas keeps for himself a mass of treasure that rightfully belongs to the throne. When the duke visits Archas to force this treasure from him, he demands another treasure as well—he commands the general to send to court his two beautiful daughters, Honora and Viola.

Archas's daughters display their virtue by their reluctance to obey this summons. Viola's "treasure," she asserts, is the virtue inculcated in her at home (III.ii.12–19). Honora, the more high-spirited of the two, protests sarcastically that they should have been sent to court younger, when their maidenheads would have been valued "at a higher rate" (III.ii.29). Archas, however, reminds them that virtue must be proved and that "Great things through greatest hazards are achieved still" (III.ii.61), and Honora responds with a militant spirit:

> I thank you, sir, you have made me half a soldier;
> I will to court most willingly, most fondly:
> . . . .
> . . . . Come, be valiant, sister:
> She that dares not stand the push o' th' court, dares nothing,
> And yet come off ungrazed.—Sir, like you, we both
> Affect great dangers now, and the world shall see
> All glory lies not in man's victory.
>
> (III.ii.66–67 ;78–82)

The language of treasure and of military life equates the trial of female chastity with the trial of male fealty. Similarly, elsewhere in the play masculine honor is described in terms usually reserved for descriptions of feminine honor. Archas's unblemished honesty is described as "a virgin" (I.v.68). Captain Putskie, using a term regularly associated with exemplary chastity, declares that the duke should have "sainted" the soldiers for defending their country (II. i.274).

Immediately after the scene of the summons to court, we see another young lady defending her honor from court wiles. Alinda is approached by the duke, but she turns aside his advances with witty answers. The jealous Petesca causes Olympia to misinterpret this scene. Assuming that Alinda has fallen from virtue, the princess dismisses her loyal servant, falsely accusing her of adultery. Thus the disguised young Archas is cast off by the duke's sister as old Archas has been cast aside by the duke. Since Olympia is an entirely virtuous woman misled by a malicious counselor, the analogy with the main plot prepares us to forgive both her and her brother when they see through their evil advisors.

Young Archas has one more task to perform while still in disguise as Alinda. He conducts a chastity test of his sisters, Honora and Viola, when they arrive at court. Alinda approaches the newcomers and pretends to instruct them in courtly wantonness. Honora denounces this "instruction" in court customs, thus pleasing and reassuring Alinda:

> Honora. A woman of your tenderness, a teacher,
> Teacher of these lewd arts! of your full beauty!
> A man made up in lust would loathe this in ye,
> The rankest lecher hate such impudence.
> (III.vi.89–92)

The assumption behind Honora's speech is the assumption implicit in the double standard and in the convention of pretended wantonness, namely, that men seek to corrupt innocent women but are then shocked by corrupt women. Honora, like Florimell in *The Maid in the Mill,* remembers this lesson and turns it to advantage when she confronts the duke.

The duke's attempt to corrupt Honora and Viola with a fulsome and flattering speech is met with a sarcastic denunciation from

Honora and shy pleadings from Viola. His asides direct audience response to the proper admiration and show an awakening moral sense: "What a sweet modesty dwells round about 'em/ And, like a nipping morn, pulls in their blossoms!" (IV.iii.39–40). His remarks continue as moral pointers: "A brave-spirited wench" (IV.iii.63); "She amazes me" (IV.iii.70); "Here are truly fair souls" (IV.iii.84). When Honora offers to die rather than let her shyer sister suffer wrong, he exclaims, "Another Archas!" Her reply, "His child, sir, and his spirit" (IV.iii.93), again emphasizes the connections between the various strands of the plot. When the duke, in spite of this display of resolute spirit, continues his addresses, Honora changes her tactics and affects wantonness. Calling him the handsomest man she ever looked on, she kisses and embraces him, urging her modest sister to do likewise. This pretended looseness brings about the desired revulsion in the would-be seducer:

> Fie Honora!
> Wanton Honora! is this the modesty,
> The noble chastity, your onset shew'd me;
> At first charge beaten back? away!
>   (IV.iii.113–16)

Honora thanks him and heaven, too; with her honor safe, she tells the duke, "Now you are thus,/ What shall become of me let Fortune cast for't" (IV.iii.123–24). The duke has passed a moral turning point in his life and vows:

> I'll be that fortune, if I live, Honora:
> Thou hast done a cure upon me counsel could not.
>   (IV.iii.125–26)

This turning from sexual vice is followed by a turning from political evil when the wicked Boroskie exceeds his warrant for the arrest of Archas and proceeds to torture the old general. The young duke, revolted by this open dishonesty and sadism, undergoes a complete reformation.

This reform, then, has two sources, the parallel forces of loyalty and chastity—masculine and feminine modes of honor. What is most interesting from the point of view of this study is that the duke's reformation begins first in admiration of the chastity of Honora rather than of the loyalty of Archas. (As the duke repents his base suspicions of Archas, so Olympia repents her suspicions of Alinda when she sees young Archas in his own person.) In contrast, Boroskie, who is unrepentant until faced with death, is portrayed as a confirmed lecher, indirectly in III.v, when the soldiers offer to sell him potatoes as an aphrodisiac, and directly in IV.ii, when the court bawd assumes that he sends for a courtesan. Chaste love, then, is the road to all virtues, and lechery is the invariable associate of all vices.[2]

That the portrayal of the beneficent effects of exemplary chastity is one of Fletcher's main purposes in *The Loyal Subject* appears beyond doubt when one compares the play with its sources, Bandello's story of Ariobarzanes, translated by Painter (Tome II, novella 4), and Heywood's adaptation of the story in *The Royal King and the Loyal Subject*. Both the original story and Heywood's play describe a contest of generosity between sovereign and subject.[3] Fletcher not only changes the basic nature of the conflict between the duke and Archas, he also adds all the scenes that contrast lechery and chastity. Indeed, the adaptation of source material resembles the adaptation of Chaucer's *Franklin's Tale* into *The Triumph of Honor*. In both cases a tale of courtesy has been transformed into a play of chastity.

Eugene Waith was the first critic, so far as I am aware, to perceive a thematic connection among the various threads of the plot. Waith, however, sees the main theme as a contrast between the honor of Archas and the Machiavellian materialism of Boroskie;[4] therefore he is unable to explain the purpose of Honora's denunciation of court life or of her pretended wantonness. He falls back on the old explanation that "Honora's immodest talk" is an example of Fletcher's "delight in the piquant flavor of situations where chaste men and women are made to 'talk bawdy'. . . ."[5] My interpretation

<hr/>

2. As suggested by the *Homily Against Adultery* (see above, chap. 3).

3. There is a comprehensive discussion of Fletcher's sources in Variorum 3:225-28. See also Waith, p. 207, for the play's indebtedness to the Senecan *controversiae*.

4. Waith, "A Tragicomedy of Humours," p. 309.

5. *Ibid.*, p. 309. Waith repeats his interpretation of the play in *The Pattern of Tragicomedy in Beaumont and Fletcher*.

of *The Loyal Subject* will supplement Waith's excellent discussion of the play by explaining these scenes.

There can be no reasonable doubt that *The Loyal Subject* glorifies chastity. This is also true of *The Custom of the Country* (1619–1623),[6] in spite of the fact that no Fletcherian play, with the exception, perhaps, of *The Captain,* has been so often and so violently denounced as lewd. *The Custom of the Country* is a chastity play, and one of the most lively and amusing in its genre. This Fletcher-Massinger collaboration has a complex and skillfully organized plot. In the main plot the hero and heroine experience a hair-raising series of trials of their chastity, and by their constancy they convert their persecutors. The hero's brother, Rutilio, undergoes an equally sensational series of adventures which convert him from libertinage, and provide occasion for the heroics and conversions of his foes. The notorious scene in which Rutilio is an inmate of a male stews has so shocked critics that they have missed the point of this second plot.

As Act I opens, the hero, Arnoldo, is distraught because, upon his impending marriage to Zenocia, Count Clodio plans to exercise his *droit de seigneur* and take her maidenhead. Arnoldo's irrepressible older brother Rutilio, a professed libertine, is mightily impressed with Clodio's prerogative:

> Rut.   How might a man achieve that place?—a rare custom!
>   An admirable rare custom!—And none excepted?
> Arn.   None, none.
> Rut.   The rarer still! how could I lay about me
>   In this rare office!—Are they born to it, or chosen?
>
> (I.i.33–37)

Although the heroic resolves of the romantic lovers occupy most of the act, Rutilio's high-spirited comments form a delightful counterpoint to relieve the tedium of declaimed virtue. Doubtless he is intended to function as a spokesman for the response of a large section of the audience to the initial premise of the action. Further, his

---

6. Ed. R. Warwick Bond, Variorum 1. The play is specifically praised as chaste by Richard Lovelace in the commendatory verses quoted above, chap. 1.

arguments on behalf of his brother against the *droit de seigneur* are amusing in themselves, based as they are on considerations entirely amoral. He is much taken with Zenocia (so much so that he wishes he could farm out the count's custom) and considers her too delicate a piece to be given to "a wild fellow," "a cannibal, that feeds on the heads of maids" (I.i.154–55). Besides, Clodio has had more than his fair share; he has had "more handsome bits/ Than a hundred honester men, and more deserving" (I.i.263–64). Rutilio's expression of admiration for the "stallion" (I.i.257), as he calls Clodio, goes beyond the bounds of decorum and is punished when in Act IV he comes himself to the "base stallion-trade" (IV.iv.133).

Although Rutilio is by far the most amusing and vivid character in the play, the structure of events clearly revolves around the trials of the romantic lovers. The opening scene alone is so constructed as to allow Zenocia to defend her chastity at length three times. She first rebuffs the arguments of her father, Charino, for a marriage to the tyrant. Charino is somewhat mysteriously under the domination of Clodio, apparently for the purpose of initiating this speech. Her next defense is made in response to a chastity test by Arnoldo. To try her resolve, he emphasizes their difficulties and continues:

> Say you did render up part of your honour,
> (For, whilst your will is clear, all cannot perish,)
> Say, for one night you entertain'd this monster;
> Should I esteem you worse, forced to this render?
> (I.i.209–12)

Her indignant reply in part foreshadows Arnoldo's own later trial:

> Should you lay by the least part of that love
> Y'ave sworn is mine, your youth and faith has given me,
> To entertain another, nay, a fairer,
> And,—make the case thus desp'rate,—she must die else;
> D' ye think I would give way, or count this honest?
> (I.i.230–34)

The scene ends with an encounter between Zenocia and the count, who makes the standard speech of seduction of a proud nobleman, but provokes only defiance.

The second scene opens with the deliberately sensational effect of the bride's own father decking a bedchamber with black hangings for the ravishment of his daughter. The lovers escape to sea, but face new hardships in Act II when their ship is captured by a Lisbon captain who takes Zenocia captive and presents her as a gift to Hippolyta. Arnoldo and Rutilio escape but are separated, and the two plot lines begin to move separately.

Act III is built around a great temptation for Arnoldo, corresponding to the danger to his wife in Act I. The wealthy Hippolyta, having by chance seen this handsome stranger, summons him to her house, where he is presented with a sumptuous banquet, delicate wines, and "lusty song." After this preparation, the lady herself appears to Arnoldo, and uses all blandishments to seduce him. He is shaken ("Hold fast, good honesty!/ I am a lost man else" (III. ii.113–14), but he recovers sufficiently to deliver a sermon to her, with a rhetorically ingenious use of the premises of double-standard morality:

> Be honest, and be virtuous, I'll admire ye;
> At least, be wise; and where ye lay these nets,
> Strow over 'em a little modesty;
> 'Twill well become your cause, and catch more fools.
> (III.ii.145–48)

When Hippolyta promptly takes this advice, reversing the convention of pretended wantonness, Arnoldo murmurs aside:

> How I stagger!
> She is wise as fair; but 'tis a wicked wisdom;
> I'll choke before I yield.
> (III.ii.170–72)

So weakened is he, that he fears she will enjoy him in spite of himself, a weakness which she perceives and presses: "Upon my conscience, I must ravish thee;/ I shall be famous for the first example" (III.ii.183–84). After a prolonged seduction scene, Arnoldo at last overcomes temptation: "My strength! away, base woman, I abhor thee!" (III.ii.186). Hippolyta is left discontented because she has not the charms of Circe and because Arnoldo is "more than Ulysses" (III.iv.29). She later says of him:

> If chastity
> In a young man, and tempted to the height too,
> Did e'er deserve reward or admiration,
> He justly may claim both.
>
> (III.v.53–56)

The lovers face their climactic trial together in Act IV. Arnoldo has caught a glimpse of Hippolyta's new waiting-woman and fears for Zenocia's good behavior in such a house. Similarly, Zenocia suspects that he has succumbed to the lure of her lady and forgotten her. This situation of mutual suspicion is contrived to allow each of the lovers to make a set speech in defense of his chastity. Hippolyta overhears their reunion; her wrath and offended vanity produce the climax of the play, an ingenious inversion of the central situation of *Measure for Measure*.[7] Hippolyta threatens to kill Zenocia unless Arnoldo becomes her lover. Zenocia, unlike Claudio in *Measure*, refuses to accept this sacrifice, which Arnoldo, unlike Isabella, is willing to make. Zenocia emphasizes that this is the greatest trial they have so far encountered:

> Do not do this;
> To save me, do not lose yourself, I charge you;
> I charge you by your love, that love you bear me,
> That love, that constant love you have twined to me,
> By all your promises;—take heed you keep 'em;
> Now is your constant trial.
>
> (IV.iii.163–68)

Arnoldo rises to his "constant trial" (i.e., constancy's trial) by scorning Hippolyta's threats, but her revenge is frustrated when the lovers are rescued by Clodio, who has arrived in Lisbon after a miraculous change of heart.

The hero and heroine face one more trial in Act V when Zenocia is stricken with a mysterious and fatal illness caused by a magic spell

---

7. Leech, p. 58.

commissioned by the still-vengeful Hippolyta. So great, however, is the sympathy between man and wife that Arnoldo is dying also. This unforeseen development so moves Hippolyta that she orders the charm to be removed, and the lovers are allowed to live not only happily but wealthily ever after: Hippolyta, in recompense for their pains at her hands, confers a dowry of a hundred thousand crowns upon her rival. Clodio, likewise humbled in the face of such extraordinary goodness, ends the barbarous custom of the country, since it was the original source of all their misfortunes. Arnoldo draws the moral:

> And the unspotted progress of our loves
> Ends not alone in safety, but reward;
> To instruct others, by our fair example,
> That, though good purposes are long withstood,
> The hand of Heaven still guides such as are good.
>   (V.v.232–36)

Clodio predicts that to their memory "chaste wives and virgins/ Shall ever pay their vows" (V.iv.111–12), concluding a series of images that indicate that Arnoldo and Zenocia are to be viewed as saints of love and martyrs to chastity. In the opening scene, for example, Charino tells his daughter that the beauty of her soul and her "saint-like modesty" (I.i.73) have so wrought upon Clodio's "wild mind" (I.i.74) that the count wishes to be her husband. Her good influence as his wife will no doubt banish the "base and barbarous" (I.i.83) custom of the country and as a result

> All virgins too shall bless your name, shall saint it,
> And, like so many pilgrims, go to your shrine,
> When time has turn'd your beauty into ashes,
> Fill'd with your pious memory.
>   (I.i.88–91)

Zenocia's steadfast loyalty to her betrothed prompts Arnoldo to exclaim: "What willing martyrdom to crown me constant,/ May merit such a goodness, such a sweetness?" (I.i.131–32). Later, when Zenocia is confronted with Hippolyta's threats, she "speaks nobly" to that "glorious Devil":

> If thou hadst studied all the courtesies
> Humanity and noble blood are link'd to,
> Thou couldst not have propounded such a benefit,
> Nor heap'd upon me such unlook'd-for honour,
> As dying for his sake, to be his martyr. . . .
> (IV.iii.152–56)

Hippolyta's wry reply continues the metaphor: "You shall not want that favour:/ Let your bones work miracles" (IV.iii.157–58). When in Act V it seems that Zenocia's only reward is to be a painful death, the reformed Clodio is outraged:

> Her life hath been so innocent, all her actions
> So free from the suspicion of crime,
> As rather she deserves a saint's place here,
> Than to endure what now her sweetness suffers.
> (V.ii.44–47)

These conventional moral pointers are used to indicate the proper audience response at certain climactic moments.

Rutilio, certainly no saint, has meanwhile been pursuing an independent set of adventures. Taunted into a duel by Duarte, a young man with a pride so excessive as to make him "like Plautus' braggart" (II.i.130), Rutilio leaves his assailant for dead and flees for his life. By chance he takes refuge with Duarte's mother, Guiomar, who swears by the laws of hospitality to protect him. She keeps her vow even when she finds that her visitor is the murderer of her only son. Rutilio next innocently runs afoul of the law and is rescued by the mistress of a male stews; she is desperate for lusty new talent, as all her regulars are exhausted. She is losing her "custom with young ladies/ And high-fed city-dames" (III.iii.24–25). Rutilio is delighted with this means of redemption; here at last is a profession exactly suited to his talents: "I am excellent at it;/ You cannot pick out such another living" (III.iii.74–75). "Now I am in my kingdom," is his gleeful cry (III.iii.87).

Rutilio makes good his boast, bringing in gold for his employer faster than she has leisure to receive it. He finds, however, to his surprise and sorrow, that the ladies of Lisbon are insatiable. Young ladies arrive by the coachful, and "old dead-palsied" ones are carried in on litters (IV.iv.27). The scene of Rutilio's discomfiture is not merely bawdy humor. It is a very clearly pointed satire on the age-old theme of the insatiable lust of women. Moreover, it has its place in the thematic structure of the play. Rutilio, like Clodio and Hippolyta, must be converted from lust and pride. His conversion falls into two parts. Here he is roundly paid for his misplaced admiration of Clodio in the opening act. Shrunken in the hams and broken-winded, he wonders, "Is this a life?/ Is this the recreation I have aim'd at?" (IV.iv.56–57). His one desire now is an honest marriage. As Rutilio laments his plight, there enter "three Men in night-caps, very faintly" (IV.iv.s.d.). These are his predecessors in the stews, who have come to see how he is bearing up:

> Second Man. We have enough on't: rest you merry, sir!
> We came but to congratulate your fortune;
> You have abundance.
> Third Man. Bear your fortune soberly;
> And so we leave you to the next fair lady.
> (IV.iv.92–95)

Rutilio is horrified at their appearance; their syphilitic noses look as if they will not endure sneezing. They are a living example of the rewards of lechery.

Rutilio is at last rescued by Duarte, who has miraculously recovered and wishes to thank the man who cured his pride. He comes in disguise, however, for he is keeping his recovery a secret in order to test his mother's chastity and to discover whether her mourning for him is genuine or hypocritical; she is, after all, a woman. Unconvincing as this motivation may be on a realistic level, it is part of the necessary thrust of the plot toward Rutilio's second conversion. He has been cured of lust, but his pride must now be humbled. Duarte and his mother are to be the agents of this change. Rutilio, vain of his good looks, imagines that Guiomar must have saved his life out of love, and solicits marriage with this rich widow. Guiomar dissembles her feelings in order to revenge herself upon her son's murderer. When Rutilio arrives for the marriage, confident of conquest, he is seized by guards. Rutilio, now rising to the occasion, throws off his trivial behavior and offers himself as a willing sacrifice to Guiomar's grief. Marriage can substitute for vengeance, however, when the now-satisfied Duarte reveals that he is still living. Rutilio has been thoroughly chastened, and with his natural courage and nobility fully revealed, he can take his place in the elevated world of the other characters.

The entire play can now be seen as a series of conversions and tests enclosed within the large frame of the ordeals of Arnoldo and Zenocia. Clodio, Hippolyta, and Rutilio are each converted from lust; Duarte, Clodio, and Rutilio are converted from pride. The trials of Zenocia are mirrored by the test of Guiomar, and both ladies emerge triumphant. All the weaknesses of motivation are deliberately used to subordinate character to the functioning of the various tests and the set defenses of chastity.

Like *The Custom of the Country, A Wife for a Month* (1624)[8] has been considered one of Fletcher's lewdest plays. Nonetheless, it is also a chastity play; like *Thierry and Theodoret,* it uses the theme of impotence to build elaborately to a test of chastity within marriage. The plot is one of Fletcher's most ingenious. Frederick, usurping King of Naples, attempts to seduce the chaste Evanthe with the aid of her evil brother, Sorano. Rebuffed, the king vows revenge. Discovering a love poem to Evanthe from Valerio, Frederick sentences the lovers to fulfill Valerio's poetic hyperbole:

> To be your own but one poor Month, I'd give
> My Youth, my Fortune, and then leave to live.
> (I.i;11)

Valerio is to marry Evanthe and to be executed at the end of one month. Sorano suggests to the king a further refinement of torture: Valerio is forbidden to consummate his marriage, the penalty for disobedience to be Evanthe's immediate death. The same penalty is to be exacted if Valerio reveals his dilemma to anyone. The gloatings of the villains over their plans clearly point toward a test of Evan-

---

8. Glover and Waller, vol. 5.

the's chastity. Sorano is sure that Evanthe "will run mad to miss"
her expected joys (III.i;30), for "women once deluded are next
Devils" (III.i;31). Audience anticipations of Evanthe's behavior
are further heightened by the characterization of the heroine as hot-
tempered.

The center of the action occurs in Act III when Valerio pretends
impotence to his bride in order to save her life. It is this wedding-
night encounter and the preceding sequence of actions that are considered so offensive. The bridegroom is characterized as "sensual,"
and the bride anticipates the joys of consummation with "unmaiden-
ly" eagerness. Actually, characterization here is a function of the
plot, building suspense as to how the lovers will behave in their
dilemma. Evanthe's anticipation will make her disappointment all
the more acute.[9] For example, after the wedding ceremony, Valerio
must stand by and overhear Evanthe express her eagerness, which
he knows he must disappoint. She tells the queen:

> I am so taken up in all my thoughts,
> So possest Madam with the lawfull sweets
> I shall this night partake of with my Lord,
> So far transported (pardon my immodesty).
>   (III.i;34)

Valerio's anguish is even more acute when the couple are left alone.
Puzzled by his seeming coldness toward her, Evanthe is made almost
to force him to bed, to suggest medical remedies, and to suggest that
perhaps he has "a better Mistris" (III.i;37).

For post-Freudians and other Romantics, Valerio's pretense of
impotence is the key element in this scene. But this modern reading
twists the emphasis askew. Because of their religious and social pre-
occupations with female chastity, the primary emotional peak of this
scene for Jacobeans surely must have been, not Valerio's declaration
of impotence, but Evanthe's resolution to live with her husband in
continence:

> Now you shall know 'tis not the pleasure Sir,

---

9. Appleton, pp. 68-69, discusses the effectiveness of this characterization.

(For I am compell'd to love you spiritually)
That women aim at, I affect ye for,
'Tis for your worth. . . .

(III.i;38)

As in *Thierry and Theodoret,* this is the supreme trial for the heroine.
The preceding emotional sequence and the emphasis upon the eagerness and anticipation of the lovers portray the strong natural impulses
that are overcome by a brave will to chastity. Evanthe's courageous
response to this trial is to be measured by the strength of her natural
physical desires, not her physical desires by some Victorian standard
of "maidenly" behavior and expression. She is to be regarded in the
light in which she appears to the other characters. Valerio wonders
at her chastity:

> You appear the vision of a Heaven unto me,
> Stuck all with stars of honour shining clearly,
> And all the motions of your mind Celestial. . . .

(IV.i;57)

She is the "honour'd sweet Maid," "the Lady that the wonder goes
on" (V.i;72).

The wedding-night encounter of Act III is framed by four other
trials, which further prove the chastity of Valerio and Evanthe.
Evanthe's right to the epithet "the chaste" is established immediately
in the opening scene when she is lured to the king's private lodgings.
There Frederick promises "wealth, ease, and honours" (I.i;5) to
her and to her friends if she will become his mistress. She scorns the
ability of his power and riches to make "wantonness confirm'd/ By
Act of Parliament an honesty" (I.i;6). Evanthe defends her chastity
with the "Tongue of an Angel, and the truth of Heaven" (I.i;7)
and so brings down upon herself the wrath and revenge of the king.

After the ill-fated wedding night, Valerio and Evanthe are both
repeatedly tempted, which emphasizes their heroic endurance of their
forced continence. First, Frederick tempts Valerio, offering to remit
his sentence of death and bestow upon him riches and favor if
Valerio will yield up his wife to him. Assuming Valerio's acquiescence,

the king expatiates on the methods by which he could pimp for his wife. Valerio's pretended submission makes his denunciation of the king all the more electrifying for the audience. His heroism is emphasized by the reminder that tomorrow is the last day of the allotted month. Next, we see Evanthe beseiged by the bawd Cassandra. Her argument plays on the *Measure for Measure* dilemma: "Two precious lives may be redeem'd with nothing,/ Little or nothing; say an hours or days sport" (IV.i;47). Cassandra compares seduction by threats to "a kind of Rape": "That keeps you clear, for where your will's compell'd/ Though you yield up your Body you are safe still" (IV.i;47). The bawd, with sophistical wit, appeals to the great archetype of chastity as a precedent for lust:

> Had Lucrece e'r been thought of but for Tarquin?
> She was before a simple unknown Woman,
> When she was ravish'd, she was a reverend Saint. . . .
> (IV.i;48)

Cassandra, however, presents no temptation to Evanthe, who dismisses her with a stinging tirade, the conventional reprehension of the bawd by the heroine.

Just at this moment Frederick enters, and his arguments cause Evanthe her most serious doubts in the play. He asserts that Valerio has pretended impotence to save his own skin; Frederick threatened him with death "in policy to try his spirit" (IV.i;51). The hot-tempered Evanthe is furious at such cowardice. Immediately, however, her faith in Valerio reasserts itself: "Sure there is some trick in't: Valerio ne'r was Coward" (IV.i;51). This doubt of Frederick is confirmed when the king, elated at her anger, overreaches himself by further asserting that Valerio set Cassandra on his own wife in order to please the king; indeed, he would have been a bawd himself. Evanthe can now "smell the malice" of this too palpable lie: "Shall my anger make me whore, and not my pleasure?" (IV.i;52). Her denunciation of the king shows her meeting the trial of her loyalty as she had earlier met the trial of her continence; her language equates the two:

Take thou heed, thou tame Devil,
Thou all Pandora's Box in a Kings figure,
Thou hast almost whor'd my weak belief already,
And like an Engineer blown up mine honour. . . .

                                    (IV.i;52)

She has successfully passed the final trial of her chastity.

Evanthe now knows that Valerio's impotence was only a pretence, but when she learns the true reason, that it was to save her life, she is greatly insulted at his thinking she would have feared the penalty:

And was not I as worthy to dye nobly?
To make a story for the time that follows,
As he that married me?

                                    (IV.i;56)

The lovers' difficulties are at last brought to an end in Act V when Alphonso, rightful king of Naples, takes the throne from his wicked brother. As in *The Custom of the Country,* a pair of lovers married early in the play are allowed to consummate their marriage only after they have been tried at the hands of devilish villains.

These villains are explicitly and repeatedly called devils, in keeping with the morality-play grouping of characters into the very good and the very bad. Frederick is "a Devil in a Kings shape,/ Such a malignant Fiend" (IV.i;47). When Sorano forbids Valerio to consummate his marriage, Valerio calls him a "Devil" and declares: "This tyranny could never be invented/ But in the school of Hell, Earth is too innocent" (III.i;29). Later he tells the king that his "unheard of malice,/ No heart that is not hired from Hell dare think of" (IV.i;43). At the same time, however, "No man can ever come to aim at Heaven,/ But by the knowledge of a Hell" (II.i;23). That is, Evanthe and Valerio are tried and proved in an earthly purgatory and thus are to be seen, like all of Fletcher's heroes and heroines of chastity, as martyrs and saints. "Sanctity" itself would "dote on" Evanthe (I.i;14). She is a "Paradise" (I.i;15). Valerio is certain that "if I dye for her,/ I am thy Martyr, Love, and time shall honour me" (I.i;13).

In *A Wife for a Month,* as in other plays, Fletcher avoids a too-rigorous grouping of characters into good and evil by including elements of burlesque. These elements anticipate and forestall criticism by incorporating it into the play itself. Fletcher here uses the knavish fool, Tony, as a wry commentator on the premises of the action. According to Tony, if Valerio insists upon dying for love, he can help him to a diseased wench who "should have kill'd him in three weeks, and sav'd the sentence" (II.i;16). There are whores in the suburbs who could do the job in two hours, and "There be also of the race of the old Cockatrices,/ That would dispatch him with once looking on him" (I.i;16). While he is acting as doorman for the bridal masque, Tony comments on the appeal of the action to the salaciously minded: "And with what joy the women run by heaps/ To see this Marriage! they tickle to think of it" (II.i;22). This scene repeats the main plot in miniature. Tony admits three young city wives as spectators, but refuses to admit their husbands. When the citizens seek admittance to protect their wives from the lascivious courtiers, the lords are outraged: "Bold Rascals, offer to disturb your wives?" (II.i;25).

Though Fletcher can burlesque himself, he is nonetheless serious about the basic theme of his play. This very bridal masque is probably a cue to his conception of the play. The masque is a dramatization of the masque of Cupid witnessed by Britomart in Book III of *The Faerie Queene*.[10] In Spenser, this masque precedes the appearance of Amoret, the virgin-wife stolen from her husband on her wedding night and kept in torment by the lustful villain Busirane because she will not give in to his evil demands. So Fletcher's masque heralds the torments of the virgin-wife Evanthe at the hands of the lustful Frederick, who, in a manner of speaking, steals her from her husband on her wedding night.

The fourth of the major plays, *The Humorous Lieutenant* (1619?),[11] is the lightest in tone and the most delightful of Fletcher's chastity dramas. Unfortunately, because of the play's concern with chastity and its satire of court procuring, it has not received unmixed

---

10. Leigh Hunt, p. 258.
11. Ed. R. Warwick Bond, Variorum 2.

praise, nor has it, to my knowledge, been anthologized. This play deserves to be better known; the conventional testing of the heroine is here handled with a naturalness and good humor not found elsewhere in Fletcher. In this play he avoids an oppressive atmosphere of excessive concern for chastity, largely through the characterization of the heroine, Celia, who defends her chastity with high spirits and wit. A second factor in the sunny quality of the play is that a good half of the action is taken up with the chivalric military exploits of the hero, Prince Demetrius. Thirdly, there is an excellent control of tone, achieved partly by switching from the main plot, whenever any ominous development threatens, to the laughable adventures of the title character. The large pattern of the play shows Prince Demetrius proving his valor on the battlefield while Celia proves her chastity in the boudoir. The humorous lieutenant, fundamentally a coward, proves himself on the battlefield precisely because he has proved himself in the boudoir—the symptoms of his venereal disease are so painful that battle comes as a positive relief.

As the play opens, King Antigonus graciously gives his son, Demetrius, sole command of his army so that the young prince may have a chance to prove his valor. Unfortunately, Antigonus sees his son taking a loving farewell of a poorly dressed but beautiful maid. This is Celia, taken captive as a prisoner of war and now living in retirement under the protection of the prince, who plans to marry her. Demetrius intends to conceal Celia, however, until his father dies, for Antigonus, though in every other way a virtuous king, is an old man with young desires who makes his court a paradise for bawds and panders. Antigonus, fearful that his son is throwing himself away on a fortune-hunter, decides during Demetrius's absence to test Celia's character and chastity:

> I would have her tried to the test: I know
> She must be some crack'd coin, not fit his traffic;
> Which when we have found, the shame will make him leave her. . . .
> (III.i.16–18)

To test Celia, Antigonus calls upon his bawds and panders.

As in *Valentinian,* the three male panders are rather inept and

turn for aid to the shrewder and more experienced she-bawds.
Fletcher here produces one of the most brilliant comic scenes in his
career. The bawd Leucippe has made herself indispensable to court
life by turning procuring into big business. She appears in her office
as the executive harrassed by the demands of her job:

> What would you have? I cannot furnish you faster than I am
> able. . . . At least a dozen posts are gone this morning for
> several parts of the kingdom; I can do no more but pay 'em and
> instruct 'em.
>
> (II.iii.86–90)

Paper work is as necessary and as tedious in this business as in any
other; Leucippe has to resort to a filing system:

> Cloe, Cloe, Cloe—here I have her—*Cloe,*
> *The daughter of a country gentleman;*
> *Her age upon fifteen:* now her complexion—
> *A lovely brown*—here 'tis—*eyes black and rolling;*
> *The body neatly built; she strikes a lute well,*
> *Sings most enticingly:* these helps consider'd,
> Her maidenhead will amount to some three hundred,
> Or three hundred and fifty crowns; 'twill bear it handsomely.
>
> (II.iii.14–21)

It is the straight-faced quality of the scene which makes the satire
of court looseness so telling. Leucippe is merely the hard-pressed
victim of circumstances, an efficient and intelligent woman trying to
make her way in the world by offering the court the services it
requires.

With the aid of Leucippe, Celia is lured to court under the impression that Demetrius has returned from the wars and awaits her
there. This ruse, and the entire sequence of court temptations, parallel
the court temptations in *Valentinian*. According to the usual pattern,
Celia's chaperone is cut off in the anteroom (III.iv.30ff.), and she
herself is met by the court bawds and panders. Unlike Lucina, however, Celia faces her predicament not with timorous fears but with a
high-spirited determination to outwit her would-be corrupters. Antigonus, on a balcony watching her poised arrival, is himself caught

by the sight of her beauty and spirit. At this point, the king's intention to test Celia becomes a desire actually to seduce her. He is further inflamed by the reports of her modesty: "She studies to undo the court, to plant here/ The enemy to our age, Chastity" (IV.i.13–14). The king disguises himself in order to see her, and offers her rich jewels. Celia recognizes the king through his disguise and, to embarrass him, affects to believe that he is a merchant attempting to sell her the jewels. When he insists that the jewels are a gift to her beauty, Celia, instead of spurning them in outrage, takes them up with wit:

> Celia. I'll never look a horse i' the mouth that's given:
> I thank you, sir: I'll send one to reward ye.
> Antigonus. Do you never ask who sent 'em?
> Celia. Never I;
> Nor never care. If it be an honest end,
> The end's the full reward, and thanks but slubber it:
> If it be ill, I will not urge the acquaintance.
> (IV.i.72–77)

The king is nonplussed. He is even further discomfited when she pretends to take him for a decayed soldier and lectures him on the baseness of earning his living as a pimp. Celia is highly amused at the whole proceeding and reflects: "If I stay longer,/ I shall number as many lovers as Lais did" (IV.i.33–34).

When Demetrius returns from the wars and discovers that Celia has gone to court, Antigonus resorts to the usual weapon of the rebuffed seducer and slanders Celia, declaring that she has been put to death as a confessed witch. Antigonus now turns to witchcraft of his own; he commands a magician to prepare for Celia a love philtre that will make the drinker dote upon the king. By mistake, the potion is drunk by the lieutenant, whose sudden and extravagant passion for the king amuses both court and city. Antigonus, unaware that the potion has gone astray, confronts Celia again.

To defend herself, she uses Hamlet's technique for dealing with foolish old men. She enters reading a book and quotes to the "royal devil":

I am reading, sir, of a short treatise here,
That's call'd *The Vanity of Lust:* has your grace seen it?
He says here that an old man's loose desire
Is like the glow-worm's light the apes so wonder'd at,
Which, when they gather'd sticks and laid upon't,
And blew and blew, turn'd tail, and went out presently. . . .
                                             (IV.v.28–33)

She goes on with the maiden's conventional arguments to a seducer of high degree. She points out that the conquest of a poor maid is a weak triumph for a powerful king (IV.v.46ff.) and urges him, as a great man, to set a good example: "Be, as your office is, a god-like justice" (IV.v.54). The king's last resort is a threat: "Say I should force ye?/ I have it in my will" (IV.v.59–60). Celia assures him that she "dare die" first and reminds him of heavenly wrath: "Do you know who dwells above, sir,/ And what they have prepared for men turn'd devils?" (IV.v.68–69). The king is now completely converted by her goodness, which he perceives is greater than his power:

> Virtue commands the stars.—Rise, more than virtue!
> Your present comfort shall be now my business.
>   (IV.v.91–92)

During the remainder of the play Antigonus professes his shame for having "wrong'd her innocence" (IV.vii.2) and works to reconcile Celia and Demetrius.

The prince is now suffering the anguish of jealousy and upbraids Celia as a "subtle Circe" (IV.viii.98) and a "serpent" (IV.vii.110). Celia's defense of her chastity in the face of Demetrius's jealousy is one of the most natural in the canon, for she is indignant and hurt as well as self-righteous. Fletcher here avoids the "chaste fury" that so often mars the representation of his virtuous heroines. Antigonus removes Demetrius's suspicions by confessing his trial of Celia, and complete harmony is restored when Celia is revealed as a princess. Celia, who undergoes all possible trials of her chastity, is, like all Fletcher's chaste heroines, praised as a saintly exemplum:

Heaven's holy light's not purer.
The constancy and goodness of all women,
That ever lived to win the names of worthy,
This noble maid has doubled in her honour:
All promises of wealth, all art to win her,
And by all tongues employ'd, wrought as much on her
As one may do upon the sun at noon-day
By lighting candles up. Her shape is heavenly,
And to that heavenly shape her thoughts are angels.
                                        (IV.viii.159–67)

Conclusion

This survey of the Fletcherian chastity plays should explain why the authors of the Folio commendatory verses praised Fletcher for his morality. Surely it is no longer necessary to suppose that Caroline Englishmen were hardened voluptuaries because they praised Fletcher in these terms:

> Thou, like thy Writings, Innocent and Cleane,
> Ne're practis'd a new Vice, to make one Sceane,
> None of thy Inke had gall, and Ladies can
> Securely heare thee sport without a Fanne.[1]

In play after play Fletcher created exemplary chaste heroines intended to surpass the ancient archetypes of female virtue. The plays show a preoccupation with marriage and constancy, the majority of these chaste heroines being wives (Dorigen, the Lady of Orleans, Lucina, Ordella, Oriana in *The Knight of Malta,* Zenocia, Juliana, Calista, and Evanthe) or troth-plight wives (Amoret, Celia, Aspatia, Merione).

To glorify these heroines, Fletcher compares them explicitly and implicitly to classical archetypes. The plot of *The Double Marriage* implies that Juliana is of greater fortitude than the Roman Portia, and the plot of *Thierry and Theodoret* implies that Ordella is a modern Alcestis. "The fortitude of all their sex, is Fable/ Compar'd to" Juliana, and Ordella is one in whom is found all that "Athens,

---

1. Glover and Waller, 1:xlviii.

Rome, or warlike Sparta,/ Have registered for good in their best Women." The Lady of Orleans defies her husband to compare her behavior with Penelope's. Dorigen, because of the type names in *The Triumph of Honor,* is implicitly found superior to the masculine virtues of ancient Athens and Rome. Celia doubles the "constancy and goodness of all women,/ That ever lived to win the names of worthy."

The emotion that such extraordinary heroines are intended to evoke in the audience is wonder. Honora "amazes" the Duke of Moscovia by her chaste behavior, Oriana is a "miracle," Evanthe is "the Lady that the wonder goes on," and Juliana is "the wonder of her Sex." Chaste heroes are equally to be wondered at. Arnoldo deserves "admiration" for refusing Hippolyta's illicit overtures; Miranda is to be "admir'd."

These exemplary characters are specifically designated as saints. Like all saints, their lives will be venerated by posterity, since they beget "A great example to mens continence." These saintly creatures are persecuted by or contrasted with characters who are "devils." This opposition of saintly and devilish characters frequently produces a morality-play structure, as we have seen in *The Knight of Malta* and *The Triumph of Death.* This is noticeable also in *The Faithful Shepherdess, Thierry and Theodoret,* and *A Wife for a Month.*

Fletcher's audience believed chastity to be a gift of grace, but one that must be proven in action. True chastity, like "true nobility" or "true wit," other qualities similarly debated during the Renaissance, must be tested before it may be said to exist. Fletcher's heroines, like Painter's "Lady Falselie Accused," rejoice in the "resistaunce of the assaultes of love," for "the croune is not due but to her that shall lawfully combate to the ende" (Painter, I.215–16).

All of the chastity plays are built around certain conventions designed to prove virtue and to elicit a set speech in defense or praise of chastity. This type of speech is the distinguishing characteristic of a chastity play. Among the conventional situations that elicit such speeches are the chastity test (*The Woman Hater, The Honest Man's Fortune, The Custom of the Country, The Humorous Lieutenant, Women Pleased, The Knight of Malta, The Faithful Shep-*

herdess, The Loyal Subject), the pretense of wantonness (*The Maid in the Mill, The Faithful Shepherdess, The Loyal Subject, The Triumph of Honor*), and the summons to court (*The Triumph of Death, The Loyal Subject, The Humorous Lieutenant, The Woman Hater, Valentinian*). Situations are contrived to create mutual suspicion between lovers (e.g., Celia and Demetrius, Zenocia and Arnoldo) so as to allow each to declare his or her innocence. Well-meaning characters attempting to convert whores from their wicked lives make speeches dissuading them from lechery (*The Captain, The Maid's Tragedy, Thierry and Theodoret*). The archetypal situations of rape, seduction, and slander (Lucrece, Penelope, and Susanna) call for speeches in defense of chastity from the heroines. Oriana's detention in a brothel is part of Gondarino's schemes to slander her honesty and thus elicits from her an appropriate statement of principle. To these standard conventions, Fletcher adds impotence, real or pretended (*Thierry and Theodoret, A Wife for a Month*), mismarriage (*The Maid's Tragedy*), and divorce (*The Double Marriage*). All of these devices are used for the same purpose as the other conventional situations, namely, to elicit a set speech about chastity.

Fletcher, like Greene and Spenser before him, tries to combine a number of these trying situations in the experience of each heroine, on the principle that if Lucrece was immortalized by her rape and suicide, if Susanna was famous for defying slander, and if Penelope earned glory for resisting seduction attempts, then a heroine who successfully passed the trials of rape, slander, seduction, and whatever embellishments the author could provide besides, was proportionately more exemplary than any one of the great archetypes taken individually. Fletcher displayed a sometimes incredible ingenuity in piling trial upon trial for his heroines. Though he often had difficulties constructing a whole plot, his contrivance of individual situations is brilliant.

The conventional situations that Fletcher uses have two very important things in common. First, they comprise the so-called prurient episodes criticized in the Beaumont and Fletcher canon, and second, none of them is psychologically "true to life." All these situations subordinate the portrayal of character to the requirements of fable and moral. The crucial point is that these scenes have been judged prurient precisely because they are not concerned with psychologically accurate characterization. The Romantic objections to these scenes go hand in hand with the Romantic emphasis on character as the most important element in drama. It is easy to imagine the consternation of a Romantic critic looking for subtle and delicate portrayal of feminine character and finding instead the following: young ladies reared in country seclusion denouncing the lewdness of court life in explicit detail, faithful and sheltered wives denouncing the lusts of tyrants and the haunts of bawds, and innocent virgins pretending to be practised whores in order to avoid ravishment. Certainly it is not "realistic" for these heroines to have such a detailed knowledge of evil. The Romantics, assuming that drama's primary purpose was to portray character, logically deduced that these chaste heroines were being delineated as "strumpets in their imaginations and wishes." This conclusion of Coleridge's has been reinforced by Freudian analyses of personality. The whole *raison d'être* of such scenes, however, is not the portrayal of character, but rather the speeches denouncing lust and defending the principle of chastity. This being so, the chaste heroines are given whatever knowledge is necessary to deliver such speeches. This is a very simple stylization of character designed to fit the requirements of fable and moral. Pre-Romantics were not particularly troubled by these scenes because of their recognition of the importance of fable in drama.

It is true, however, to meet another Romantic criticism, that fable and situation are more extreme in Fletcher and his contemporaries than in Shakespeare and his other predecessors. This was almost inevitable after "the Shakespearian moment," because the conventional themes and situations of Elizabethan drama had been worked and reworked. (Even Shakespeare, in his last plays, offers more extreme fables than in his earlier works.) To take but one example, the girl-page, disguised in order to win her true love, had appeared so often that it is not surprising to find Beaumont and Fletcher reintroducing this figure in Euphrasia-Bellario, the girl disguised as a page because of a platonic attachment, and Veramour, the supposed girl disguised as a page but, comically enough, really only a faithful boy after all. Fletcher showed a remarkable ingenuity in reworking the stock Elizabethan themes and conventions. This is doubtless one of the reasons why his audiences hailed him as the "Monarch of Wit" and "King of Poets."[2] The Folio commendatory verses specifically praise Fletcher for devising "fresh matters" which "soare above old Theames."[3]

Ingenious variants of shopworn themes were devised not only to make plays more entertaining and up-to-date, and to revitalize old situations by the witty infusion of new ideas, but also, and equally importantly, to reinforce the traditional moral lessons. The plays are designed not only to entertain by these novel situations but to instruct by moving the audience to admire exemplary figures faced with extreme moral dilemmas. A case in point is Fletcher's reworking of an earlier play that shows a painful moral dilemma, *Measure for Measure* (a play that some modern audiences consider too extreme), into the even more extreme *Queen of Corinth, The Custom of the Country,* and *A Wife for a Month.* This procedure is designed to test moral attitudes and standards *in extremis* and thus has the effect of testing the moral preconceptions of the audience (see the discussions of *Valentinian, The Lovers' Progress,* and *The Knight of Malta*). Doubtless these extreme situations are intended to provoke discussion and speculation in the audience.

The type of discussion Fletcher anticipated may perhaps be indicated by *Four Plays in One.* It will be remembered that in *The Triumph of Honor* the chaste Dorigen, in order to punish Sophocles for his ignoble suspicions of her, pretends that she has already lost her honor to Martius. Dorigen's behavior in this episode is the subject of discussion in the stage audience of the frame play, King Emmanuel and Queen Isabella:

> Emmanuel. Here was a woman, Isabel.
> Isabella.   I, my Lord,
>   But that she told a lye to vex her husband;

---

2. *Ibid.,* 1:xlv.
3. *Ibid.,* 1:xxxvii.

Therein she fail'd.

Emmanuel. She serv'd him well enough;
He that was so much man, yet would be cast
To jealousie for her integrity.
This teacheth us, the passion of love
Can fight with Soldiers, and with Scholars too.

. . . .

What hurt's now in a Play, against which
          some rail
So vehemently? thou and I, my love,
Make excellent use methinks: I learn to be
A lawful lover void of jealousie,
And thou a constant wife.[4]

This passage is unusual only in its length; everywhere in the chastity plays one finds moral pointers inserted to direct audience response to an evaluation of conduct that remains exemplary under extreme duress.

If this study is accurate in its analysis of Fletcher's aims and techniques, and in the inferences drawn about the probable responses of sophisticated Jacobean audiences, it might be appropriate to speak, not of the "prurient" Fletcher, but of the "fabulous" Fletcher, the master contriver of ingenious and entertaining situations designed to provoke the audience to moral speculations about virtue *in extremis*.

---

4. *Ibid.*, 10:312.

Appendix A

CHRONOLOGY OF THE FLETCHERIAN CHASTITY PLAYS

Date	Title	Author	Limits	Type	Auspices	Discussion in Text
1606	*The Woman Hater*	Beaumont Fletcher	1606	Comedy	Paul's	42–44
1608	*The Faithful Shepherdess*	Fletcher	1608–1609	Pastoral	Queen's Revels (?)	134–50
1608	*Cupid's Revenge*	Beaumont Fletcher	c. 1607–1612	Tragedy	Queen's Revels	191–95
1609	*Philaster*	Beaumont Fletcher	1608–1610	Tragicomedy	King's	181
1609	*The Coxcomb*	Beaumont Fletcher	1608–1610	Comedy	Queen's Revels	195–98
1610	*The Maid's Tragedy*	Beaumont Fletcher	c. 1608–1610	Tragedy	King's	176–78
1611	*A King and No King*	Beaumont Fletcher	1611	Tragicomedy	King's	179–81
1612	*The Captain*	Beaumont Fletcher	1609–1612	Comedy	King's	198–200
1612	*Four Plays in One*	Fletcher Beaumont or Field	c. 1608–1613	Moral	unknown	30–41
1613	*The Honest Man's Fortune*	Fletcher Field Massinger	1613	Tragicomedy	Lady Elizabeth's	45–47
1614	*Valentinian*	Fletcher	1610–1614	Tragedy	King's	151–56

Date	Title	Author	Limits	Type	Auspices	Discussion in Text
1617	The Queen of Corinth	Fletcher Field Massinger	1616–c. 1618	Tragicomedy	King's	156–63
1617	Thierry and Theodoret	Fletcher Beaumont Massinger	1607–1621	Tragedy	King's	166–71
1618	The Loyal Subject	Fletcher	1618	Tragicomedy	King's	205–10
1618	The Knight of Malta	Fletcher Field Massinger	1616–1619	Tragicomedy	King's	185–90
1619	The Humorous Lieutenant	Fletcher	1619 (?)	Tragicomedy	King's	222–27
1619	The Little French Lawyer	Fletcher Massinger	1619–1623	Comedy	King's	201–4
1620	Women Pleased	Fletcher	1619–1623	Tragicomedy	King's	200–201
1620	The Custom of the Country	Fletcher Massinger	1619–1623	Comedy	King's	210–17
1620	The Double Marriage	Fletcher Massinger	1619–1623	Tragedy	King's	171–76
1623	The Maid in the Mill	Fletcher Rowley	1623	Comedy	King's	163–66
1623	The Lovers' Progress	Fletcher	1623; rev. Massinger, 1634	Tragicomedy	King's	181–85
1624	A Wife for a Month	Fletcher	1624	Tragicomedy	King's	217–22

The factual information in this appendix is compiled from Harbage, *Annals of the English Drama*; Bentley, *The Jacobean and Caroline Stage*; and Chambers, *The Elizabethan Stage*.

Appendix B

ELIZABETHAN CHASTITY LITERATURE PRIOR TO
THE FAITHFUL SHEPHERDESS

There are other poems, stories, and plays about chastity besides those discussed in chapters 4 and 5. Related plays include Whetstone's I and II *Promos and Cassandra* (1578), Heywood's I and II *Edward IV* (1599) and *A Woman Killed with Kindness* (1603), Marston's *Sophonisba* (1605), *The Revenger's Tragedy* (1606), and the anonymous *Locrine* (1591) and *Edward III* (1590). A number of lost plays have suggestive titles: *Lady Barbara* (1571) was probably a version of the popular "Lady of Bohemia"; *Chariclea* (1572) suggests a dramatization of the trials of the chaste heroine of the *Aethiopica;* the lost *Diocletian* (1594) perhaps dealt with the persecutions of the virgin-martyrs. The connections are obvious between the Fletcherian chastity plays and *Much Ado About Nothing, All's Well That Ends Well, Measure for Measure, Troilus and Cressida, Pericles,* and *Othello. Cymbeline* and *The Winter's Tale* appeared after *The Faithful Shepherdess.*

Related prose pieces include Whetstone's *An Heptameron of Civill Discourses* (London, 1582), a discussion of marriage cast into a form that seeks to imitate *The Courtier.* W. Averill's *A Dyall for dainty Darlings, rockt in the cradle of Securitie* (London, 1584) has as its second subtitle "A Myrrour for vertuous Maydes." This euphuistic piece opens with a tirade against "unshamefastnesse," which leads to "utter disdaine of all vertue" (sig. B1^r). R. Southwell's *Marie Mag-*

dalens funeral teares (London, 1591) is a prose complaint with Mary as the speaker; the pamphlet is curious but strangely moving.

There are a number of poems about chastity. *A Paradise of Dainty Devices* (1576) includes "A Young Man of Egypt and Valerian," which tells how a Christian youth resisted carnal temptation by the distraction of biting out his own tongue; "Spurina and the Roman Ladies," which describes how a virtuous young man avoided lustful women by disfiguring his face with wounds; and "Zaleuch and his Son," which gives an example of the Locrensian law, mentioned in the *Homily on Adultery,* which punished adulterers with blindness. *The Second Part of the Mirror for Magistrates* (1578) by Thomas Blennerhasset includes "The Lyfe of Lady Ebbe," who flayed her face to avoid being raped by the invading Danes and persuaded her sister nuns to follow her example. George Peele's "The Praise of Chastity" was printed in *The Phoenix Nest* (1593). Richard Niccols's *The Cuckow* (London, 1607) is a debate between Philomel, representing chastity, and Dan Cuckow, representing unchastity. Also in 1607 W. N. (Nicholas Breton) published *Barley-breake, or a warning for wantons;* this pastoral poem tells of the disastrous fate of the shepherdess Euphema when she ignored her father's advice to be chaste.

Bibliography

I. EDITIONS OF THE BEAUMONT AND FLETCHER PLAYS

Alden, Raymond M., ed. *The Knight of the Burning Pestle and A King and No King.* Boston, 1910.

Bowers, Fredson, gen. ed. *The Dramatic Works in the Beaumont and Fletcher Canon.* 2 vols. Cambridge, 1966–70.

Bullen, A. H., gen. ed. *The Works of Beaumont and Fletcher: Variorum Edition.* 4 vols. London, 1904–12.

Darley, George, ed. *The Works of Beaumont and Fletcher.* 2 vols. London, 1840.

Dyce, Alexander, ed. *The Works of Beaumont and Fletcher.* 2 vols. Boston, 1854.

Gerritsen, J., ed. *The Honest Man's Fortune.* Groningen, Djakarta, 1952.

Glover, A. and Waller, A. R. *The Works of Beaumont and Fletcher.* 10 vols. Cambridge, 1905–12.

Hunt, Leigh, ed. *Beaumont and Fletcher.* London, 1855.

Turner, Robert K., ed. *A King and No King.* Regents Renaissance Drama Series. Lincoln, Neb., 1963.

II. OTHER SOURCES

Appleton, William W. *Beaumont and Fletcher: A Critical Study.* London, 1956.

Augustine. *The City of God.* Translated by Marcus Dods. New York, 1950.

Ault, Norman, ed. *Elizabethan Lyrics.* London, 1925.

Averill, W. *A Dyall for dainty Darlings.* London, 1584.

Barnfield, Richard. *Poems 1594–1598.* Edited by Edward Arber. *The English Scholar's Library,* vol. 14. London, 1882.

Beecham, Sir Thomas. "John Fletcher." The Romanes Lecture, 7 June 1956. Oxford, 1956.

Bentley, G. E. *The Jacobean and Caroline Stage.* 7 vols. Oxford, 1941–1968.

Bentley, Thomas. *The Monument of Matrons.* London, 1582.

Bertram, Paul. *Shakespeare and The Two Noble Kinsmen.* New Brunswick, N.J., 1965.

The Bible. Geneva edition. London, 1560.

Bond, R. Warwick. "On Six Plays in *Beaumont and Fletcher, 1679.*" *RES* 11 (1935) : 257–75.

Boyle, Robert. "On Massinger and *The Two Noble Kinsmen,*" *The New Shakespeare Society Transactions* 8, 1st ser. (1882) : 371–99.

Breton, Nicholas. *Works in Verse and Prose.* Edited by A. B. Grosart. 2 vols. Edinburgh, 1879.

Brooke, Rupert. *John Webster and the Elizabethan Drama.* London, 1916.

Brooke, Tucker. *The Renaissance.* Vol. 2 in *A Literary History of England,* ed. Albert C. Baugh. New York, 1948.

———. "Willobie's *Avisa,*" *Essays in Honor of Albert Feuillerat,* ed. Henri M. Peyre. New Haven, 1943.

Brustein, Robert. "Italianate Court Satire and the Plays of John Marston." Ph.D. dissertation, Columbia University, 1957.

Bush, Douglas. *Mythology and the Renaissance Tradition in English Poetry.* Minneapolis, 1932; repr. New York, 1957.

———. "The Petite Palace of Pettie His Pleasure," *JEGP* 27 (1928) : 162–69.

Camden, Carroll. *The Elizabethan Woman.* Houston, 1952.

Certayne sermons or homilies. . . . London, 1576.

Chambers, E. K. *The Elizabethan Stage.* 4 vols. Oxford, 1923.

Chaucer, Geoffrey. *Works,* ed. F. N. Robinson. 2d ed. Cambridge, Mass., 1957.

Churchyard, Thomas. *Churchyard's Challenge*. London, 1593.

Clark, Alice. *Working Life of Women in the Seventeenth Century*. London, 1919.

Coleridge on the Seventeenth Century. Edited by Roberta Florence Brinkley. Durham, 1955.

Collier, J. Payne, ed. *Illustrations of Old English Literature*. 3 vols. London, 1866; repr. New York, 1966.

Colse, Peter. *Penelopes Complaint*. London, 1596.

Craig, Hardin. *The Enchanted Glass*. Oxford, 1965.

Danby, John F. *Poets on Fortune's Hill*. London, 1952.

Daniel, Samuel. *The Complete Works in Verse and Prose*. Edited by A. B. Grosart. 4 vols. London, 1885.

Davies, John. *Orchestra*. Edited by E. M. W. Tillyard. London, 1947.

Donne, John. *Biathanatos*. Reproduced by the Facsimile Text Society. New York, 1930.

Drayton, Michael. *Works*. Edited by J. William Hebel, K. Tillotson, and B. H. Newdigate. 5 vols. Oxford, 1931–41.

Dryden, John. *Essays*. Edited by W. P. Ker. 2 vols. Oxford, 1900.

Dunn, T. A. *Philip Massinger, The Man and the Playwright*. London, 1957.

Edwards, Philip. "Massinger the Censor," *Essays on Shakespeare and Elizabethan Drama,* ed. Richard Hosley. Columbia, Mo., 1962.

Ellis-Fermor, Una. *The Jacobean Drama*. 4th ed. rev. London, 1957.

Elyot, Sir Thomas. *The Defence of Good Women*. Edited by E. J. Howard. Oxford, Ohio, 1940.

Englebert, Omer. *The Lives of the Saints*. Translated by Christopher and Anne Fremantle. New York, 1951.

Erasmus. *Encomium Matrimonii*. Translated by Richard Tavernour. London, 1530.

Fenton, Geoffrey. *Certaine Tragicall Discourses*. Tudor Translation Series, gen. ed. W. H. Henley. London, 1898; repr. New York, 1967.

Frank, Grace. *The Medieval French Drama*. Oxford, 1954.

Frere, W. H. *The English Church in the Reigns of Elizabeth and James I*. London, 1904.

Gairdner, J. *The English Church in the Sixteenth Century*. London, 1902.

Garter, Thomas. *The Most Virtuous and Godly Susanna*. Malone Society Reprints. Oxford, 1936.

Gayley, Charles Mills. *Beaumont, the Dramatist*. New York, 1914.

Gifford, Humfrey. *A Posie of Gilloflowers*. London, 1580.

A Gorgeous Gallery of Gallant Inventions. Edited by Hyder E. Rollins. Cambridge, Mass., 1926.

Greene, Robert. *Life and Works*. Edited by A. B. Grosart. 15 vols. London, 1881–86.

Greg, Walter W. *Pastoral Poetry and Pastoral Drama*. London, 1906.

Haller, William and Malleville. "The Puritan Art of Love," *The Huntington Library Quarterly* 5 (1941–42) : 235–72.

Harbage, Alfred. *Annals of the English Drama*. 2d. ed. rev. Samuel Schoenbaum. Philadelphia, 1964.

———. *Shakespeare and the Rival Traditions*. New York, 1952.

Harrison, G. B. *A Jacobean Journal*. London, 1941.

Hatcher, Orie Latham. *John Fletcher*. Chicago, 1905.

Heliodorus. *Aethiopica*. Translated by Sir Walter Lamb. London, 1961.

Heywood, Thomas. *The Dramatic Works*. 6 vols. Pearson Reprints. London, 1874.

Homer. *Odyssey*. Translated by E. V. Rieu. London, 1946.

Hotson, Leslie. *I, William Shakespeare*. London, 1937.

Howell, Thomas. *Howell's Devises*. Edited by Walter Raleigh. Oxford, 1906.

Hoy, Cyrus. "The Shares of Fletcher and his Collaborators in the Beaumont and Fletcher Canon," *Studies in Bibliography* 8, 9, 11–15 (1956–1962).

Hunter, Robert G. *Shakespeare and the Comedy of Forgiveness*. New York, 1965.

Johnson, Jean E. "The Persecuted Heroine in English Renaissance Tragicomedy." Ph.D. dissertation, Columbia University, 1969.

Johnson, S. F. "The Tragic Hero in Early Elizabethan Drama." *Studies in the English Renaissance Drama*. Edited by J. W. Bennett et al. New York, 1959.

Jonson, Ben. *Sejanus*. Edited by W. F. Bolton. London, 1966.

Kelso, Ruth. *Doctrine for the Lady of the Renaissance*. Urbana, Ill., 1956.

Lamb, Charles. *Specimens of the English Dramatic Poets*. 2 vols. London, 1844.

Lawrence, W. J. "The Date of *Four Plays in One*," *TLS* (11 December 1919), p. 740.

Leech, Clifford. *The John Fletcher Plays*. Cambridge, Mass., 1962.

Lewis, C. S. *The Allegory of Love*. Oxford, 1936.

———. *English Literature in the Sixteenth Century*. Oxford, 1954.

Lodge, Thomas. *The Complete Works*. 4 vols. London, 1883; repr. New York, 1963.

Lowell, James Russell. *The Old English Dramatists*. Cambridge, Mass., 1892.

Macaulay, G. C. "Beaumont and Fletcher," *Cambridge History of English Literature* 6. Cambridge, 1910.

———. *Francis Beaumont*. London, 1883.

Makkink, H. J. *Philip Massinger and John Fletcher—A Comparison*. Rotterdam, 1927.

Mason, Eudo C. "Satire on Women and Sex in Elizabethan Tragedy," *English Studies* 31 (1950): 1–11.

Massie, William. *A Sermon Preached at Trafford*. Oxford, 1586.

Maxwell, Baldwin. *Studies in Beaumont, Fletcher, and Massinger*. Durham, 1939; repr. New York, 1966.

McKeithan, D. M. *The Debt to Shakespeare in the Beaumont and Fletcher Plays*. Austin, Tex., 1938.

Middleton, Thomas. *The Ghost of Lucrece*. Edited by J. Q. Adams. New York, 1937.

Mincoff, Marco. "The Social Background of Beaumont and Fletcher," *English Miscellany* 1 (1950): 1–30.

The Mirror for Magistrates. Edited by Lily B. Campbell. Cambridge, 1938.

Mizener, Arthur. "The High Design of *A King and No King*." *Modern Philology* 38 (1940–41): 133–54.

More, Paul Elmer. "Beaumont and Fletcher—II," *The Nation* (1 May 1913), pp. 436–38.

N., W. (Nicholas Breton). *Barley-breake, or a warning for wantons*. London, 1607.

Nearing, Homer. *English Historical Poetry 1599–1641*. Philadelphia, 1945.

Nelson, William. *The Poetry of Edmund Spenser*. New York, 1963.

Niccols, Richard. *The Cuckow*. London, 1607.

Notestein, Wallace. "The English Woman, 1580–1650." *Studies in Social History*. Edited by J. H. Plumb. London, 1955.

Oliphant, E. H. C. *The Plays of Beaumont and Fletcher*. New Haven, 1927.

Ornstein, Robert. *The Moral Vision of Jacobean Tragedy*. Madison, Wis., 1960.

Overbury, Sir Thomas. *A Wife*. London, 1614.

Ovid. *Metamorphosis*. Translated by Arthur Golding. Edited by W. H. D. Rouse. London, 1904.

Painter, William. *The Palace of Pleasure*. Edited by Joseph Jacobs. 3 vols. London, 1890.

The Paradise of Dainty Devices. Edited by Hyder E. Rollins. Cambridge, Mass., 1927.

Parts Added to the Mirror for Magistrates. Edited by Lily B. Campbell. Cambridge, 1946.

Peend, T. de la. *The moste notable historie of John Lord of Mandosse*. London, 1565.

Peter, John. *Complaint and Satire in Early English Literature*. Oxford, 1956.

Pettie, George. *A Petite Palace of Pettie His Pleasure*. Edited by Herbert Hartman. London, 1938.

Phoenix Nest. Edited by Hyder E. Rollins. Cambridge, Mass., 1931.

Powell, Chilton Latham. *English Domestic Relations 1487–1653*. New York, 1917.

Pruvost, René. *Matteo Bandello and Elizabethan Fiction*. Paris, 1937.

Rich, Barnaby. *The Excellency of Good Women*. London, 1613.

———. *The Honestie of This Age*. Edited by Peter Cunningham. Percy Society Reprints, vol. 11. London, 1844.

———. *Riche His Farewell to Military Profession*. Edited by T. M. Cranfill. Austin, Tex., 1959.

Ristine, F. H. *English Tragicomedy*. New York, 1910.

Robinson, Richard. *The Rewarde of Wickednesse*. London, 1574.

Rogers, Katharine M. *The Troublesome Helpmate*. Seattle, Wash., 1966.

Rosenbach, A. S. W. "The Curious-Impertinent in English Dramatic Literature before Shelton's Translation of *Don Quixote*," *MLN* 17 (1902) : 357–67.

Savage, James E. "Beaumont and Fletcher's *Philaster* and Sidney's *Arcadia*," *ELH* 14 (1947) : 194–206.

Schelling, Felix. *Elizabethan Drama 1558–1642.* 2 vols. Boston, 1908.

Shakespeare, William. *The Complete Works.* Edited by Hardin Craig. Chicago, 1951.

———. *Henry VIII.* Edited by R. A. Foakes. New Arden Shakespeare. Cambridge, Mass., 1957.

———. *The Poems.* Edited by Hyder E. Rollins. New Variorum Edition. Philadelphia, 1938.

Smith, Henry. *Works.* Edited by Thomas Fuller. 2 vols. Edinburgh, 1866.

Southwell, R. *Mary Magdalens funeral teares.* London, 1591.

Spenser, Edmund. *The Poetical Works.* Edited by J. C. Smith and E. de Selincourt. London, 1912.

Spivack, Bernard. *Shakespeare and the Allegory of Evil.* New York, 1958.

Sprague, A. C. *Beaumont and Fletcher on the Restoration Stage.* Cambridge, Mass., 1926.

Staton, W. F. and Simeone, W. E. *A Critical Edition of Sir Richard Fanshawe's Translation of Giovanni Battista Guarini's Il Pastor Fido.* Oxford, 1964.

Stone, Lawrence. *The Crisis of the Aristocracy 1558–1641.* 2 vols. Oxford, 1965.

Swinburne, Algernon Charles. *Studies in Prose and Poetry.* London, 1894.

Symonds, J. A. *In the Key of Blue.* London, 1893.

Thomas, K. V. "Women and the Civil War Sects," *Past and Present,* no. 13 (April 1958), pp. 42–57.

Thorndike, A. H. *The Influence of Beaumont and Fletcher on Shakespeare.* Worcester, Mass., 1901.

Tilney, Edmund. *A brief and pleasant discourse of duties in Mariage, called the Flower of Friendshippe.* London, 1568.

Tottel's Miscellany. Edited by Hyder E. Rollins. 2 vols. rev. ed. Cambridge, Mass., 1965.

Utley, Francis Lee. *The Crooked Rib.* Columbus, Ohio, 1944.

Waith, Eugene. *The Pattern of Tragicomedy in Beaumont and Fletcher.* New Haven, 1952.

———. "The Sources of *The Double Marriage* by Fletcher and Massinger," *MLN* 64 (1949) : 505–10.

———. "A Tragicomedy of Humors: Fletcher's *The Loyal Subject,*" *MLQ* 6 (1945) : 299–311.

Wallis, Lawrence B. *Fletcher, Beaumont and Company*. New York, 1947.

Ward, A. W. *A History of English Dramatic Literature to the Death of Queen Anne*. 2d. ed. 3 vols. London, 1899.

Watson, C. B. *Shakespeare and the Renaissance Concept of Honor*. Princeton, 1960.

Whetstone, George. *An Heptameron of Civill Discourses*. London, 1582.

————. *The Rock of Regard*. Edited by J. Payne Collier. London, 1870.

Willobie, Henry. *Avisa*. Edited by G. B. Harrison. London, 1926.

————. *Avisa*. Spenser Society Publications, no. 42. Manchester, 1886.

Willson, D. H. *King James VI and I*. New York, 1956.

Wilson, E. C. *England's Eliza*. Cambridge, Mass., 1939.

Wilson, Violet A. *Society Women in Shakespeare's Time*. London, 1924.

Wolff, S. L. *The Greek Romances in Elizabethan Prose Fiction*. New York, 1912.

Wright, Louis B. *Middle-Class Culture in Elizabethan England*. Ithaca, 1935.

Index